ANCIENTS AND MODERNS

General Editor: Phiroze Vasunia, Reader in Classics, University of Reading

How can antiquity illuminate critical issues in the modern world? How does the ancient world help us address contemporary problems and issues? In what ways do modern insights and theories shed new light on the interpretation of ancient texts, monuments, artefacts and cultures? The central aim of this exciting new series is to show how antiquity is relevant to life today. The series also points towards the ways in which the modern and ancient worlds are mutually connected and interrelated. Lively, engaging, and historically informed, *Ancients and Moderns* examines key ideas and practices in context. It shows how societies and cultures have been shaped by ideas and debates that recur. With a strong appeal to students and teachers in a variety of disciplines, including classics and ancient history, each book is written for non-specialists in a clear and accessible manner.

DENISE EILEEN McCOSKEY is Associate Professor of Classics and an affiliate in Black World Studies at Miami University, Ohio. She has written extensively on the politics of race in antiquity, and in 2009 she won the American Philological Association Award for Excellence in Teaching at the College Level.

ANCIENTS AND MODERNS SERIES

RACE
ANTIQVITY AND ITS LEGACY

DENISE EILEEN McCOSKEY

OXFORD
UNIVERSITY PRESS

Oxford University Press, Inc., publishes works that further Oxford University's objective of excellence in research, scholarship, and education.

Oxford New York
Auckland Cape Town Dar es Salaam Hong Kong Karachi
Kuala Lumpur Madrid Melbourne Mexico City Nairobi
New Delhi Shanghai Taipei Toronto

With offices in
Argentina Austria Brazil Chile Czech Republic France Greece
Guatemala Hungary Italy Japan Poland Portugal Singapore
South Korea Switzerland Thailand Turkey Ukraine Vietnam

First published by I.B.Tauris & Co. Ltd. in the United Kingdom

Published by Oxford University Press, Inc.
198 Madison Avenue, New York, New York 10016

www.oup.com

Library of Congress Cataloging-in-Publication Data

McCoskey, Denise Eileen, 1968-
Race : antiquity and its legacy / Denise McCoskey.
p. cm. — (Ancients and moderns)
Includes bibliographical references and index.
ISBN 978-0-19-538094-1 (hardcover) — ISBN 978-0-19-538188-7 (pbk.) 1. Greece—Race
relations—History. 2. Rome—Race relations. 3. Race discrimination—Greece—History—
To 1500. 4. Race discrimination—Rome. 5. Greece—Civilization—To 146 B.C. 6. Rome—
Civilization. 7. Race. 8. Race relations. 9. Civilization—Greek influences. 10. Civilization—
Roman influences. I. Title.
DF135.M36 2012
305.800938—dc23   2011031285

ISBN (HB): 978-0-19-538094-1
ISBN (PB): 978-0-19-538188-7

Typeset in Garamond Pro by Ellipsis Digital Limited, Glasgow
Printed and bound in Great Britain by CPI Group (UK) Ltd, Croydon, CR0 4YY

CONTENTS

ACKNOWLEDGEMENTS

This book would have been impossible without the involvement of many people to whom I want to extend my deepest gratitude. To begin, I wish to express my sincere thanks to Alex Wright and Phiroze Vasunia for giving me the opportunity to write this book, as well as for their confidence in my efforts and continuing patience as I brought it to completion. I wish also to thank the anonymous reviewers, whose wisdom substantially improved the work. I am grateful to Miami University for two Summer Research Appointments that allowed me to research many parts of the book, and to Fitzwilliam College (University of Cambridge) for a Visiting Fellowship many years ago that allowed me the luxury of time to think. My colleagues and students in Classics and Black World Studies at Miami have been subjected over the years to much of this material in less advanced form; I thank them for their role in helping me develop it further.

I would never have become (or remained) a classicist without Judith Ginsburg, whose support for me as an undergraduate was fierce and unrelenting; David Halperin, whose intervention at a key moment in my graduate career was of inestimable value; and Lawrence Richardson, jr, who, in addition to his keen intelligence and enormous generosity of spirit, shared with me his Propertius – one of my most precious possessions. 'I am Larry Richardson's student' is surely one of the happiest sentences in the English language.

I am very grateful for the support of many colleagues in classics, whose own work has been a constant source of inspiration, especially: Alessandro Barchiesi, Mark Buchan, Peter Burian, Joy Connolly, Judith de Luce, Simon Goldhill, Charlotte Goldy, Kathryn Gutzwiller, Jonathan Hall, Tom Hawkins, Benjamin Isaac, David Mankin, Julia Nelson-Hawkins, Kirk

Ormand, Kevin Osterloh, Kent Rigsby, Chris Spelman, Zara Martirosova Torlone, Steve Tuck, and Victoria Wohl. I am especially thankful to Willy Clarysse, Traianos Gagos, Peter van Minnen, and Dorothy Thompson for so generously opening the world of papyrology to me (all errors remain my own). I cannot express enough my admiration for, and gratitude toward, Gerry Kearns, Stuart Lane, and Stephen Legg, who made me feel so much at home in historical geography when I needed it most. Friendship with Sarah Meer has been a wonder. The beginnings of this book can be traced in large part to Katya Gibel Azoulay, who insisted long ago that I needed to learn more about race in the ancient world. I am also thankful to Mary Jean Corbett for introducing me to Virginia Woolf's wonderful short story.

Friends and family in the UK have played a profound role in my life, for which I can never thank them enough: Bob, Jean, Paul, Andrea, Ben and Sophie Watson, Charlotte Ellis, Helen Parkins, Lynn Shouls, Helen Wood, and all the wonderful people in Chester-le-Street who accepted me so warmly as one of their own. I feel extremely lucky to know the following, all of whom have left strong imprint on me and my work: Cathie Arnold, Kim Blue, Mitchell Brown, Mercè Caballero, Edgar Gonzalez, Carolyn Haynes, Chloe Hogg, Erik Jensen, Ann-Marie Knoblauch, Marc Loy, Beth McCarty, Terri McCarty, Pablo Ojeda-O'Neill, Francisco Ortiz, Jutta Pfleger, Axel Pohlmann, David Rutherford, Maureen Sullivan, Lisa Weems, and Ann Wood. It is impossible to put into words the enormous gratitude I feel toward Ron Becker for his reassuring presence and constant encouragement throughout the writing of this book.

I wish to thank my family for all the love and support they have shown me, especially my parents, who have been meticulous in knowing when to ask (and not) about my progress on this book; I treasure every day the history they have given me. I am likewise grateful to Mary Margaret Meyer for her enthusiasm, as well as her infectious laugh. I have been inspired by my niece Allie's great love of Egypt, and hope this work will also one day find its way to Jake, Maddie, Bronwyn and Freya. Most of all, I wish to thank my sister Suzanne, who has been an essential part of my life from our very first moments together. Finally, I give my thanks to the Cincinnati Reds, without whose constant radio company – including a thrilling run to the NL Central Division title in 2010 – this book would have been much more difficult to write.

This book is dedicated to the memory of my grandparents.

FOREWORD

Ancients and Moderns comes to fruition at a propitious moment: 'reception studies' is flourishing, and the scholarship that has arisen around it is lively, rigorous, and historically informed; it makes us rethink our own understanding of the relationship between past and present. *Ancients and Moderns* aims to communicate to students and general readers the depth, energy, and excitement of the best work in the field. It seeks to engage, provoke, and stimulate, and to show how, for large parts of the world, Greco-Roman antiquity continues to be relevant to debates in culture, politics, and society.

The series does not merely accept notions such as 'reception' or 'tradition' without question; rather, it treats these concepts as contested categories and calls into question the illusion of an unmediated approach to the ancient world. We have encouraged our authors to take intellectual risks in the development of their ideas. By challenging the assumption of a direct line of continuity between antiquity and modernity, these books explore how discussions in such areas as gender, politics, race, sex, and slavery occur within particular contexts and histories; they demonstrate that no culture is monolithic, that claims to ownership of the past are never pure, and that East and West are often connected together in ways that continue to surprise and disturb many. Thus, *Ancients and Moderns* is intended to stir up debates about and within reception studies and to complicate some of the standard narratives about the 'legacy' of Greece and Rome.

All the books in *Ancients and Moderns* illustrate that *how* we think about the past bears a necessary relation to *who* we are in the present. At the same time, the series also seeks to persuade scholars of antiquity that their own pursuit is inextricably connected to what many generations have thought, said, and done about the ancient world.

Phiroze Vasunia

INTRODUCTION

Radical simply means 'grasping things at the root.'

Angela Davis

Few other features of modern life are as central to our experience as race. From the government forms we fill out to the films we watch to the company we keep, race remains essential to the ways we locate ourselves in, and make meaning of, the world around. As David Theo Goldberg explains, 'Modern social subjects have become unselfconscious in establishing racial characteristics. They take for granted the recognition of racial difference: they make racial claims, assert racial truths, assess racial value – in short, create (fabricate) racial knowledge. In this sense, racial knowledge is integral to the common sense, to the articulation, of modernity's self-understanding.'[1] The very ubiquity of race encourages most of us to take its existence for granted, to accept the power it exerts as completely natural and to allow the process by which it has assumed such authority to remain unquestioned. Yet it is precisely because we too often perpetuate the power of race by such passive acceptance that Michael Omi and Howard Winant insist 'the task . . . is to explain this situation.'[2]

This simple charge stands as the inspiration for the work that follows, for I want to help explain the position of race today by unveiling its relation to structures of thought and practice in the past, and more specifically, those of classical antiquity. This study will thus attempt both to account for the role of race in the classical world and also trace the intricate ways Greek and Roman racial ideologies continue to resonate in modern life.

1

I do not aim to provide a comprehensive history of race *per se*, but rather to examine the historical operation of race via a very specific juxtaposition: the ancient world and our modern one, the latter a world that remains inexorably shaped not only by a deep sense of its own 'classical inheritance,' but also by the sweeping events and intellectual movements of the more recent eighteenth and nineteenth centuries.

Before turning to the continuities and discontinuities that characterize ancient and modern versions of race, however, it might be useful to define more clearly the object of study by posing a deceptively simple question: what is race?

Racial formation

At its most basic, race is an ideological structure that organizes and classifies perceived human variation. Race thus allows the division of people into broad categories that presume to demarcate according to fundamental differences, such as 'black' and 'white'. As the primary role of skin colour in defining race today suggests, racial differences have traditionally been attributed to biological characteristics, implying that racial categories emerge inherently from the human body. But, as Omi and Winant write, '(a)lthough the concept of race invokes biologically based human characteristics (so-called "phenotypes"), selection of these particular human features for purposes of racial signification is always and necessarily a social and historical process.'[3] Race, in other words, does not derive passively from human anatomy, but is dependent on social intervention, on the formulation of theories that designate the surface of the human body as the primary vehicle of race and also determine exactly *which* physical features 'matter' in determining racial groups. Race's dependency on social and historical forces – a dependency concealed behind seemingly objective criteria – emerges when we consider, for example, the changing racial identity of 'black' Irish immigrants over time in the United States, a group whose 'whitening' in racial terms had very little to do with somatic pigmentation and very much to do with the changing socioeconomic power of the Irish in relation to African Americans.[4]

Just as race's roots stretch beyond the mere biological, racial structures of thought generally extend past simple biological classification to ascribe a wider set of characteristics and capacities to every member of a group. Thus, 'blackness' and 'whiteness' have long been used to 'predict' qualities as far removed from skin colour (or, to be more precise, from the level of melanin in skin) as intellectual capacity and moral tendency. The designation of such racial 'characteristics' – what we might call stereotypes – can, in turn, be used to justify a range of social outcomes, such as disparate access to economic opportunities. The closer we look, then, the more it becomes evident that race does not define us, we define race, and in contexts that are constantly changing. As James Donald and Ali Rattansi explain: '(t)he issue is not how *natural* differences determine and justify group definitions and interactions, but how racial logics and racial frames of reference are articulated and deployed, and with what consequences.'[5] Omi and Winant likewise provide an invaluable framework by using the terminology 'racial formation' rather than 'race', meaning the 'sociohistorical processes by which racial categories are created, inhabited, transformed, and destroyed.'[6]

Historicising the workings of race is crucial, not least because race has often been treated as not merely objective, but also universal – a form of classification that has remained fixed and unchanging throughout human history. In recent years, however, historians have sought to identify the myriad forms race has assumed across time and place, as well as its intersections with other prominent entities, such as the nation.[7] In demonstrating the sheer agility of race – its ability to adapt to countless social, political, and historical contexts – scholars have come to increasing consensus that the dominant view of race today, one adamantly linked to skin colour, is not some universal response to human variation, but rather the specific 'product of popular beliefs about human differences that evolved from the sixteenth through the nineteenth centuries.'[8] Modern ideas about race were thus initiated within the specific context of European exploration, which brought Europeans into greater contact with populations in both Africa and the Americas, and led to the employment of a range of ideas and texts

– including both the Bible and the ancient environmental theory – in explaining the differences perceived in such encounters. Often premised on alleged empirical observation, these racial structures of thought allowed European writers to account for a range of traits they perceived as vastly different from their own, including the degree to which other groups seemed more or less 'civilized.' Such theories were soon readily harnessed to claims of European superiority, casting Europeans as racially superior (therefore 'naturally' superior) and providing an important rationalization in the rise of European colonialism and the African slave trade.[9]

By the nineteenth century, new scientific models of the natural world were flourishing, and these emergent theories were grafted closely onto questions of human diversity, radically transforming perceptions of both the source and meanings of race. While in the first part of the century 'mono-genesis', or the single origin of human life, had been the prevailing view – based in part on Christian doctrine – later in the century the tide would turn to 'polygenesis' or multiple origin, suggesting that a more fundamental separation had existed between racial groups from the very beginning of time.[10] With its focus not merely on asserting the superiority of certain races in 'scientific' terms, but also outlining the dangers of 'race-mixing', Joseph Arthur de Gobineau's *Essai sur l'Inégalité des Races* (1853) was critical in consolidating these major turns in racial theory in the nineteenth century. As they continued to gain the ascendant, 'scientific' explanations of race generally encompassed five basic propositions (propositions often accompanied by elaborate schemes of classification): first, that human beings *could* be divided into separate categories based on the observation of select features like skin colour; second, that these groups could be ranked according to a strict hierarchy, a hold-over from the earlier idea of the great chain of being; third, that external characteristics correlated with internal qualities, e.g., that head measurements could reveal brain capacities; fourth, that such characteristics were inherited; and fifth, that groups were innate and unchanging, created by nature or God, depending on the perspective of the author.[11]

The overall contention of such 'scientific' theories – that race was a 'natural' and unalterable phenomenon – proved to be so persuasive that the bond of race and biology acquired an unassailable authority that it continues to hold even today. Recognizing that the nineteenth century propounded a new "'scientific" racism', however, V.Y. Mudimbe insists that we distinguish it not from a time 'before' race or racism, but rather from a previous 'history of race-thinking', meaning that race existed as a structure for organizing human difference (including by writers like Voltaire and Kant) long before our particular and potent modern form took hold.[12] Can we, then, identify the structure of earlier 'race-thinking' in classical antiquity? Or, to propose a slightly different starting point, how have classical scholars traditionally approached the question of race in these earlier periods?

Blacks in antiquity

From its origins in the modern nineteenth century, the discipline of classics has been infused with contemporary racial ideologies. Indeed, as Martin Bernal has demonstrated, the initial rise of the professional study of the classical past in places like Germany was greatly fostered by explicit racial identification with the ancient Greeks.[13] Led by burgeoning theories of race, which increasingly cast race as the main engine of human development, many early classical scholars consciously aimed to uncover a racial genealogy closely linking the European past and present, claims that – absent the physical remains of ancient peoples or evidence of 'real' bloodlines – were demonstrated primarily through language clusters or language 'families.' Trying to explain who the Greeks and Romans had been from how they had spoken thus became closely linked to asserting claims about which modern European groups could lay claim to being their 'legitimate' descendants, conclusions fraught with racial overtones.

Assumptions about race inundated contemporary social and anthropological writing well into the twentieth century,[14] and they continued to find expression in ancient studies as well, including an unsettling focus on 'race-mixture', a topic intimately related to concerns about 'deterioration' and 'decline'. In 1937, Aubrey Diller published *Race Mixture Among the*

Greeks Before Alexander. Outlining the two sides traditionally taken in response to de Gobineau's work, Diller asserted '(t)he problem begins and ends in history. For it was first raised when it began to appear that races had a history and functioned in history, and the results of the argument must in turn be applied to the interpretation of history'.[15] Later he added that '(a)ll combatants in the field of race theory recognize Greece and Rome as their chief bone of contention',[16] a belief about the importance of classical antiquity to wider debates about race that still, as we shall see, often holds true today. Reiterating at the end of his study that '(t)he significance of race in civilization . . . is largely a matter of opinion' since both positive and negative claims about race 'remain incapable of proof or disproof',[17] Diller concluded overall that 'the problem of race was not conceived as vividly among the Greeks before Alexander as in modern times', and, more specifically, that '(f)or the historical period before Alexander . . . we must conclude that there was not much race mixture'.[18]

Contemporary racial ideologies were generally far more explicit when applied to the case of Rome, especially given the frequent attempts to cast Rome's infamous 'fall' in terms of racial practices or racial character. In 1916, the historian Tenney Frank disturbingly employed race when trying to determine the cause of Rome's so-called decline, seeking to calculate from inscriptional evidence the amount of 'race mixture' between Romans and others. Arguing that 'the whole empire was a melting-pot and that the Oriental was always and everywhere a very large part of the ore,' Frank described the negative effect of such mixing in wholly racist terms, proposing that 'what lay behind and constantly reacted upon all such causes of Rome's disintegration was, after all to considerable extent, the fact that the people who built Rome had given way to a different race'.[19] Between the wars, A. Duff similarly applied the question of 'race-mixing' explicitly to the 'problem' of contemporary immigration, chillingly lamenting also the absence of eugenic strategies in the earlier Roman custom of slave manumission.[20]

Not all classicists of this period agreed with such views, however; in 1926, the Russian émigré Michael Rostovtzeff in his masterful study *The Social and Economic History of the Roman Empire* vehemently rejected

Frank's proposition. Acknowledging that 'theories of degeneration and race-suicide have been applied to the ancient world', Rostovtzeff countered 'I see no criterion for distinguishing between inferior and superior races. Why are the Greek and Latin races considered the only superior races in the Roman Empire?'[21] Rostovtzeff sought instead to recast the question in terms of class. Arnold Toynbee likewise devoted a lengthy section of *A Study of History* to the problem of race, seeking aggressively to debunk colour as a source of racial classification. Conceding that the 'Black Race' had yet to demonstrate its capacity for civilization, Toynbee refuted those who interpreted that lack as innate rather than circumstantial:

We can attribute these retardations to the interplay between a Human Nature which is common to all Mankind and certain exceptionally unfavourable circumstances in the local environments of some sections of the human family during certain periods of time; and we need seek no further than this in order to explain why it is that within these first six thousand years, the Black Race has not helped to create any civilization, while the Polynesian White Race has helped to create one civilization, the Brown Race two, the Yellow Race three, the Red Race and the 'Nordic' White Race four apiece, the 'Alpine' White Race nine, and the 'Mediterranean' White Race ten.[22]

Toynbee's phrasing (as well as concomitant 'score-card') clearly yields considerable discomfort today, yet he was aiming to undermine the racial logic frequently applied to classical antiquity by insisting that environmental factors and not race *per se* lay behind what he and others perceived as differential rates in the development of human civilization. Promoting the notion of a universal 'Human Nature' and 'human family', Toynbee later went even further in confronting contemporary racial theories by observing that, in actuality, 'nearly half the civilizations that have emerged hitherto have been created by a mixture of races', forcefully repudiating any modern equation of racial mixture and deterioration.[23] Soon after, the consequences of Nazi racial ideology would shock classicists – like everyone else – into facing the consequences of such theorising (it is impossible today to read Diller's speculation about a 'final solution of the problem' of racial theory without utter nausea, even if such phrasing might have seemed innocuous at the time of his writing[24]) and in classical studies, as elsewhere, the experiences of World War II would cause major shifts in approaches to collective identity.

In the post-war period, a number of classical scholars – including some specifically based in Africa – started employing the concept of race not to draw conclusions about racial origins, racial character or 'decline', but rather to determine how 'race relations' (a patently different framework for evaluating contact between groups than 'race-mixture') were conducted in antiquity.[25] This question held manifest significance in a world witnessing both the rise of independence efforts in Africa and the civil rights movement in the United States. Given such dramatic global events, these studies often addressed the role of skin colour, at least in passing, usually denying it the primacy it held in the modern world. By the 1970s, commensurate with the politics of the time, however, the study of race in classics had begun to focus almost exclusively on the question of 'blacks' in antiquity, treating 'blackness' and black skin colour as the primary locus for investigating race and racial difference of every era. Frank M. Snowden, Jr., one of the few African–American classicists of his generation, led the way in defining such an approach with his two major studies: *Blacks in Antiquity: Ethiopians in the Greco-Roman Experience* (1970) and *Before Color Prejudice: The Ancient View of Blacks* (1983).

In his work, Snowden was candid about the contemporary pressures that drove his research, insisting that '(t)he relationship of blacks and whites continues to be a critical problem of the twentieth century. Not without meaning for the vital question is the experience of the Ethiopian in classical antiquity – the first major encounter in European records of blacks in predominately white society'.[26] By demonstrating that the Greeks and Romans did not systematically discriminate against those with black skin colour, Snowden sought to call attention to the significant differences between past and present racial systems of thought. Lloyd Thompson, based at the University of Ibadan in Nigeria, similarly cited such contrasts in his work *Romans and Blacks*, arguing that 'Roman attitudes . . . even at their most negative, have nothing to do with the familiar modern phenomenon of *race* (*sic*) and are of a kind very different from those commonly described by social scientists by the terms "racist", "racial prejudice", "colour prejudice", and "racism"'.[27]

In groundbreaking ways, such research on 'blacks in antiquity' helped strengthen and circulate more widely an assumption that had become standard for many ancient historians, namely that skin colour was negligible in defining racial identity in antiquity. Even more, in drawing such conclusions, many authors sought to levy powerful blows against the racism that characterized their own societies. Underlining the fact that the modern preoccupation with skin colour was not necessarily how things 'had always been done', such scholars forcefully asserted that our current investment in skin colour remained a sign of our own modern limitations and discriminatory impulses, our own psychoses. Yet, paradoxically, such work – even as it sharpened our reading of modernity – too often obscured our understanding of antiquity, leading most readers to assume that the Greeks and Romans did not employ racial structures of any kind.[28] From there, the presumption often followed that Greek and Roman society was inherently more enlightened than our own. Indeed, since that time, with only a few notable exceptions, classical historians have completely avoided the language of race when discussing ancient structures of identity and difference.[29]

This book is founded on the belief that the concept of race remains essential to the study of antiquity. It is necessary first, though, to pinpoint with greater precision what was actually demonstrated by Snowden and others before picking up the trail from there. For one, such scholarship, in unanimously arguing for the insignificance of skin colour, did not in point of fact demonstrate that the ancients did not think racially, only that they did not endorse one particular brand of racial ideology. In making this distinction – that only skin colour and not race *writ* large was shown to be insignificant in antiquity – I do not mean in any way to discount or minimize the contributions of this earlier research; rather I want to build on the efforts of Snowden and others by pursuing what I consider the requisite follow-up question: if skin colour was not the basis of racial difference in antiquity, what forms or versions of racial formation might the Greeks and Romans have actually used?

But even as we may seek greater clarity in shaping a historically accurate approach to race (one that can excavate the racial ideas and practices that pre-existed our modern nineteenth century), it remains a thorny task to try to distance perceptions of classical antiquity from modern experience. For one, scholarly recognition that race is not consistent across time and place has yet to dent the longstanding habit of applying modern racial formations to the past. As Diller notes, modern audiences often rely heavily on notions of race to aid their interpretation of history. Central to such efforts has been the attempt to identify 'white' versus 'black' cultures in earlier eras and to determine what each racial group was able to achieve over time. Such approaches have granted paramount explanatory power to the surface of the body, that is, in such contexts it is generally presumed that the 'whiteness' of 'white' civilizations is directly related to their historical accomplishments, as is 'blackness' to 'black' civilizations. That such beliefs are central to 'modernity's self-understanding', moreover, is clear from the seamless fusion of ancient and modern in many such debates.

Succinctly illustrating just such a practice, Martin Bernal once asserted provocatively of the ancient Egyptians that '(f)ew . . . could have bought a cup of coffee in America's Deep South in 1954'.[30] At first glance, this loaded image – with its allusions to the profoundly segregated American South of the pre-civil rights era, a time in which African–American use of public space was strictly regulated – is both provocative and incongruous, and useful precisely because of the discomfort it generates. Yet such a 'translation' of ancient Egyptian racial identity to our modern experience ignores a question perhaps more salient to the ancient Egyptian themselves: whether they could have 'bought a cup of coffee' in their own historical setting, the history of coffee notwithstanding. Around no historical figure has the modern desire to 'assess racial value' or 'create racial knowledge' been more insistent than the Egyptian queen Cleopatra, whose continuing resurgence in popular culture attests, in no small way, to the unrivalled position of classical antiquity in the modern imaginary, while also demonstrating at closer look the considerable hazards of eliding ancient and modern too carelessly.

Lost in translation

> ANTONY: I have a fondness for almost all Greek things . . .
> CLEOPATRA: As an almost Greek thing – I'm flattered.

From the moment Cleopatra sprang out of a rolled-up carpet before the startled eyes of Julius Caesar in 48 BCE,[31] her appearance has tantalized western audiences. Indeed, Cleopatra's popularity in the latter part of the twentieth century would be impossible to separate from Joseph Mankiewicz's epic film *Cleopatra* (1963), whose glamorous leading lady, Elizabeth Taylor, helped solidify the ancient queen's status as a modern style icon. Keen interest in Cleopatra's real life invariably attends her modern appearances, but Mankiewicz chose mainly to address the question of who she was in cagey terms, as the brief exchange from the movie above suggests.[32] In what way, the audience might wonder, could Cleopatra, legendary queen of Egypt, possibly be considered 'almost Greek'?

In 332 BCE, Alexander the Great had conquered Egypt as part of his massive campaigns, and, following his early death in 323, Egypt was ruled by the Ptolemaic dynasty for nearly three hundred years. The Ptolemies, descended from Alexander's general Ptolemy, were Macedonian in origin, like Alexander himself – a category often conflated with Greek, although not without strain, as we shall see in the next chapter. During their long reign, the Ptolemies would become embroiled in numerous internecine struggles, and Caesar had arrived in October 48 to resolve the dispute between Cleopatra (actually Cleopatra VII) and her brother/husband Ptolemy XIII over control of Egypt, an enmity that had ignited into open warfare. Siding with Cleopatra, Caesar was eventually able to suppress the civil conflict, and, after a leisurely cruise up the Nile during which he allegedly impregnated the queen, he left Cleopatra along with her younger brother Ptolemy XIV in possession of Egypt's throne.

These political manoeuverings within the Ptolemaic royal family are generally overlooked in modern accounts of Cleopatra – as is her participation in the Ptolemaic practice of brother-sister marriage – yet Mankiewicz, in his film's dialogue, sought to convey some of the political complexity and frequent instability of Ptolemaic rule in Egypt.[33] The visual aspects of the movie, however, consistently returned to a simplified and familiar Hollywood vocabulary of 'ancient Egyptian', a style that fused the image of a timeless or eternal Egypt with various modern touches.[34] Despite the sly identification of Taylor's Cleopatra as 'almost Greek', then, the queen's attire and taste in interior décor did little to explain that claim: 'there is nothing in the design of Cleopatra's wardrobe that suggests the clothing of a Graeco-Roman noblewoman; the look is purely Egyptian, but with a reflection of 1960s aesthetic, in particular the tightly clinched corseted waists and Christian Dior-style tailoring techniques, so perfectly suited to Elizabeth Taylor's voluptuous figure.'[35] Presented as a visual feast, Taylor's own pale skin notably refused to signify any racial difference between herself and the Roman men in the film. Appearing in US theatres in a year when Martin Luther King, Jr. would be arrested in Birmingham, Medgar Evers murdered, and four young black girls killed in a church bombing, Mankiewicz presumably chose not to disconcert the white members of his audience by addressing the volatile subject of Cleopatra's 'actual' racial identity.

Cecil B. DeMille's earlier film (1934), on the other hand, explicitly raised the spectre of Cleopatra's racial difference – only to ridicule and immediately diffuse it when a Roman woman's query whether the queen was black is greeted by laughter. The fact that Cleopatra was played by the luminously white actress Claudette Colbert served to underline the presumed ludicrousness of the proposition. Key to Colbert's casting was the range of commercial tie-ins that accompanied release of the film.[36] As Maria Wyke notes '(w)omen in the audiences of DeMille's historical film were thus encouraged to identify with the Cleopatra on screen and to carry over that identification into their lives outside the cinema through the purchase of

Cleopatra gowns and other "style accessories"'[37] In short, the goal of the film was not to alienate its white female audience by reminding them of any gap, racial or otherwise, between themselves and the Egyptian queen, rather to assure them that they, too, could be Cleopatra with the right accoutrements. This reliance on Cleopatra to stoke female consumption (as well as male fantasy, surely) makes Mankiewicz's designation of her as a commodity, 'an almost Greek *thing*', seem particularly apt.

Assumptions about Cleopatra's fundamental whiteness recur throughout western art and literature, yet other traditions run counter to this view. Indeed, it could be said that DeMille's smug scene records the existence of alternative traditions precisely to disparage them. The African–American classicist Shelley Haley writes that her grandmother insisted, 'Remember, no matter what you learn in school, Cleopatra was black.' Haley explains: 'In the Black oral tradition, Cleopatra becomes a symbolic construction voicing our Black African heritage so long suppressed by racism and the ideology of miscegenation. When we say, in general, that the ancient Egyptians were Black and, more specifically, that Cleopatra was Black, we claim them as part of a culture and history that has known oppression and triumph, exploitation and survival.'[38] Such views of Cleopatra at times point specifically to modern experiences of miscegenation, as Haley intimates, calling attention to the fact that the identity of Cleopatra's paternal grandmother, a mistress of Ptolemy IX, has never been conclusively established. The classical scholar Alan Cameron argued some years ago that this grandmother might have been Egyptian or Ethiopian.[39] But does filling the gaps in Cleopatra's official lineage or reconstructing her bloodline get us any closer to defining her racially in ways that would have made sense to her?

The continuing fascination with Cleopatra's racial origin – a question steeped in conjecture about her skin colour – is closely related to long-standing debates about the skin colour of the ancient Egyptians themselves, a debate that derives its power from the successive, and highly publicized, discoveries of the physical remains of ancient Egyptians: mummies.[40] One writer has fittingly called mummies 'the ancient human body *par excellence*' and professes that they have 'been utilised as an object of western "pornography."'[41] We can witness the eager interest in putting ancient Egyptian bodies under a modern microscope (literally and figuratively) in the recent attempts to solve the 'mystery' of King Tut's death, endeavours whose popular appeal seems to fall somewhere between Agatha Christie's *Death on the Nile* and television's *C.S.I.* With even greater urgency, Egyptian mummies have been forced to speak the modern scientific language of race – their remains have been unwrapped, their DNA analyzed, and their head sizes measured, interrogations premised on the assumption that the biological remains of ancient Egyptians can be used to categorize them racially, one we will revisit in the final chapter.

Dissenting views of Cleopatra's own racial identity burst into the American mainstream media on September 23, 1991 when the magazine *Newsweek* bluntly asked on its cover 'Was Cleopatra Black?' Historians inside the magazine were, like DeMille, roundly dismissive of the question, pointing to the fact that Cleopatra was part of the Ptolemaic dynasty. Still, the answer they routinely proffered, 'No, she was Greek,' disingenuously shifted the terms of the debate from 'black' and 'white' to 'Greek,' a tactic that served only to reinforce the misleading form of the original question. Such attempts to align 'Greekness' with whiteness have been surprisingly resilient, even as they belie the ancient evidence itself; ancient ideology, as Snowden and others have demonstrated, grants skin colour nothing like the racial force we give it today. It cannot be repeated often enough that the ancient Greeks and Romans would be quite perplexed by our glib tendency to lump them into the category of 'dead *white* men.' Indeed, Mankiewicz's '*almost* Greek' provides a far more instructive opening for thinking about ancient notions of race and the ways they rebut our modern expectations since his 'almost Greek' locates race within a range of possible identifications rather than via strict binaries. 'Greek' and 'Egyptian,' as it turns out, might not be as mutually exclusive as 'black' and 'white,' especially in the case of Egypt's last queen.

While the Ptolemaic dynasty strongly identified as Greek in many public settings, as the rulers of Egypt they moved between Greek and Egyptian identifications with a kind of relay that should be familiar to students of later European dynastic history, which features many kings and queens ruling outside their country of origin. The Ptolemies, in fact, continued to support the construction of Egyptian temples,[42] and recent underwater excavations off the coast of Alexandria have demonstrated that they exhibited traditional Egyptian art throughout their capital city.[43] The modern decipherment of ancient Egyptian hieroglyphics can actually be traced to this Ptolemaic 'bilingualism', since the famous Rosetta stone – discovered in 1799 – dates to the Ptolemaic period. In 196 BCE, the stone was inscribed to record the achievements of Ptolemy V, and its repetition of the same text in a number of ancient languages, including Greek, helped modern scholars unlock the meaning of individual hieroglyphs.[44] Cleopatra, moreover, seems to have been especially devoted to the pursuit of a hybrid performance of both Greek and Egyptian practices. She was a prominent worshipper of the Egyptian goddess Isis, and was also credited with being the first in her family to speak the Egyptian language.[45] With presumably little cognitive dissonance to herself or others, then, Cleopatra could appear on coinage and perhaps portrait busts in the clothing and hairstyle of a typical Greek woman,[46] while portraying herself with all the traditional regalia of an Egyptian pharaoh on the side of the temple of Hathor at Dendera.[47]

Such a fluid public image has been essential to Cleopatra's afterlife and its many distortions. Llewellyn-Jones suggests that in representing Cleopatra 'Hollywood does not know what to make of a hybrid culture'[48] and until recently other modern outlets proved little better. The television series *Rome*, a lavish co-production of Home Box Office (HBO) and the British Broadcasting Corporation (BBC) first broadcast in 2005, however, chose to present a more racially indeterminate Cleopatra, one whose short haircut and thin frame aggressively defied audience expectations. Its representation of the Egyptian setting likewise eschewed standard Hollywood conventions by creating a markedly hybrid vision of the Ptolemaic royal court, 'resulting in a style so bizarre that it appears alien and grotesque even to the Romans, and certainly to the viewing audience.'[49] Defining well the disorientation of *Rome*'s visual design, Gregory Daugherty's treatment of the Roman gaze within the programme as parallel to that of the viewer external to the programme is not coincidental, for it is from the Romans that we inherit a vision of Cleopatra as 'essentially' Egyptian and so fundamentally different and exotic. Indeed, Roman accounts of Cleopatra allow us to witness the process of 'racial formation' in action, since the Romans promoted Cleopatra's alleged 'Egyptianness' in response to very specific historical circumstances.

Prior to Caesar's liaison with Cleopatra, the Romans had long been aware of the Ptolemies; as the Romans were conquering the Greek kingdoms in the former territories of Alexander the Great, Ptolemaic Egypt had remained the last holdout – although, as Caesar's presence suggests, the Romans were exerting ever-increasing influence behind the scenes. Throughout their dealings with Egypt, the Romans clearly considered the Ptolemaic royal family either Greek, a perception not without negative connotations for the Romans, or Macedonian, a more positive label given its continuing associations with Alexander the Great. In 46 BCE, Cleopatra herself came to Rome as Caesar's mistress. Her arrival in the city is generally portrayed in opulent terms in modern cinema. As Wyke argues of DeMille's staging, such excess seems to mark contemporary unease about urbanization and the heightened public presence of both 'foreigners' (immigrants) and women in American cities. Part of the pleasure was thus the audience's awareness that Cleopatra's grandiose display of power and wealth was only transitory: she would soon be returned to Egypt (where she belonged), and punished there by Rome for this transgression and many others.[50]

Yet ancient sources record much less fanfare and anxiety surrounding Cleopatra's presence in the eternal city. We know only that she settled into Caesar's estate in Trastevere, presumably accompanied by the young child she claimed as Caesar's son. Cleopatra either remained there continuously for over a year or left the city, only to return in time for Caesar's assassination in 44 BCE, when it became prudent to leave Rome permanently.[51] In the rare mentions of Cleopatra during her actual stay, Roman sources treat her fairly mildly. She draws ire for an unnamed insult from the Roman statesman Cicero (106–43 BCE), for example, but while he expresses blunt hatred of her in one of his letters, he calls her only the queen ('*regina*'), avoiding any other qualifier, racial or otherwise.[52] Accusations that Cleopatra was already dreaming the conquest of Rome during her time there would only later be inserted into historical memory as part of the widespread attacks against her. In a poem written after her defeat, the Roman poet Propertius (born between 54 and 47 BCE) thus memorably claims that Cleopatra had demanded Rome from Antony as a wedding present, then imagines her stretching her 'mosquito nets' on the Capitoline Hill and sitting in judgment among the city's ancient statues.[53]

It was Cleopatra's involvement in the lengthy confrontations between Mark Antony and Octavian (Caesar's great-nephew and adopted heir) following Caesar's assassination and the final breakdown of the two men's fragile alliance, that led pro-Octavian sources to portray Cleopatra as an aberration and manifold threat to Roman order, a strategy that would increasingly draw on racial imagery for its impact. Access to Egypt's resources was clearly central to Antony's alliance with Cleopatra, but it was the sexual affair between the two and their – supposedly – related appetites that served to epitomize their dangerous bond in Roman propaganda. Attributing to Cleopatra an excessive hunger that was both material and sexual, Octavian relentlessly framed her as the Roman enemy *par excellence*, a device that was designed, in more pragmatic terms, to allow him to treat what was essentially a civil war with Antony as a foreign war against the overreaching Egyptian queen. Significantly, the actual declaration of war in 32 BCE was directed only at Cleopatra.[54]

This newfound insistence on Cleopatra's 'Egyptianness' was central to Roman demonization of her. Egypt was now no longer merely the site of Cleopatra's political authority – one possible meaning of 'Egyptian queen' – but, drawing on longstanding stereotypes about Egypt and Egyptians, Egypt became the perfect expression of her debauched essence. The increasing use of Egypt as a racial identifier, moreover, served only to reinforce her sexual difference; as one Roman writer succinctly phrased it: when Cleopatra fled from Actium, site of the decisive battle with Octavian, she did so 'true to her nature as a woman and an Egyptian'.[55] As they sought in increasingly hostile terms to categorize Cleopatra as racially 'other', Roman authors markedly never relied on the colour of her skin to feed animosity and prejudice against her. There is little reference to her actual physical appearance in contemporary sources, and when her presumed attractions are explained by the later writer Plutarch (born before 50 CE), he declares that her beauty was not exceptional, but rather her stimulating conversation, her behaviour and presence, and her facility speaking an array of languages were the source of her tremendous attraction.[56]

The relative silence surrounding Cleopatra's body – remarkable from a modern perspective that has made physical beauty her defining feature – was no longer possible after her death. Having defeated the lovers decisively at Actium, Octavian pursued them to Egypt, where they evaded final capture in 30 BCE by taking their own lives; Cleopatra's suicide, by some accounts, dramatically involving asps. His living prey eluding him, Octavian emphatically paraded an effigy of Cleopatra in his triumph back at Rome, initiating a voyeuristic tradition by which Cleopatra's body would signify both the allure of the exotic 'other' and its inevitable defeat and containment.[57] From this point on, Octavian (who was awarded the title Augustus in 27 BCE by which he is more commonly known) would herald Egypt as the cornerstone of his rise to power, and both Egypt and Cleopatra herself, in allusions subtle and not so subtle, would reverberate throughout Augustan state art and architecture. Roman sources attest, for example, that Augustus adorned a statue of Venus in the newly-dedicated Pantheon with earrings made out of one of Cleopatra's enormous pearls in 25 BCE.[58]

Even more, Augustus would use one of the ancient obelisks he had taken from Egypt as the pointer or gnomon for an enormous sundial he erected in 10 BCE, adding to it an inscription reminding the Roman audience of Egypt's conquest.[59] Such public displays fanned a chronic desire for the appropriation of Egypt that would recur throughout all levels of Roman society. As James Stevens Curl notes, such gestures were not restricted to the pronouncement of state power nor even limited to the consumption of 'real' or 'authentic' objects from Egypt: 'Egyptianising rather than genuine Egyptian works occur in great numbers in Italy, pointing to the growing importance of the Egyptian cults and to the Egyptomania among fashionable Romans for a suitably exotic décor in private houses.'[60] Not content to possess Egypt as a province, the Romans, thus, fashioned their own 'Egyptianising' forms and practices – including popular worship of the goddess Isis – through which they could define their status as Romans, as well as articulate a range of public and private aspirations. Later, the Roman emperor Hadrian (117–138 CE) would famously employ Egyptianising sculptural styles when portraying his dead lover Antinous, who had tragically drowned in the Nile. Over the next centuries, 'Egyptianising' fads would continue to resurface in western culture – from Mozart's *Magic Flute* (*Die Zauberflöte*) to, more recently, the Bangles' 1986 hit song encouraging listeners to 'walk like an Egyptian'.[61]

In his influential work *Orientalism,* Edward Said outlines the distinct set of discursive practices historically used by the west to define the east, describing 'Orientalism' as 'a way of coming to terms with the Orient that is based on the Orient's special place in European Western experience.' Said expands further on the meaning of this particular site of contact:

> The Orient is not only adjacent to Europe; it is also the place of Europe's greatest and richest and oldest colonies, the source of its civilizations and languages, its cultural contestant, and one of its deepest and most recurring images of the Other. In addition, the Orient has helped to define Europe (or the West) as its contrasting image, idea, personality, experience. Yet none of this Orient is merely imaginative. The Orient is an integral part of European *material* civilization and culture.[62]

Egypt provided a major conduit for Greek and Roman fantasy and self-definition, but Said's emphasis on the material dimensions of Orientalism is also crucial, for the Romans profited enormously from the Egyptian grain supply even as they sought to entrap Egypt within a restrictive vocabulary that repudiated such dependency. In a speech to the Roman emperor Trajan (98–117 CE), Pliny the Younger (c. 61–112 CE) openly cautions the Egyptians, a 'vain and haughty people', not to consider their grain a necessity for Rome, but rather Egypt's rightful tribute to its rulers; 'we do not need Egypt', Pliny succinctly avows 'rather Egypt needs us'.[63] At other times, Egypt's 'innate' exoticism would be paired with its ostensible 'timelessness', a strategy that firmly relegated Egypt's relevance to the distant past. Such discursive treatment shaped European contact with Egypt for centuries, perpetuating a practice of looking on Egypt as a historical relic rather than modern state, a dynamic reinforced by its lengthy colonial status.

Focusing on the role of the visual in nineteenth-century western encounters with Egypt, Timothy Mitchell contends that there was an active disconnect between non-European visitors to Europe and the public exhibits (often demeaning) of 'otherness' they found there, reductive and exotic displays like those of the Paris World Exhibition of 1889 that, as Mitchell phrases it, emerged from the 'particularly European concern with rendering things up to be viewed'.[64] Similarly calling attention to the priority of the visual in Howard Carter's dramatic discovery of the tomb of Tutankhamen in 1922 – when asked if he could see anything as the tomb was first breached, Carter recorded that he had breathlessly responded only 'yes, wonderful things' – Elliott Colla argues that Carter's discovery 'pushed the largely scholarly interest in the Pharaonic past and its artefacts into the forefront of the mainstream political and expressive cultures of modern Egypt' by 'yield(ing) tangible objects and indelible images of what an Egyptian sovereign *might look like*'(my emphasis).[65] Needless to say, while King Tut and his tomb shaped perceptions of the past within Egypt itself, the boy king eventually made his way to the exhibit cases of the west, reaffirming both stock images of Egypt's past and the extreme pleasures to be experienced by looking upon it – and its ancient inhabitants. With such an eagerness for gazing upon Egypt and Egyptians building over thousands of years, a gaze magnified and refracted by centuries of colonialism and tourism (two different, albeit mutually reinforcing, ways of seeing and consuming),[66] is it any wonder that our fascination with the sight of Egyptians, and Cleopatra herself, is so acute – and, at the same time, so over-determined, given our simultaneous reliance on visual criteria in assigning race?

In the work that follows I want to provide a suitable backdrop against which to better examine racial formations among the Greeks and Romans. While I will leave Cleopatra's own racial identity open (in seeking firm conclusions, we would need to acknowledge first and foremost that the vast majority of surviving 'evidence' comes from her enemies), I want to underline two points we can take from her example. First, while negative values are often attached to Cleopatra's prospective identification as 'Egyptian' (i.e. certain historians treat it as an 'insult' to consider Cleopatra Egyptian when she was 'really' Greek), that does not mean that the Romans invented her status as Egyptian out of whole cloth. Given what we know of her own performances, Cleopatra, it seems to me, would be far more open to the racial label 'Egyptian' than many modern scholars admit. But that does not mean she would simultaneously refuse the label 'Greek' or would even see the terms as mutually exclusive. Second, and more significantly, Cleopatra's case invites awareness of a tension between essence (equated here with her appearance) and performance, one that will recur throughout this study. Why should we assume that Cleopatra's physical form – what we might find on the surface of her body – defined her racially, as we so desperately want it to today? Could it be rather the actions she undertakes, and not least her variant cultural performances, that defined her racially in her own context, as they also defined her beauty, i.e. that she herself actively created and pre-formed her own racial identity apart from the gaze of others?

Shifting from the external observer to the racial subject him or herself allows us to acknowledge a distinction that has been important in critical theory – namely the difference between a racial *category*, i.e. a racial group whose members are assigned from the outside, and a racial *identification*, i.e. a racial label actively claimed or asserted by the subject or group itself. Greater attention has traditionally been paid to the historic impact of racial categories (not least because the production of racial categories, especially when bolstered by state power, has had such catastrophic consequences), but the concept of racial identification allows us to consider the complementary possibility of individual agency: the act of 'taking on' race, of asserting one's own racial identity from the inside out, as it were. Both processes contribute to racial formation, even when, or perhaps because, they are frequently in tension with one another. What happens, for example, when subjects identify racially in ways that go against external perceptions or even racial laws? Such conflicts might range from the assignment of racial labels – whether a person considered 'black' or 'white' by others would concur with that designation – to disagreement over the meaning of labels or categories – whether 'white' or 'black' might mean something else to members of the group itself. In the latter case, we can witness attempts not to repudiate a modern racial label, but rather to reclaim and reinterpret it via slogans like 'black is beautiful'.

Finally, even our persistent fascination with Cleopatra and the ancient Egyptians – a fascination that situates Egyptians as the predominant racial 'other' of the Greeks and Romans – reveals the considerable distortions of our modern lens. For it was actually the ancient Persians associated with modern Iran who first dominated the ancient Greek racial imaginary, and it is from the series of Greek and Persian wars that the potent notion of the 'barbarian' would emerge. Given recent world events, western audiences have started to probe the relationship between the Greeks and cultures to the east for possible ancient parallels.[67] On March 18, 2003, touting his presence at Troy (located in modern Turkey), the *New York Times* columnist Nicholas Kristof, for example, drew a striking corollary between the impending invasion of Iraq and the ancient Trojan War, proposing that 'on the eve of a new war' 'the remarkably preserved citadel of Troy is an intriguing spot to seek lessons.' Later Kristof concluded: 'We Americans are the Greeks of our day, and as we now go to war, we should appreciate not only the beauty of the tale, but also the warnings within it.'[68]

The battle between the Greeks and Persians was itself recently portrayed in the blockbuster film *300* (2007), which recounted the legendary stand of the three hundred Spartan warriors who briefly held off a massive Persian invasion of Greece, despite being vastly outnumbered. *300*, based on Frank Miller's graphic novel, used a dramatic visual style to portray the Persians as racially different from the Spartans, portraying many of the Persian forces as physically monstrous, even sub-human. While Leonidas, the bearded Spartan king, was given that must-have sign of twenty-first century masculinity, a seriously well-defined set of abdominal muscles, the towering Persian king Xerxes, in contrast, was shown as both decadent and sexually ambiguous with a nearly naked body that was simultaneously stripped of hair and draped in jewellery. Such devices did little to reflect actual ancient Greek representations of Persians, although they might be said to 'translate' Greek ideology in its most extreme form, including the Greek penchant for portraying the Persians as effeminate and excessively obedient to authority. Not surprisingly given the timing of its release, *300* was received less positively in many global markets, sparking considerable controversy about its underlying 'message' and even inciting riots in Iran.[69]

Such representations of, as well as disputes over, the meaning of classical antiquity today illustrate a recurring theme of this study – namely, the ways our racial imagination about the past has been conditioned by our own methods for seeing and experiencing the world, methods that have themselves been crafted by the exigencies of our own personal and collective histories, not to mention the conventions of our own popular culture. In order to apprehend race on its own terms in classical antiquity, it will be necessary, then, to leave behind our preconceptions and modern racial frameworks, even though we may glimpse the origins of some of our own racial systems in the making. Before embarking further, though, I want to define more explicitly my method in the chapters that follow.

Sight unseen

To reiterate: race in no way pivots around 'whiteness' and 'blackness' in antiquity, despite the centrality of those categories to racial thought today. While such a statement captures well the current consensus among classical historians, it nonetheless requires some clarification. As the range of ancient vocabulary for skin colour pigmentation suggests, the Greeks and Romans were in no way 'colour-blind' – they patently perceived differences in skin colour, and not only demarcated those differences in language, but also portrayed them in a wide array of visual arts, as we shall see. Nor was the perception and representation of black skin colour itself always value-neutral; Snowden cites an ancient superstition that treated the sight of a black person as an omen of bad luck.[70] Still, the Greeks and Romans did not promote any fundamental racial opposition between 'whiteness' and 'blackness'. Indeed, they apparently did not consider themselves 'white.' Thus, in the *Satyricon*, a comic novel by the Roman writer Petronius (first century CE) when two characters contemplate disguising themselves, they note that they could darken themselves to appear Ethiopian or lighten themselves to look like Gauls.[71] So the question is not so much whether the Greeks and Romans at times noticed and reacted to physical features different from their own nor even whether skin colour held particular connotations in and of itself, but whether skin colour provided the foundation for an entire racial system of thought, and there is little evidence for that in antiquity. This does not mean that ancient Greek and Roman writers did not seek to understand the cause of skin colour variation, but the attempt to identify a source of somatic difference or even a propensity for finding such difference peculiar is not the same as imbuing that difference with wide-ranging consequences, including the unequal distribution of social and political power.

Skin colour therefore does not stand at the centre of this study – although, given the occasional reference to skin colour in ancient literature and art, I will return at various points to consider what racial meaning it might have held. My aim instead is to uncover the assorted frameworks that organized and classified human diversity more fundamentally in antiquity. In doing so, I utilize Omi and Winant's concept of 'racial formation', terminology that situates race as a series of strategies or processes by which fundamental differences are asserted in light of specific historical dynamics. In that sense, I nowhere attempt to state categorically that race meant 'x' (i.e. only one thing) in antiquity, but try to take into account when it held certain meanings, how, and why. This approach means that it will be possible to track the emergence of racial formations in the plural, and not simply propose a standard meaning of race that remained constant across centuries and despite significant historical shifts.

In antiquity, as in later centuries, increasing knowledge of the world and its various populations remained fundamental to the emergence of new racial formations. My discussion therefore calls particular attention to the ways in which the Greeks and Romans experienced the world, and what kinds of racial formations such knowledge – whether accurate or not – produced. Crucial to such a method is the acknowledgement that one's source of knowledge about the world and its inhabitants, whether derived at a distance from books (or today, television and movies) or at closer range through economic exchange or warfare, contributes greatly to both the form and intensity of racial thought. In this way, the manner and tenor of contact between groups plays a vital role in shaping racial formations; the Persian Wars ultimately generated very different formations from those developed during Roman imperial expansion, for the Persian Wars encouraged the Greeks to posit a fundamental distinction between 'Greek' and 'barbarian', while the building of the Roman empire demanded that the Romans account for their relationship to a wider range of populations, leading them to conceive of racial difference along a scale rather than through a strict binary. Even more, although the ancient Germans were as racially different as the Ethiopians from the Roman point of view, given the more torturous history of Roman contact with the Germans, representations of German difference were invariably more loaded for a Roman audience, that is, any categorical 'explanation' of German character necessarily raised concerns about how threatening that made them. Ethiopians, on the other hand, were generally less consequential in political terms and so could remain the object of more removed curiosity or fantasy. (By making this distinction, I do not mean to suggest that fantasy does not have real dangers for those defined by it, only to acknowledge a significant difference in the operation of various racial formations.)

Racial formation by definition situates two or more groups in relation to one another: it does not simply allow a dominant group to define an 'other' or 'others' without regard to itself. Too often today, race is treated as pertaining to – or the burden of – racial 'minority' groups alone. Thus, American Presidential candidate Barack Obama felt it necessary to explain his views of race to the American electorate in a well-publicized speech on March 18, 2008. Such a speech was presumably obligatory because Obama was black (although Obama's position at times defies easy categorization in the public sphere given that he has a white mother from Kansas and a black father from Kenya). Yet there was no corresponding pressure on the opposing candidate, John McCain, to explain his opinions about race because he was white, a presumption that would follow logically but which seems nonsensical in the context of current attitudes about race. Despite the continuing privileges that allow 'whiteness' to assume the guise of neutrality, to stand as a kind of default 'race-lessness,' however, it is only the racial partnership of 'black' *and* 'white' that has historically animated American racial formations. Much like current work in gender studies that treats masculinity and femininity as mutually constitutive (no longer demanding that women alone bear the weight of sexual difference), historians of race have therefore increasingly traced the complementary emergence and meanings of 'whiteness' in modern life.[72] I follow that same method here by not merely examining how the Greeks and Romans defined others, but also how racial structures of thought enabled them to define themselves. It is, after all, no accident that the contours of 'Greekness' were articulated against the spectre of the 'barbarian.' Collective identification as 'Greek' or 'Roman' was, in short, neither innate or value-neutral – despite our modern tendency to take these groups for granted – and the evolution of these categories remains central to any attempt to document ancient racial formations.

In establishing a putative difference between groups, the production of racial formations inevitably requires drawing a boundary delineating those inside a racial group from those outside it. Yet, the precise basis of such a line (i.e. that which actually distinguishes groups), as well as its continuing regulation, often produces considerable unease. The 'one-drop' rule in American law comprises a desperate attempt to reinforce racial boundaries by treating one drop of blood as the definitive line between 'black' and 'white', a measure taken in direct response to growing social anxiety created by phenomena like 'passing' (i.e. people who were able, based on their light-skinned appearance, to 'pass' as white despite having at least one black ancestor).[73] In the ancient world, there were seemingly many opportunities for individuals to 'pass' or to cross racial boundaries, opportunities facilitated by the changing ways in which the source of racial difference itself was conceptualized. There is, for example, a discernible shift in antiquity from the designation of geographic origin or blood descent as the basis of racial identity to an emphasis on cultural practice instead – that is, a shift from what people ostensibly 'are' to what they 'do'. At the same time, it is critical not to romanticize too fully these openings since racial categories and their attendant social hierarchies remained firmly in place, and the capacity for certain individuals to cross racial categories often seems to have produced complementary anxieties about 'unauthorized' crossings by others. This dichotomy suggests that corresponding markers of privilege (of, say, gender or class) worked alongside ancient racial formations, granting some individuals a freedom of movement across boundaries that was unavailable to others, a phenomenon still evident in modern discourses that suggest certain celebrities or sports figures – even Obama himself – can somehow 'transcend' their blackness.

It remains, finally, to spell out why I adhere to the terminology of race in this work given the overwhelming preference among classical historians today for 'ethnicity' or, even more recently, 'cultural identity'.[74] The current trend among classicists for 'ethnicity' follows not only major shifts in the field, but also broader historical developments, for while race had provided the dominant terminology for collective identity early in the twentieth century, it was vigorously challenged by the middle of that century by the emergence of ethnicity. Following on the heels of the traumatic experience of World War II and the Holocaust, Egal Feldman summed up the mood:

> As an undergraduate . . . I recall being cautioned by my professors to avoid using the word 'race' unless I knew precisely what I meant by that term. The implication was that I could employ the term 'ethnic'

27

even if I did not know the exact meaning. The reason was obvious: in the imagination of that age, genocide was employed against a 'race', not against an 'ethnic' group.[75]

The rise of ethnicity, as Feldman's experience suggests, sought to undermine the destructive power of race, in part by calling attention to the intervention of individuals in the formation of identity. Rather than an identity fixed in time and place or one imposed externally by others, ethnicity was instead understood to be premised on the internal claims of particular groups or individuals. These claims, moreover, could reference the past by positing a common lineage or place of origin or could be performed in the present by the use of shared cultural practices like language and religion. In this model, Irish people could consciously claim their Irish ethnicity by referencing their original county in Ireland or their descent from Irish ancestors and/or performing certain cultural acts, such as attending particular churches or speaking Gaelic. In all, the popularity of ethnicity was predicated on the widespread belief that it derived from the active agency of groups and individuals, a source completely different from that of race, which was still perceived as a passive product of human anatomy.[76]

In recent decades, as we have seen, the 'science' of race, including its pretence to having an objective basis in human biology, has been aggressively challenged. Scientific research disproving the biological foundation of race has now been widely disseminated, appearing not only in scientific journals but also popular magazines like *Discover*, the latter devoting an entire issue to critique of the flawed science of race in 1994.[77] Although ancient historians have lagged somewhat behind, most scholars in other fields now recognize that despite its previous status as a science or pseudo-science, race – like ethnicity – remains emphatically a product of social construction. It is therefore no longer possible to distinguish race as 'biological' from ethnicity as 'social', one based in 'objective' science, the other in 'subjective' belief, rather the two terms increasingly seem to converge. In the words of one scholar, they 'play hide-and-seek with each other.'[78]

In the case of classics, the continuing preference for 'ethnicity' can also be attributed to two additional dynamics. First, many classical historians utilize 'ethnicity' in recognition of the ancient use of the term *'ethnos'* as an alternative to the *'polis'* in early Greek social and civic organization, a distinction not without its own attendant set of value judgments among modern historians.[79] Beyond this distinction, many classicists adhere to ethnicity because of its clear linguistic roots in ancient Greek, unlike the English word 'race' which is of more recent, albeit disputed, origin.[80] 'Ethnicity' thus seems on the surface to offer greater historical accuracy – to be, unlike race, a term that was used by the Greeks themselves. Closer examination of the ancient term *ethnos*, however, suggests that its range of possible meanings was much broader than the modern one. Jeremy McInerney proposes that *ethnos* in antiquity comprised 'a conveniently loose label', one he equates with the 'vague English term "people".[81] Jonathan Hall expands that: ' . . . even the most cursory survey of ancient sources is sufficient to demonstrate that *ethnos* could embrace a wider variety of meanings than simply "ethnic group." While it certainly can describe groups of people, its use does not appear to be strictly circumscribed in any defined sociological sense.'[82] In some contexts, the Greek *ethnos* could even be used to denote a group linked solely by profession or occupation[83] – a meaning that would be very difficult to find today: would we ever now refer to accountants or teachers as an 'ethnic group'?

Conversely, ancient Greek has a word that seems at first glance to correlate closely with race: *genos*. Linguistically related to 'birth', *genos* denotes a relationship derived from descent; as C.P. Jones explains: 'the essential idea is of a group into which one enters at birth, what one *becomes* (*sic*) . . . by the fact of birth.'[84] This primary meaning makes it possible for *genos* to signify something as small as a family unit and as large as a taxonomic category, i.e. 'genus' as opposed to 'species' (*eidos*). While its connections to birth suggest a strong reliance on biology, *genos* does not, like the modern idea of race, find expression in any specific physical traits. It does mirror the modern form of race, however, in concealing beneath its ostensibly 'natural' source an adamant social foundation, for *genos* was not attained through birth or biology alone in antiquity, but also depended on *claims* of descent, whether real or fictive. Claims of bloodline thus held substantial discursive power, and blood relations – especially claims of paternity – are evoked throughout early Greek literature as a means of locating an individual's place in the world (this, in part, is what makes Oedipus' legendary ignorance of his father's identity such an acute crisis). Even more, Greek writers often created elaborately constructed genealogies tracing the roots of certain aristocratic families all the way back to prominent figures in Greek myth[85] – a practice whose relation to social power is not unlike modern American families claiming descent from people like Thomas Jefferson or Abraham Lincoln.

Despite any surface similarities, in the end, it is difficult to translate terms like *genos* and *ethnos* smoothly into modern languages without weighing the shifting meaning of such terminology in both historical contexts. Indeed, just as 'race' and 'ethnicity' overlap in modern usage, Catherine Morgan ironically highlights the ways *'genos'* and *'ethnos'* potentially elide in ancient thought when she advocates that ' . . . one should not confuse the genos, by definition constituted with regard to real or fictive shared descent, with the ethnos, which need not stress descent but may do so'.[86] Looking specifically at the meaning of the two terms in the work of the Greek historian Herodotus (deceased c. 420 BCE), C.P. Jones argues that for Herodotus an *ethnos* 'is . . . viewed as a geographical, political or cultural entity, often in relation to the time of the narrative context', while *genos* denotes 'a group viewed as united by birth, and often in relation to some point previous to the narrative time'.[87] This difference in emphasis, including whether a collective identity is grounded in the past or present, Jones argues, helps explain why Herodotus can label a single group – the Scythians – as both an *ethnos* and *genos* at different points in his work.[88] As such close reading indicates, the employment of these terms can therefore reflect a distinction or emphasis that not only changes over time, but also according to the views of individual authors or even the needs of specific parts of a single text.

By adopting 'race' and 'racial formation' as the terminology for this study, then, I do not mean to signal adherence to any specific ancient vocabulary:

I am not restricting myself solely to those dynamics labelled in ancient texts by the Greek *genos* or by complementary Latin terminology like *gens*. Nor by employing the language of race do I mean to insinuate that the collective identities under discussion are somehow 'natural' or essential; even less do I want to endorse racist assumptions about any innate hierarchy of races. Rather, I use race and racial formation as a way of acknowledging a particular set of processes that have traditionally been associated with race, including those rooted in essentialist thought (i.e. the belief that an identity is inherited and unchanging) and linked specifically to the body or the natural environment. At times, my employment of racial terminology might suggest an ambiguous line between a racial identity grounded in cultural practice and what might be labelled a 'cultural identity,' but I will briefly explain my discomfort with the term 'cultural identity' later in the discussion.

The terminology of race is also advantageous because it has tended to connote a greater degree of difference than ethnicity in modern usage – at least in American practice, where ethnicity has been used to differentiate within racial categories, to distinguish, for example, between Italian Americans and French Americans, both of whose members are assigned to the larger racial category 'white'. Race thus helps avoid a potential confusion that emerges from ancient historians' practice of using ethnicity both to name identities *among* Greeks (e.g., Athenians versus Spartans) and *between* Greeks and others (e.g., Greeks and Egyptians) – pairs that do not involve the same degree of separation in Greek thought. Still, given that the space between race and ethnicity can itself seem miniscule at times, I admit that my preference here is largely polemical. Like bell hooks and Paul Gilroy, I prefer race to ethnicity 'because it connotes, and refers investigations to, issues of power'.[89] The word race, thus, forces us to confront our all too-frequent idealization of classical antiquity, and to view more critically a variety of Greek and Roman ideologies and practices, violent facets of the ancient world that can seem too sanitized when called something else.[90]

Although not all racial formations lead to racism, we will witness in this study a recurrent link between the designation of a group as fundamentally different – as racially 'other' – and a desire to dominate it.[91] Two important studies have addressed this specific aspect of the ancient world: A.N. Sherwin-White's *Racial Prejudice in Imperial Rome* (1967) and Benjamin Isaac's more recent *The Invention of Racism in Classical Antiquity* (2004).[92] In his opening of the earlier work, Sherwin-White records that '(i)t is commonplace to assert that the ancient world knew nothing of [the] colour bar and racial prejudice'; he then quickly shifts the terminology of his approach (despite the title of his work) by continuing '(i)f there was no racial prejudice, there certainly was some culture prejudice. The question is, how much, how deep, and whether or why it became a problem in the Roman Empire.'[93] Sherwin-White's subsequent chapters skilfully explore many of the dynamics and groups considered in this present study (e.g., Germans, Gauls, Greeks, and Jews), yet his preference for the terminology of 'culture' persists throughout.

Isaac, on the other hand, emphatically places 'racism' at the centre of his analysis, distinguishing it clearly from any focus on race *per se*;[94] Isaac likewise expressly omits any consideration of the actual historical or material practice of racism, noting that his work 'traces the history of discriminatory ideas rather than acts.'[95] Providing an invaluable treatment of both racial theory in antiquity and the specific, often negative views held by the Greeks and Romans in regard to an impressive range of groups, perhaps the most significant contribution of Isaac's work is his thorough parsing of such negative attitudes, carefully distinguishing racism from other forces like ethnic prejudice or xenophobia, a distinction that relies heavily, for Isaac, on whether certain differences were perceived as inherited and unchangeable.[96] Throughout, Isaac traces the later reverberations of certain ancient ideas and, by the end, has convincingly implicated the Greeks and Romans in a larger history of western racism.

This present study, while it clearly relies on earlier research in classical studies, seeks specifically to revive the use of 'race' in the study of Greek and Roman antiquity by tracing its recurrence throughout ancient thought and practice. In pursuing this aim, I have adopted an approach that is as broad as possible in its scope, demonstrating both the influence of race on as wide a range of ancient institutions as possible and its participation in as diverse a set of cultural expressions. In addition, I attempt to highlight throughout the noteworthy intersections of race with other important social structures, such as gender and class. While I endeavour to document the fundamental role of race in the ancient world itself, I ultimately turn to the influence of ancient racial formations on the modern world as well, an influence mediated by the varied receptions and appropriations of classical antiquity. So unceasing has the use and abuse of the ancient world been that, as we shall see, it seems to have become central to the very constitution of modernity, a period that remains bound within its own fractured attempts to reconcile past and present.

The first three chapters explore specific ways in which race pertains to diverse fields of classical studies: ancient racial theory and ethnography in Chapter I, archaeology and social history in Chapter II, and art and literature in Chapter III. This organization allows readers to focus on specific areas that most appeal to them, whether, for example, Roman archaeology or ancient epic. Since I follow what seem to me the most revealing or compelling evidence and arguments in each chapter, it is important to note that the chapters do not always concentrate on the same historical periods – whereas Ptolemaic Egypt provides a compelling site for looking at racial practice, for example, I employ earlier Greek tragedy in looking at racial representations. I have attempted, however, to orient the reader by providing a brief historical overview of all the periods under discussion in Chapter I; throughout, I follow the current convention among historians for using 'BCE' instead of 'BC' and 'CE' instead of 'AD'.

Taken together, all three chapters seek to illustrate the sheer ubiquity of race and the range of ancient settings in which it both assumes and sheds its forms. Moreover, in dividing my chapters this way, I do not mean to insinuate an absolute separation of racial theory, racial practice, and the cultural representations of race – on the contrary, I want to emphasize the significant interface between them. Racial theory clearly fuels many types of social policy and practice. That Greeks received a tax exemption in Greek-ruled Egypt, for example, suggests the presence of an underlying belief that

Greeks were different in meaningful ways from other groups in Egypt, as well as a concomitant belief that this difference should be expressed in economic obligations to the state. But the tax code in Ptolemaic Egypt is not sufficient on its own to explain the portrayal of Greeks or Egyptians in literature from that period, and vice versa. In the fourth and final chapter, I utilize a series of case studies to tackle a residual paradox: namely, the persistent and often impassioned use of Greek and Roman antiquity in defining racial structures in post-classical eras, identifications that cross national boundaries and emerge even as racial formations – and the historical processes with which they collaborate – undergo significant transformations.

This study is plainly only a start; while I hope the design of the work, in particular, will provide a useful foundation for thinking more critically about race's many sites of operation in both ancient and modern eras, I hope even more that it will provoke a range of questions that go far beyond what I am able to attempt here. In that sense, I am more interested in proposing an effective structure for asking the right questions about race than providing all the answers. Ultimately, I hope to persuade every reader to become radical when it comes to race – that is, to provoke in every reader the desire to work tirelessly in grasping this most devastating notion, both past and present, at and by its very roots.

CHAPTER 1

RACIAL THEORY

An identity is questioned only when it is menaced, as when the mighty begin to fall, or when the wretched begin to rise, or when the stranger enters the gates, never, thereafter, to be a stranger.

James Baldwin

Reflecting on the ways collective identity is both formed and transformed by contact with other groups, the American writer James Baldwin presents a helpful starting point for understanding the various types and stages of ancient racial formation, including the ways the Greeks and Romans constructed a sense of self from within and also the ways they refined that sense of self and others when 'menaced' by outsiders. Even more, Baldwin alludes to the relations of power inherent in both the setting of racial boundaries and their crossing, both when energy is devoted by the 'mighty' to keeping others out and, conversely, when the 'stranger' enters the gates and is no longer strange. In this chapter, I want to examine the methods the Greeks and Romans used for explaining themselves and others, including not only the range of theories developed to elucidate human difference, but also the employment of such ideas and frameworks in their descriptions of other cultures, a practice we might call ethnography. Ancient racial theory and ethnography – both important components of racial formation – remain intimately linked to the historical contexts of their production, so I begin first by outlining how and what the Greeks and Romans knew of the world, then turn to some of the evolving meanings they made of it.

A world of difference

By the time of Eratosthenes of Cyrene (c. 285–194 BCE), widely regarded as the father of scientific geography, Greek philosophers had long pondered the earth's dimensions and its natural properties (they were well aware, for example, that the earth was spherical; only in later periods would such knowledge be 'lost' and the earth assumed to be flat).[1] In accounting for the features of the world in human terms, ancient geographers relied heavily on the concept of the *oikumene*, or 'inhabited world', an entity they generally perceived as a single land mass surrounded by water.[2] The *oikumene* was a concept rife with contemporary social and political significance, as were related cartographic conventions. Ancient geographers for example, regularly debated whether to divide the *oikumene* into two or three continents, that is, whether or not Libya (Africa today) should be considered a separate continent alongside Asia and Europe.[3] While the Greeks and Romans recognized that there were populations dwelling outside the *oikumene*, the concept of the *oikumene* (or, as the Romans would call it the *orbis terrarum*[4]) allowed an imaginary boundary to be drawn that divided the part of the world that was known from the more distant parts that were not, treating the more remote regions as a kind of undifferentiated fantasy space. The putative boundary of the *oikumene* was constantly shifting in antiquity as knowledge of the world expanded, and the enduring popularity of myths like the labours of Hercules and the voyage of Odysseus reflects an ancient audience eager to make sense of such expansion as well as the contact it brought with new lands and peoples.[5]

In general terms, we can trace the Greek and subsequent Roman knowledge of, and engagement in, the world by looking first to the north and west; then to the east; and, finally, to the south. To the immediate north, the limits of Greece itself were difficult to define precisely, with territories like Epirus and Macedonia alternately treated as part of Greece or outside its boundaries.[6] Beyond those territories lay Thrace, a nation that stretched to the Black Sea and had steady exchange with Athens, providing both a range of natural resources and a steady supply of slaves. The mythical

Hyperboreans, who enjoyed a lifestyle and closeness to the gods generally beyond mortal reach, were sometimes placed at the northern limit of the world, but more often that space was allocated to the Scythians, a group north of the Black Sea defined mostly by its nomadic lifestyle, pointedly the inverse of civilized life in the Greek city.[7] Greek knowledge of the west, in turn, was closely correlated with the practice of colonization, which began in the eighth century BCE. Although some Greek colonies were established near the Sea of Marmara and along the Black Sea in the east – as well as at Cyrene in North Africa – most Greek colonists went west to southern Italy and Sicily, with a few venturing even further to Massalia (today Marseilles) and limited parts of Spain. Archaeologists and classical historians have investigated these colonies as distinct sites of racial formation,[8] but the scale of such early colonization was much more limited than the modern experience of colonization since Greek colonies were generally linked only to their original Greek 'mother' cities, such as Megara, Miletus or Corinth, not to any larger colonial network or nation.[9]

While these colonies gave individual Greek city-states a toehold in the west, ancient writers considered the Romans' systematic opening up of the western landscape their most significant contribution to ancient geographic knowledge.[10] This undertaking corresponded, not coincidentally, with extensive Roman military campaigns in places like Spain and Gaul. Likewise, for the Romans, the perceptions of people and places to their north would shift in conjunction with their prospective military efforts throughout much of what is today eastern and western Europe, including not only Germany and Britain, but also Illyria (roughly modern Albania) and Dacia (roughly modern Romania).[11] While the Romans also utilized what we call 'colonies', these were likewise not consistent with our modern understanding of the term, but consisted of two distinct types of settlements: early 'Latin' colonies (founded until the 160s BCE), a kind of 'half-way house to Roman citizenship',[12] and, later, communities of veterans spread throughout the Mediterranean, who were given land grants as reward for their military service.

Although the Greeks had continuing contact with various groups to their north and west, they remained much more profoundly oriented towards the east. In fact, the scope of such encounters, including the degree to which Greek culture was itself formed by Near Eastern influence, has long been the subject of ardent debate, a debate we will explore more fully in Chapter IV. By the sixth century, the Greeks had very pressing reasons for looking east, for the powerful Persian empire ruled by the Achaemenid dynasty was quickly gathering steam. In 549 BCE, the Persians had conquered the Medes and soon after they defeated the Lydians, taking possession of the Ionian (i.e. Greek) city-states that had been established along the western coast of Asia Minor (modern Turkey) roughly five hundred years before as part of a series of migrations that involved the Aegean islands as well. When the Persians subsequently conquered Babylon, they had 'established sovereignty over an area stretching from the borders of India to the Hellespont.'[13]

In 499 BCE, the Ionian cities revolted against the Persians, and embroiled an alliance of Greek city-states, led by Athens and Sparta, in a series of conflicts that would forever change the way the Greeks perceived themselves and their position in the world. The Ionian revolt itself was suppressed in 494, and the Persian king Darius, pressing his advantage, then invaded Greece proper; his advance was eventually halted when he suffered a defeat at Marathon in 490 BCE. Ten years later, Darius' son Xerxes embarked on another dramatic invasion, and, following his defeat of the heroic Spartan three hundred at Thermopylae in 480, he was able to conquer much of Greece until he was finally repelled by a Greek naval victory at Salamis near Athens. In later decades, the Greek city-states – brought low by their devastating years of conflict with one another – continued to vie with Persia, although Persia would never again present the same level of threat.

Some one hundred and fifty years later, Alexander the Great invaded Asia, defeating the mighty Persian empire and taking possession of its extensive territories. At his early death, these territories were divided between three Greek dynasties (with the Antigonids receiving Macedonia, the Ptolemies Egypt, and the Seleucids Asia), whose combined influence 'extended from mainland Greece to modern-day Afghanistan and northwest India, north to south it reached from Macedonia and Thrace to Egypt and the Gulf of Arabia'.[14] These Hellenistic kingdoms repeatedly battled with one another until the Romans, having risen to prominence in the Mediterranean, conquered both Greece itself and these Greek kingdoms left in Alexander's wake. With their conquest of the Greek Seleucid dynasty and subsequent campaigns, the Romans were able to annex much of the Near East, although they had perpetual difficulty with the Parthians, the formidable successors to Persia in modern Iran. Parthia, like Germany, remained one of Rome's most stalwart enemies, and, in a clearly traumatic event for the Romans, the Parthians soundly defeated the Roman general Crassus in 53 BCE, leading to persistent calls for a campaign to recapture the lost Roman standards.

The fact that the eastern part of the empire was constructed from former Greek kingdoms would yield important differences between the two halves of the Roman empire. For one, Roman rule in the east generally took advantage of prior Greek institutions, especially Greek cities. So, too, Greek continued to serve as the official language in the eastern empire, although, attesting to the cultural complexity of the Roman east, there is also evidence for the continuing use of Aramaic, Hebrew, Phoenician, Nabataean, Palmyrene, and Syriac.[15] While Roman rule was in many ways greatly facilitated by these prior Greek structures (not to mention the presence of a Greek ruling elite that was often receptive to Roman rule), the Roman relationship to the Greeks themselves was a fraught one, exemplified by the continuing value assigned to, and also the concomitant anxiety generated by, 'Greekness' itself in Roman thought.

Even further east, India served as the putative limit of the *oikumene* and was a site of considerable allure to both the Greeks and Romans. Alexander the Great's campaigns had done much to foster Greek fascination with India, although his own progress was notoriously halted by the refusal of his troops to cross the Hyphasis in 326 BCE. Accounts of India flourished following Alexander's campaigns, greatly influenced by two earlier texts, both connected to Persian patronage: Scylax, who was presumably dispatched there by the Persian king Darius in the early fifth century and

Ctesias of Cnidus, who served as a physician in the Persian royal court nearly a century later.[16] Ctestias' *Indika* testifies to what would become a lasting focus on India's alleged 'marvels', recording 'a sense of an enormously complex landscape crowded with anomalies at every turn. This India revealed a nature which seemed to exfoliate in a limitless series of new and unexpected forms, an exuberant and creative force which defied all Greek expectations of biological normality.'[17] During the Hellenistic period, trade routes connected India to the Greek world,[18] and markets eager for India's spices and luxury goods proliferated during the Roman period as well.[19] That India helped structure imperial aspirations post-Alexander is strongly suggested by Augustus' proud declaration that embassies from India had come to Rome for the first time under his reign.[20] Much less remarked upon in ancient sources is China's presumed awareness of the Roman empire, and vice versa.[21]

Towards the south, Africa presented continuing challenges for both the Greeks and Romans. V.Y. Mudimbe has outlined the narrative traditions by which Africa has been defined in western discourse, beginning with 'the "special place" that *agrioi* (savages), *barbaroi* (barbarians), and *oiorpata* (women killers of men) occupy' in the Greek and Roman conceptual map of the continent.[22] Noting that in Pomponius Mela' s *Chorographia* (c. 37–41 CE) Africa 'is a land full of empty spaces, impenetrable areas, misleading landscapes and deadzones', Rhiannon Evans asserts succinctly: 'In the geographical imagination, Africa is an area of confusion and disorientation for Rome'.[23] Testifying to just such *aporia* (an *aporia* that seems to anticipate more modern labelling of Africa as the 'dark continent'[24]), there was a persistent confusion of terminology applied to Africa in antiquity. While the Greeks called the entire continent 'Libya', that name could also refer in a more restricted way to the northern part of Africa, west of Egypt. The Romans, in turn, were the first to use 'Africa' of the continent, but that was likewise the name of their province on the coast. As with India, Africa's seeming spatial remoteness was often associated with unpredictability and perpetual novelty; a common proverb associated Libya with the incessant production of new things.[25] In comparing ancient attitudes towards Africa and India, however, James S. Romm suggests that Greek perceptions of Africa were in many ways the inverse of those attached to India: where India seemed boundless (it had, after all, defied Alexander's attempts to reach its limits), Africa had been circumnavigated around 600 BCE according to Herodotus.[26] Romm expands: ' . . . the Greeks tended to look on their penetration of the Asiatic frontier as a daring assault on the terrors of distant space . . . Explorations of Africa, by contrast, were most often targeted as a mystery of interior rather than exterior space'.[27]

Greek knowledge of Africa was initially connected to sea-faring, as Greek travel and transport more generally. Euthymenes, from the Greek colony of Massilia allegedly reached Senegal or The Gambia sailing along the western coast of Africa around 550–525 BCE.[28] So, too, a popular Greek translation of the voyage of Hanno, a fifth-century Carthaginian sailor, survived well into the Roman period, detailing an alleged expedition – perhaps as far as Sierra Leone – that featured an encounter with a fierce band of 'hairy men' he calls 'gorillas'.[29] Further inland, Alexander the Great evidently sent an expedition to find the source of the Nile, a perennial obsession for the Greeks,[30] and the Greek Ptolemies became involved in both numerous attempts to found trade routes along the Red Sea and elephant hunts in Somaliland.[31] Substantial Greek and Roman presence in Africa was nonetheless mainly confined to a band along the northern coast from Egypt to the Maghreb, territory that, unlike the Sahara to its immediate south, offered a more regular water supply.

The Greek colony Cyrene, in modern Libya, had been founded in the seventh century,[32] although the Phoenicians, a powerful ancient sea empire, had arrived in Africa some time before. The most important Phoenician colony was at Carthage, near modern Tunis, which became the centre of Phoenician power after the fall of Tyre, located in what is today Lebanon, in 574 BCE. Having weathered a series of conflicts with Greeks in the west and two previous wars with the Romans – the First and Second Punic Wars, which featured, among other notable events, Hannibal's crossing of the Alps with elephants in 218 BCE – Carthage was brutally destroyed by the Romans in 146 BCE. From 112 –106 BCE, the Romans waged war against Jugurtha of Numidia,[33] and, in the years following, North Africa and its various strongholds were drawn into the Roman civil wars, culminating in Caesar's victory at Thapsus in 46 BCE and Cato the Younger's dramatic suicide at Utica shortly after. The Romans would later gain control of Mauretania, although they faced a series of obstacles, including the outbreak of a revolt under Tacfarinas in 17 CE. Further east, sources suggest that Lucius Cornelius Balbus made incursions into the Sahara when fighting the Garamantes in 19 BCE.[34]

Despite these notable events to the west, there was nowhere in modern-day Africa more consequential to both the Greeks and Romans than Egypt, although it is imperative to note that the Greeks and Romans did not typically associate Egypt with the rest of Africa. The Greeks had been in contact with Egypt since the Bronze Age (c. 3000–1150 BCE), and its influence on the development of Greek culture is a topic of great controversy, a controversy to which we will return in Chapter IV. A Greek trade city, Naucratis, had been established in the Nile delta in the seventh century BCE, probably during the reign of Psammetichus I, and, in the early sixth century, Greek mercenaries testified to their presence by leaving graffiti at Abu Simbel (many centuries later, under the Romans, a series of graffiti would likewise be written on the leg of one of the colossal statues of Memnon[35]). In 525 BCE, the Persians added Egypt to their empire and they held it until they were forced out by a revolt in 404 BCE; they later regained it in 343 BCE only to yield it to Alexander the Great in 332. After the defeat of Antony and Cleopatra in 31 BCE, Egypt became a formal Roman possession.

Further south of Egypt, in the upper Nile Valley, stood the civilization of Kush as it was called by the Egyptians, although the region was also referred to as Nubia in antiquity, and its people as Nubians; it would eventually become known as Ethiopia to the Greeks and Romans, who were most familiar with the last Kushite capital Meroë, which had emerged by around 250 BCE.[36] While the Ptolemies in Egypt had experienced occasional conflict with Meroë – Plutarch notes that Cleopatra could speak to Ethiopians without the aid of a translator[37] – such outbreaks became more pronounced in the Roman period. In 29 BCE, the first Roman governor of Egypt, Cornelius Gallus, settled an Ethiopian revolt in the Thebaid. A few years later, when the Romans were distracted by Aelius Gallus' ill-fated campaign in Arabia, the Ethiopians once more attacked, leading the Romans to respond with two further invasions of their territory. The terms of the Romans' eventual settlement with the Ethiopian queen Candace, however, have been much disputed.[38] Roman sources suggest that the emperor Nero later sent an expedition that reached the Sudd in 61–63 CE, 'a point . . . not to be reached again by Europeans until 1839–40'.[39] This southern frontier continued to present a strategic concern for the Romans throughout the rest of the imperial period, and, significantly, Greek and Roman ideas would penetrate Africa even further than they themselves had. Maynard W. Swanson notes that in the modern era, late nineteenth-century visitors to the impressive stone ruins of Great Zimbabwe (located in Zimbabwe, formerly the colony of Rhodesia) 'labelled it "The Acropolis" with all the classical connotations that implies.'[40] Throughout the colonial period, many racist theories would expressly credit the construction of Great Zimbabwe to external (i.e. non-African) sources, believing native civilizations incapable of such efforts[41] – a judgment that would also be applied to ancient Egyptian civilization, as we shall see in Chapter IV.

Even as the Greeks and Romans learned more about territories south of Egypt, a noteworthy lack of precision continued to attend their use of the label 'Ethiopian' itself. From the beginning, the exact space inhabited by the Ethiopians was not clearly defined in ancient thought. Homer associates them with the edges of the earth by the streams of Oceanus, where they were often visited by the gods, and also professes that the Ethiopians were split in two.[42] Snowden argues that the Greeks' first widespread encounter with black Africans was during the Persian Wars, when they presumably served in Xerxes' army.[43] Around that time, the Athenian tragedian Aeschylus was the first extant Greek writer to put the Ethiopians 'definitely in Africa'.[44] The alleged home of Ethiopians was then associated with various parts of Africa until they were increasingly located in the kingdom of Meroë. Still, the term 'Ethiopian' continued to convey a range of meanings for Greek and Roman writers, denoting in different contexts a political identity (i.e. an association with the political state of Meroë), a geographic origin more loosely understood, or a physical type defined primarily by black or dark skin colour. Diodorus of Sicily (active c. 60–30 BCE) presents one of the most extensive accounts of the Ethiopians, and his work reveals well 'a tension between his mythical reading of Ethiopian genesis and his ethnographical interpretations of local habits and customs', capturing the frequent elision of mythic and ethnographic discourse in ancient discussions of the Ethiopians.[45]

It is useful to define the Greek and Roman worldview by looking north, south, east, and west since ancient discussions of the *oikumene* placed considerable weight on the identification of the *oikumene's* limits in each direction, as well as giving special attention to the people thought to reside at the furthermost point of each. In the fourth century, Ephorus of Cyme (c. 405–330 BCE) specifically associated Celts with the extreme west, Scythians with the north, Indians with the east, and Ethiopians with the south,[46] and ancient writers would continue to treat these groups as emblematic of human life in each direction. Notably, there was a frequent conflation of Ethiopia and India in ancient thought, suggesting that the geographic extremes of east and south often blurred in the ancient worldview. Overall, such a scheme served to posit not a single racial binary, but two pairs of opposing extremes defined in relation to a central group (initially the Greeks, then later the Romans), a group allegedly superior precisely because of its geographic 'middle' position.[47]

The north and south opposition was especially popular in certain intellectual contexts. The Presocratic philosopher Xenophanes (born in approximately 570 BCE), for example, used the polar opposition of Thracians and Ethiopians to illustrate what he considered a truism, namely that every group imagines gods in their own image: 'The Ethiopians say that their gods are snub-nosed and black, the Thracians that theirs have light blue eyes and red hair'.[48] Rosalind Thomas similarly notes that the contrast of cold and wet Scythians with hot and dry Libyans was commonplace in ancient medical literature.[49] While northern and southern peoples would be subjected to judgments about their relative stage of development – including stereotypes attached to northern 'hardness' and southern 'softness' – the corresponding difference between west and east also became resonant in certain contexts, with the west generally perceived as 'under-civilized' and the east 'hyper-civilized'. Such a distinction lasted into the Roman period, when it mapped effortlessly onto the difference between previously unconquered territories in the west and those steeped in Greek culture in the east. Epitomizing nicely such structures of thought and stereotype, Pliny the Younger expresses surprise at finding bookshops in the city of Lugdunum in Gaul,[50] presumably akin to the shock some New Yorkers might feel at finding a Starbucks in Arkansas.

Vaguely aware of populations residing beyond the boundaries of their *oikumene*, the Greeks and Romans used that space to amplify their racial theories, dwelling in large part on the presumed curiosities and idiosyncrasies of those populations.[51] (Reflecting a similar mindset, later mapmakers would infamously write on the periphery of their maps: 'here be monsters'.) Indeed, as Greek and Roman knowledge of the world increased, certain mythic populations were 'relocated' precisely so that they remained outside the *oikumene*'s putative boundaries. Wm. Black Tyrrell writes of such tendencies in ancient accounts of the Amazons, a mythic tribe of warrior women: 'As the known world expanded, Amazons were moved outward from Ionia to Phrygia and from the Thermodon River to Lake Maeotis and the Caucasus Mountains'; one writer even placed them in Libya.[52] Given that ancient views imposed a strong correlation between geographic distance and the relative 'likeness' or 'strangeness' of a culture, to some extent it mattered less where exactly certain populations were thought to reside and more how far away or remote it was. As with the Ethiopians and Amazons, ancient writers over time also 'moved' the ancient pygmies – who served as 'a sort of prehistoric premise to the human condition'[53] – placing them alternately in India, Scythia, and Africa.

The ancient environmental theory

In addition to their focus on populations at the edge of the *oikumene* and beyond, ancient philosophers and geographers pondered other geographic explanations of human variation. At one point, the *oikumene* was divided into a series of latitudinal bands or zones called '*klimata*', a method that would last well into the Renaissance,[54] and racial characteristics were eventually attributed to groups living in each zone. When attempting to explain how human diversity correlated with such zones, ancient writers usually referenced the relative exposure of each to the sun's heat and its purported effects on the human body (a view related to the ancient theory of humors).[55] While emphasis was placed on the sun's ostensible effects on internal features, such as blood, ancient authors also posited that black skin colour itself was the result of the sun's heat. In fact, the Greek word '*Aithiops*' connotes an appearance that has been burnt, and Pliny the Elder (23/24–79 CE) pointedly wrote of the 'scorching' of the Ethiopians in his account of the impact of climate on human development.[56] Significantly, this 'explanation' of black skin colour stood well into the modern nineteenth century.[57] In linking human variation closely to geographic placement, such environmental theories – much like modern racial ideology – ranged far beyond mere biology to assert a series of extended claims about human capacity and overall societal development. The Roman geographer Strabo perfectly encapsulates such tendencies when he connects the 'savagery' in Ireland to its cold climate.[58]

The Hippocratic essay *Airs, Waters, Places* provides the most extensive surviving ancient treatise on environmental theory. The essay itself belongs to a collection of medical writings loosely associated with the legendary medical practitioner Hippocrates,[59] and some scholars have suggested that its goal is to provide a 'scientific' explanation for the Greek victory over the Persians, thus allowing it to be tentatively dated to the second half of the fifth century BCE.[60] Although the sections on Libya and Egypt have been lost, the surviving parts of the essay make clear that one of its primary objectives was to assert a fundamental division between the continents of

Asia and Europe, linking the differences between the inhabitants of each to their respective climates. Summing up its method, the essay grandly asserts near the end that 'as a general rule . . . the constitutions and the habits of a people follow the nature of the land where they live'.[61]

In detailing the consequences of climate, *Airs, Waters, Places* maintains that a moderate climate is not necessarily beneficial, for while it may produce large people and crops, it also produces an inclination for luxury and ease. Later the essay becomes even more pointed about the consequences of the temperate climate in Asia, professing that it leads to 'mental flabbiness and cowardice as well'.[62] When it arrives at Europe, the essay spends considerable time outlining the deficiencies of the Scythians, crediting such qualities to their geographic remoteness and the climate of their region, while also briefly discussing the special cases of the Sauromatae – a Scythian tribe whose women allegedly possessed characteristics much like those of the Amazons (indeed some scholars have suggested they are the source of the Amazon myth)[63] – and the Scythian upper-class Anarieis. In the rest of Europe, however, where there are significant climate changes, the people show greater variation and, following the difficulties of their climate, have a toughness or hardness that makes them more courageous than people in Asia.

While *Airs, Waters, Places* argues broadly for the role of climate in determining racial difference, it also cites the impact of cultural practice and customs (*nomoi*), especially political structure. Thus, people in Asia are feeble not only because of their climate, but also because they are governed by monarchy.[64] Europeans, on the other hand, are more courageous because they experience the benefits of self-rule, a mode of government that encourages greater risk-taking by making individuals more invested in the outcome of their efforts.[65] As it develops its argument, then, the essay seems to endorse two distinct sources of human variation: climate and government (and we could add the influence of class as well given the discussion of the Anarieis[66]). Yet the author does not specify the relative weight of each, making the overall theory difficult to reconstruct with any precision. Rosalind Thomas phrases it well: '(Hippocrates) has two contradictory agenda: (a) to show that climate is crucial; and (b) to show that continent is crucial . . . In addition he stresses a third point (c), that *nomoi* are also crucial – which confounds all.'[67]

In creating such ambiguity, *Airs, Waters, Places* seems to be grappling with an important phenomenon that environmental theories would increasingly confront, namely the spread of certain populations beyond their presumed place of geographic origin: what happens, in other words, when 'Greeks' no longer live in Greece – or even in Europe? *Airs, Waters, Places* attempts to alleviate this dilemma by insisting that certain people living in Asia retain a capacity for valour, writing that 'the most warlike men in Asia, whether Greek or barbarians, are those who are not subject races but rule themselves' – presumably an attempt to distinguish those living in the Ionian cities that dotted the coast of Asia Minor from other parts of the continent. Conversely, monarchy remains a perpetual threat no matter where a person is from, given that 'even if a man be born of brave and of stout heart, his character is ruined by [it]'[68] – a claim that intensifies the prospective threat posed by the Persians by suggesting the Persian Wars endangered not only Greek sovereignty, but also Greek character itself.

Because the climate theory at closer look offers some manoeuverability, scholars have often contrasted it with modern methods for constructing race, suggesting that a system of identification linked to the environment is inherently more supple and therefore less violent than one based in human anatomy.[69] While true at the theoretical level, it is critical to remember that the Romans cited the possibility of change – i.e. the alleged capacity for political structure to transform human nature – when justifying their entire imperial project. As the logic went, blessed with their own pre-eminent geographic position, the Romans were charged with improving the condition of other, less favourably situated groups by placing them under the civilizing mantle of Roman rule. In effect, climate theory was evoked both to explain the 'natural' superiority of the Romans and to rationalize the continuing extension of their imperial reach.[70]

While the environmental theory and related concepts like the *oikumene* helped give structure to ancient views of the 'other', mapping racial difference in ways that allowed the Greeks and Romans to anticipate the proclivities of other groups in a range of encounters, peaceful and otherwise, it is important to consider the process that complements such procedures: the consolidation of the Greek and Roman 'self'. I have so far been employing 'Greek' and 'Greeks' in ways that are familiar to a modern audience – that is, to designate the group of people we confidently call the 'ancient Greeks' – but it is time to investigate more fully when and how such a category was formed in the world of classical antiquity itself.

Becoming Greek

In seeking the racial roots of Greek civilization, modern scholars have often turned to Greek mythology, the earliest type of Greek narrative, one that survives in recognizable form beginning in the Archaic Period (c. 750–480 BCE). Since Greek myth ostensibly conveys for the Greeks a series of stories about their own past, scholars have often assumed it contains important historical traces of the earlier Bronze Age. Gaps in our surviving evidence, however, make reconstruction of these early periods sketchy at best, and the Bronze Age often seems to serve as a repository for modern fantasies about early Greek history. Sigmund Freud, for example, memorably treated the Bronze Age Minoan and Mycenaean cultures as a kind of pre-Oedipal stage to the rest of Greek history.[71] Despite the quixotic attempts of early classicists like Heinrich Schliemann to 'verify' episodes from Greek myth by finding their physical proof – Schliemann infamously claimed to have found the 'death mask' of the mythic king Agamemnon[72] – just how Greek myth connects to early Greek history remains a barbed question, as we will see in Chapter IV. But even if we have difficulty in identifying the historical basis of Greek myth, the Greeks clearly 'believed' in these stories in complex and evolving ways.[73] The question is how such beliefs worked and what they actually tell us about the Greeks' understanding of their own racial origins.

Despite the prominent role of geography in ancient racial theory, Greek myth itself does not rely on assertions of any original connection between the Greeks and Greek territory; indeed, Greek myth at times names other indigenous dwellers of Greece, such as the 'Leleges' and 'Pelasgians', groups who connote for the Greeks a category of earlier, more primitive inhabitants of Greece. The subsequent 'arrival' of the Greeks in Greece and ostensible displacement of these earlier populations, while a burning question for modern scholars, is actually somewhat murky in the Greeks' own telling. There is no single account of the influx of the Greeks, although some myths dramatize the arrival and dispersion of smaller groups within Greek territory, often by focusing on their legendary founders. In one prominent myth, Danaus, having been promised the territory of Libya by his father, quarrels with his brother Aegyptus and flees to the Greek city of Argos accompanied by his daughters where he is eventually made king.

With its provocative geographic nomenclature and insistence on Danaus' origin outside Greece, the myth of Danaus raises important questions about Greek conceptions of civic foundation and racial identity. Assuming an historical basis to such myths, Martin Bernal sees such narratives as indicative of the Greeks' open acknowledgement of early foreign influence, as we shall see in Chapter IV. Yet it is not entirely clear what Danaus' 'foreign origin' would signify for its ancient Greek audience when set against the primary affiliation he forges with his new territory. Jonathan Hall states outright that '(i)t is not the *place of departure* which is as important as the *fact of arrival*, and this is because the Greeks had great difficulties in "thinking their origins"'.[74] To place the question of departure versus arrival (or start versus finish) in a very different context, we could note how quickly American founders or 'forefathers' 'lost' their English heritage in American historical memory. Thus, despite being a first-generation American (his father having immigrated, albeit to a British colony, in 1683), most versions of American history would not hesitate to identify Benjamin Franklin as unequivocally 'American'; so, too, despite later idealized attachments to American soil evident in folk songs like 'This Land is Your Land, This Land is My Land', many historians find it easy to overlook the brutal displacement of America's own indigenous inhabitants, treating them as entirely marginal to the ultimate 'American' story. To return to Greek myth: many figures wander in

Greek myth, not just city founders, but that does not mean that the mythic landscape defines them in ways that are equally legible – or even hold the same connotations – at every time and place, and for every ancient audience. Edith Hall has argued, in fact, that the world of early Greek myth was 'homogenously heroic'; she has further posited that it was only later in the fifth century – in Aeschylus' *Suppliant Women* (a play we will return to in Chapters III and IV) – that the 'Egyptianness' of Danaus and his daughters took on meaningful ethnic or racial connotations.[75]

Most ancient historians today believe that identity in Greece was originally local or regional in nature and often closely linked to membership in a particular city-state or *polis*. Historical evidence therefore suggests that a collective identification as 'Greeks' ('Hellenes') was established only after smaller groups in Greece had come into being, including those associated with the three major dialect groups: Dorian, Aeolic, and Ionian.[76] On the other hand, a myth naming Hellen as the original ancestor of all Greeks – known as the 'Hellenic genealogy' – had emerged by the end of the sixth century and was used to suggest that a unified Greek identity had existed from a very early point in time. In presenting such early unity of the Greeks, the Hellenic genealogy, in essence, projected into the past a shared origin that, while it may have been a desirable belief by the sixth century, would presumably not have been conceivable in those earlier periods.[77] Still, the very production of narratives like the 'Hellenic genealogy' demonstrates what Jonathan Hall has called the 'aggregative mode' of Greek identity formation, that is, such stories reveal a clear attempt in later centuries to underline the affiliation between certain Greek groups by tracing (or inventing) bloodlines and family structures stretching all the way back to the mythic era.[78] Moreover, the continuing expressive power of such mythic genealogies is evidenced by a later story that the Persians had attempted to gain sympathy from the Greek city-state of Argos by evoking their alleged mutual descent from the mythical Perses, son of Andromeda and Perseus.[79]

The promotion of such mythical genealogies – the primary aim of texts like the Hesiodic *Catalogue of Women* – connected disparate Greek groups through claims of shared ancestors, but any unity implied by Hellen's alleged paternity could also at times be offset by placing greater emphasis on the descent of different groups from Hellen's various sons, Doros, Xouthos, and Aiolos.[80] In effect, the myth provided a mode of both unification and distinction depending on the context. Such dynamics illustrate well the thorny and recurring problem of the 'proximate other' for the Greeks. Using the example of Scottish and English identities, Jonathan Smith argues that 'distinctions are usually drawn most sharply between "near neighbours"; he expands: '(t)he radically "other" is merely "other"; the proximate "other" is problematic, and hence, of supreme interest'.[81] In just such a way, early Greek history was driven by the shifting relationships *between* Greeks, between 'near neighbours', long before their encounters with outsiders would demand a unified identity *as* 'Greek'.

Despite modern assumptions about the Greeks and their early history, then, collective identification as 'Greek' was not an innate impulse of early populations living side-by-side in Greece. In fact, when the term 'Hellenes' does appear in early sources, it seems utilized in a more restricted way geographically. Appearing infrequently in the Homeric epics (dated roughly to the eighth century BCE), the term 'Hellenes' there seems to denote only the residents of a specific region south of Thessaly.[82] When the *Iliad* and *Odyssey* seek to name a broader collective group – often in relation to the unified (what we today loosely call 'Greek') military force fighting at Troy – the poems instead use labels like 'Achaians', 'Argives', and 'Danaans', terms that designate populations from specific spaces in Greece, treating those areas as a kind of synecdoche for the whole. It is as if the term 'New Yorkers' had been employed to refer to all early residents of American soil, a term that would certainly be recognizable in its intentions (even today spaces like New York hold remarkable power in encapsulating the image of American life abroad), but would nonetheless fail to denote the range of meanings and claims – and so also exclusionary force – inherent in the historical emergence of collective identification as 'American.'

We can go even further in thinking about what the absence of a sense of collective 'Greekness' might mean in this early period, for, given their preconceptions about what was at stake in this epic encounter, modern readers are often surprised at Homer's portrayal of the Trojan War. Far from any archetypal clash of 'west' and 'east' – as the Trojan War has been read in later eras – Homer, in fact, emphasizes the fundamental sameness of the two sides, calling attention again and again to the many ties the warriors share. The 'Achaians' and Trojans fight not to assert their categorical differences with one another, but rather to satisfy the demands of honour, the gods, and fate. Along the way, the two sides share the same language, the same rituals, and the same gods; some even exchange presents in ritual recognition of an affinity that crosses generations, an affinity related to their shared aristocratic status.

Approximately three centuries later, in his *History of the Peloponnesian War*, the Athenian author Thucydides (c. 455-c. 400 BCE) pointed out the surprising – from the perspective of a later Greek – omission of the term 'barbarian' from the Homeric epics. Linking it to the lack of certain structures of thought in Homer's era, Thucydides proposed that the term was absent because 'in his (Homer's) time the Hellenes were not yet known by one name, and so marked off as something separate from the outside world'.[83] As such a statement implies, by Thucydides' time, the term 'Hellenes' had expanded to connote the 'Greeks' in a wider sense that more closely approximates our own.[84] Even more, as Thucydides' formulation suggests, identification as 'Hellenes' received its primary impetus from the rise of its imagined inverse: the 'barbarian' (*barbaros*). The emergence of such a fundamental opposition was no accident, for the fifth century provided a major turning point in the construction of Greek identity, one intimately tied to the advent of the Persian Wars.[85] As Jonathan Hall phrases it, the Greeks now turned to an 'oppositional' mode of identify formation, one articulated in relation to an external group (i.e. the Persians) and progressively expressed in terms of culture rather than blood or kinship.[86]

At its most rudimentary level, collective identification as 'Hellenes' was derived from a set of shared cultural practices, especially common language and religion. The reliance on cultural features was crucial since identification as 'Hellenes' never led to the formation of a unified political state. Nor would the space occupied by 'Hellenes' ever be conclusively defined, rather the term would reach beyond Greece proper to 'designate the whole Greek-speaking world from Sicily to the Black Sea, including the islands and free eastern cities'.[87] The term 'barbarian', on the other hand, had previously been used to label non-Greek speakers with somewhat limited connotations (its syllabic repetition of 'bar-bar' evidently recording the nonsensical sounds of other languages from the Greek perspective). But against the backdrop of the Persian Wars, the term was soon applied directly, and with greater animosity, to the Persians themselves. Later the 'barbarian' would also encompass the range of peoples the Persians had added to their own empire (e.g., Egyptians, Phoenicians, and Thracians) and ultimately it would connote all non-Greek peoples.[88] This collapsing of all human variation into a single racial opposition – Greek vs. barbarian – is the closest parallel in antiquity to the modern racial binary of 'black' and 'white'.

Given the specific threat to Greek sovereignty the Persian Wars presented, the barbarian was defined first and foremost by the propensity for a particular mode of government, a theme central, as we have seen, to *Airs, Waters, Places*. Whereas barbarians displayed a natural inclination for subservience and tyranny, as the theory went, Greeks were characterized by a commitment to democratic rule and the equality of citizens. Notoriously advocating the idea of the 'natural slave', Aristotle likewise proposed that barbarians, as opposed to Greeks, were inherently servile.[89] By imposing the categories Greek and barbarian onto master and slave, Aristotle's formulation demonstrates the significant convergence between the idea of the barbarian and ancient notions of slavery.[90]

A variety of types of servitude existed in antiquity, but chattel slavery, a form of slavery that viewed slaves as possessions, had become the most prominent by the sixth-century BCE.[91] Slaves in this system were generally acquired by force through war, piracy, and kidnapping; thus, the geographic origins of slaves varied over time as sites of conflict shifted. For classical Athens,

> the majority of slaves were derived from regions to the north and
> east – Thrace, the lower Danube, the coasts of the Black Sea, and

Asia Minor . . . For Rome, the military campaigns . . . provided slaves in vast quantities . . . from North Africa, Sicily and Spain during and after the Punic Wars, from Gaul and Britain as a result of Caesar's campaigns, and intermittently thereafter from campaigns on the Rhine and Danube, and in Judaea and Parthia.[92]

During the Roman period, conquest fuelled a constant supply of slaves,[93] and although ancient sources promoted the benefits of 'house-born' slaves as well,[94] the degree of actual reliance on this latter source of slaves is difficult to determine.[95]

Emphasis on the diverse geographic origins of ancient slaves is not meant to obscure the sheer brutality of the institution, only to make the point that – unlike more modern versions – ancient slavery in no way derived from a single geographic source nor corresponded categorically with any physical trait, such as skin colour. Many ancient sources make clear that slaves, in fact, could not be distinguished from non-slaves by physical appearance alone. Slaves' feet were at times whitened with chalk at auctions 'to distinguish them from those of local origin,'[96] and physical descriptions provided in notices of runaway slaves in Roman Egypt cite a range of skin colours, with one explicitly calling an escaped slave 'pale-skinned.'[97] Suggestive of the later stock Roman visual stereotype of slaves, slave characters in Roman comedy evidently wore red wigs as part of their costume.[98] Even as black Africans could be enslaved, then, so also could Germans, Gauls, Syrians, Jews, and Greeks. In fact, Syria was an especially popular source and close study of slave names suggests three-fifths of all slaves may have come from Asia Minor.[99]

Given their diverse origins, slaves were frequently categorized by stereotypes attached to their specific homelands (stereotypes which could also dictate the kind of work they were assigned, as well as their presumed economic value), and perceptions of slaves, perhaps the most intimate form of contact with the 'other' for most Greeks and Romans, likewise contributed to evolving racial ideologies. Given that the practice of manumission played a prominent role in slavery at Rome, the Romans would later view slavery more as a condition or circumstance than natural state.[100] Slaves who had been formally manumitted (called 'freedmen') were even eligible for Roman citizenship, although they often remained bound to their former masters by economic obligations and could also be restricted in more informal ways by social stigma and negative stereotypes.[101]

In addition to a presumed propensity for servitude (entailing both literal enslavement and, as the Greeks saw it, enslavement to monarchy[102]), other alleged qualities underlined the distinction between Greeks and barbarians: barbarians demonstrated excess rather than restraint, passion rather than self-control, emotion rather than reason, and cowardice rather than bravery. In turning to such contrasts, the construction of the barbarian frequently borrowed from gender stereotypes, explicitly casting barbarians as effeminate and insinuating that barbarians were to Greeks as women to men. The Greek and barbarian dichotomy, moreover, did not die out with the end of the Persian Wars; its residue would continue to structure ideas of racial difference in the Greek and Roman world for centuries to come, ultimately making its way, with significant alterations, into our own modern era. But by the end of the fifth century, the opposition of Greek and barbarian would be only part of a larger arsenal of racial formations.

The Athenian fifth century

Opening with the glorious union of 'Hellenes' against Persians, Greek identity in the fifth century had entered a 'transitional phase during which both the form (aggregative > oppositional) and the content (ethnic > cultural) of Greek identity underwent a profound . . . development',[103] meaning that whereas Greek identity had previously been formed internally – among Greeks – and structured around claims of descent and bloodline, Greek identity was now increasingly expressed as a unified response to external groups and its source linked to cultural traits and cultural practices. The replacement of one mode by the other, however, was never absolute, and we can observe their persistent co-existence in the discursive strategies of the powerful city-state of Athens itself. On one hand, even after the conclusion of the Persian Wars, many Athenian intellectuals continued to perpetuate an ideology opposing Greeks and barbarians. So prominent was this idea in the post-war years, in fact, that many scholars have suggested that the 'barbarian' was employed with conspicuous intensity precisely to conceal Athenian attempts to exert its growing hegemony over its fellow Greek city-states.

At the same time, Athens developed newer methods for defining 'Athenian' against other Greeks, a more proximate 'othering' than that required by the Persians. Promoting a myth of its own autochthonous origin, Athens started to insist that its citizens were not merely linked by political bond, but had emerged from the same soil – a type of romantic attachment to land generally absent in Greek thought.[104] In similar terms, Pericles' citizenship law of 451 BCE made Athenian parentage (i.e. descent on both the paternal and maternal side) a prerequisite for citizenship, a stipulation that seemed designed to curb the tendency, especially among the Athenian elite, for marrying foreign women.[105] In other contexts, though, the Athenians turned to culture and social practice in defining themselves, features that were levied with particular intensity against the Spartans against whom the Athenians waged the brutal Peloponnesian War from approximately 431 to 404 BCE. In his funeral oration of 431 (a speech recorded and perhaps elaborated by Thucydides), Pericles, a leading Athenian statesman, markedly 'eschews the topics of common lineage and autochthonous origins and places the entire emphasis on common values and traits of character that distinguish the Athenians' way of life from that of their Spartan enemies'.[106]

As we have seen in Jones' analysis of Herodotus' use of *ethnos* and *genos* in discussing the Scythians, the Greek historian Herodotus directly referenced both sources of identity in his work, drawing at times on ancestry or genealogy in defining a group, while at others on cultural features like religion or social practice.[107] In a famous passage near the end of his work, Herodotus pointedly combined both modes of identification, proposing that Greek identity was founded on 'the community of blood and language, temples and ritual; our common way of life'.[108] Many scholars have interpreted this passage as recording the rising authority of cultural features in Greek self-definition; nor would Herodotus' influence be confined to his articulation of the shifting vocabulary of 'Greekness', but his entire approach to racial and cultural systems would structure anthropological and ethnographic methods for centuries to come.

The rhapsode of the *oikumene*

Herodotus was born around 480 BCE in Halicarnassus, a city on the coast of Asia Minor. His *Histories* takes as its primary subject the Persian Wars, although – given its presumed date of composition around the 450s–420s – it has also been interpreted as addressing the growing crisis among the Greek city-states in the latter part of the fifth century, tensions that would eventually erupt into the Peloponnesian War. The scope of Herodotus' work, which provides not merely an account of the Persian Wars, but also a wide range of ethnographic and geographic argument, was unprecedented in antiquity. Thomas, for example, has pointed out that Herodotus shares certain racial structures of thought with contemporary science and medical writers, who sought to explain human variation as part of a larger account of the workings of the world and did not generally politicize such differences *per se*.[109] She and others have compared Herodotus' work to *Airs, Waters, Places*, contending that, despite significant parallels, Herodotus adheres to a much looser reading of environmental theory. As Charles Chiasson concisely phrases it, unlike *Airs, Waters, Places*, Herodotus posits 'analogy rather than aetiology between the natural and cultural spheres';[110] patterns of nature, in other words, are used as a way of illustrating human phenomena without necessarily standing as their root cause. In a perfect example of such methods, Herodotus uses climate and the reverse flow of the Nile as a parallel for the 'strangeness' of the Egyptians themselves, writing: 'Not only is the Egyptian climate peculiar to that country, and the Nile different in its behaviour from rivers elsewhere, but the Egyptians themselves in their manners and customs seem to have reversed the ordinary practices of mankind.'[111]

Herodotus spends considerable time presenting the build-up of Persian power, focusing largely on the territories and peoples already subjected to it. Such ethnographic discussions serve both to define the Greeks in relation to these other groups and to intimate reasons why the Greeks, in contrast, were able to withstand the Persian onslaught.[112] As François Hartog notes, this dual focus gives voice to 'two Herodotuses, one the historian of the Persian Wars, and another who is primarily the Herodotus of "others", of non-Greeks;' later Hartog poetically terms the latter Herodotus 'a surveyor of otherness and a rhapsode of the *oikumene*'.[113] Herodotus' actual ethnography uses a number of general methods. Echoing ancient geographic theory, Herodotus employs space and geographic distance to help classify racial groups, moving 'from the orderly and complicated system of the central region, especially Greece, through the simple, but still related ways of the nomads, to the primitive anarchy of the fringes'.[114] In addition, Herodotus relies on concepts like symmetry and inversion to structure his account; in this view, one reflective of the Greek reliance on binaries more generally, racial groups are not just different from one another, but stand in exact opposition.[115] While Herodotus describes Persian customs at one point in his narrative,[116] he devotes more effort to drawing an extended contrast between the Scythians and Egyptians, illustrating what James Redfield terms Herodotus' opposition between 'hard' and 'soft' peoples, one in which '(s)oft peoples are characterized by luxury, the division of labour, and complexity of *nomoi*, especially in the sphere of religion; (while) hard peoples are simple, harsh, and fierce.'[117]

Herodotus recognizes that cultures influence one another – that groups, including the Greeks, often borrow customs (*nomoi*) from other groups. In doing so, Herodotus emphasizes the Greek capacity for seriously evaluating *nomoi* before adapting them and 'calls upon the Greeks to be critical assimilators, to experience cultural change not as mere diffusion but as a thoughtful choice between options'.[118] The issue for Herodotus, in other words, is not so much *whether* groups should take such practices from others, rather *how* such borrowing is conducted.[119] A number of important points follow from Herodotus' treatment of such phenomena. For one, as Thomas argues, this emphasis on cultural appropriation does not mean that Herodotus imagined collective identity itself as being unstable; on the contrary, even as the features or practices of a group might change, for Herodotus the group itself remained constant[120] – Greeks did not stop being Greek just because they borrowed certain gods from the Egyptians. Even more, Herodotus' characterization of such dynamics has exerted tremendous influence over modern debates about the nature of Greek cultural achievement, leading some scholars, for example, to assign an innate 'strength' or 'mastery' to Greek culture premised on its presumed ability to take on the practices of others without losing its own 'integrity'. Conversely, given all the cultural features the Greeks have allegedly borrowed (or, to use a more charged term, 'stolen'), others have seen Greek culture as fundamentally derivative: in short, where one side infers cultural vigour from Herodotus' account, the other finds only cultural dependency.

In his opening sentence, Herodotus declares that he intends to show the wondrous deeds of Greeks and barbarians, as well as what led to the wars between them. Using such categories to define his aims, Herodotus seems to draw on the standard opposition of Greeks and barbarians from the outset of his work, yet his actual employment of the binary is more complex than such initial phrasing suggests, for Herodotus undermines the viability of the opposition throughout. At one point, for example, Herodotus recognizes that Egyptians have their own *barbaroi* (i.e. that they apply the concept to those unable to speak *their* language); comparing this gesture to a similar fragment of Antiphon that professes 'we make barbarians of each other', Thomas credits both authors with express awareness of the social constructedness of the trope.[121] By suggesting at another point that the Athenians were originally descended from the Pelasgians and only later became Greek, Herodotus similarly 'implies that the boundaries between Greek and barbarian are permeable, and Greekness can be acquired' – subversively illustrating that proposition through the Athenians themselves.[122] Recognizing Herodotus' favourable portrayal of non-Greeks, Plutarch would later label him '*philobarbaros*' (a lover of *barbaroi*), a term in no way meant as a compliment.[123]

Herodotus' lengthy account of Egypt in Book 2 remains one of the most-discussed parts of his work, and it clearly falls within a larger tradition of Greek fascination with Egypt. As Herodotus phrases it, Egypt is well worth his lengthy description because it contains more 'wonders' than any other land.[124] Still, as Phiroze Vasunia argues, while the Egyptians were in many ways implicated in the emergent discourse of the barbarian, '(w)hat distinguishes Egypt from several other barbarians in Greek texts is that whereas Egyptians are not always portrayed in a negative light and do not always serve as a negative foil, they nonetheless occupy a series of different and sometimes contradictory positions'.[125] On one hand, the Greeks remained deeply impressed by Egypt's antiquity, while, on the other, they could conjure it as a site of despotism and barbarity, of gender inversion and human sacrifice.[126] Such ambivalence is captured well by Herodotus' use of time in his narrative, for, in describing Egyptian customs, Herodotus adopts a kind of indefinite 'ethnographic present', but when he switches to his account of Egyptian history, a narrative more clearly anchored in recognizable time, he stops with Cambyses' conquest – an event nearly thirty-five years before the first Persian invasion of Greece. With such dual strategies, Herodotus, in effect, produces 'a narrative that consistently archaizes Egypt and denies it coevality'.[127]

While physical descriptions *per se* occupy a fairly minor role in Herodotus' representation of Egypt, their role is worth considering briefly given our preoccupation today with the ancient Egyptian body. Herodotus' keen interest in mummification and Egyptian care of the dead, for one, prefigures our modern fascination.[128] Claiming in one passage to have visited a battlefield where the remains of Egyptians and Persians were still visible, Herodotus also anticipates the modern practice of craniometry when he observes that the Egyptians had much thicker skulls than the Persians, presumably, he explains, because they had been hardened by the sun.[129] Equally significant for modern audiences is Herodotus' mention of skin colour in describing the appearance of Egyptians. In two passages, Herodotus refers to the Egyptians as 'black', the first merely in passing, and the second when providing as evidence for the Colchians' Egyptian descent their 'black skins and woolly hair'.[130] This latter passage has fuelled continuing debate about the prospective 'blackness' of ancient Egyptians, as we shall see in Chapter IV. Frank Snowden has argued against overestimating such colour terminology, however, insisting that the 'Greeks and Romans differentiated clearly between the various gradations in the colour of dark-skinned Mediterraneans' and he asserts more specifically that Ethiopians were always understood to have darker skin than any other group.[131] Herodotus himself mentions the Ethiopians on a number of occasions. In the course of a description of the Indians, for example, he explicitly remarks on the similarity of their skin colour to that of the Ethiopians, claiming both male populations have black and not white semen – evidencing once again a mindset that saw the two geographic extremes of east and south in closely related terms.[132]

Herodotus' writings helped initiate the entire western practice of ethnography, providing a lasting structure for organizing perceptions of the 'other.'[133] His work provided a key framework for Columbus on his voyages, vying only with Marco Polo's more recent accounts of the Orient,[134] and Herodotus would even be 'drawn into controversy over an issue utterly unknown to the Father of History: the origins of racial distinctions and the justice of slavery'.[135] Isolating the more immediate consequences of Herodotus' racial representations, Vasunia has argued that Herodotus' writings formed part of a larger Greek narrative treatment of Egypt that cumulatively offered Egypt up as an appealing dish for Alexander the Great's formidable appetite,[136] helping foster a vision of empire that would change the world as Alexander and his contemporaries knew it, while expanding the workings of 'Greekness' itself.

From 'Hellenes' to Hellenism

Setting out in 334 BCE, Alexander aspired to reach the eastern edge of the *oikumene*. Although he would never achieve his goal, he would manage to introduce Greek language and culture across an immense geographic horizon, a process once grandly labelled 'Hellenization.' More recently, historians have termed this phenomenon 'Hellenism' instead, because, as G. W. Bowersock explains, Hellenism 'was a concept that the ancients talked about, whereas Hellenization was not. Hellenism did not necessarily threaten local cultures, nor was it imperialistic . . . Hellenization was a modern idea, reflecting modern forms of cultural domination.'[137] Rather than a set of static and unchanging practices imposed unilaterally by Alexander's military might, such a shift in terminology positions Greek culture as a dynamic entity, one that continually adapted to – and was shaped by – local contexts as it spread. Still, even as the actual form and content of Greek culture might be subject on the ground to the pressures of local cultural exchange, Greek culture as an idealized mode of performance increasingly furnished the means by which 'Greeks' could distinguish themselves from others throughout the Mediterranean world. In his *Panegyricus* from around 380 BCE, the Athenian orator Isocrates famously redefined 'Hellenism' in just such terms, reiterating the shift from blood to culture that we saw already starting to take hold in the previous century by professing that 'the name "Greek" no longer connotes the race but the mental attitude, and men are called "Greeks" when they share our education rather than merely our common blood'.[138]

During the Hellenistic Period (dating from approximately the death of Alexander in 323 BCE to the death of Cleopatra in 30 BCE), Greek culture would become even more prominent as a source of Greek racial identification as Greeks and Greek practices such as language, religion, and dress spread further and further afield. Yet, even as cultural practice gained increasing authority in defining racial categories, tensions and uncertainties continued to accompany this shift, producing enduring concern over the relative roles of essence and practice. Were Greeks 'Greek' now *because* they used Greek culture – the practice alone being sufficient to validate the claim – or did individuals use Greek culture because they *were* 'Greek' – meaning the performance of 'Greekness' reaffirmed an identity established by some other source, such as geographic origin or bloodline? Tim Whitmarsh captures a related dilemma when he points to the writings of Favorinus, a Roman from Gaul writing in Greek in the second century CE, for whom 'the distinction between "being (*einai*) Greek" and "seeming (*dokein*) Greek" . . . is never clear'[139] – a distinction ('being' vs. 'seeming') that was taken up in many forms of ancient thought, perhaps most memorably by the philosopher Plato.

Such unease emanates from the ambiguities of cultural performance and its putative limits, and I will turn in the next chapter to a fuller discussion of race as a form of social practice. In outlining the specific evolution of ancient racial theories here, though, it is instructive to return to Alexander the Great himself, and explore certain ideas that have taken centre stage in the ongoing debates over his legacy.

Alexander's one world?

In Alan Moore and Dave Gibbons' graphic novel *Watchmen*, the villain Adrian Veidt explicitly identifies the Macedonian general Alexander the Great as his role model. Calling his own violent attempt to force the countries of the world to come together 'the culmination of a dream more than two thousand years old', Veidt praises Alexander specifically for 'ruling without barbarism', and laments only that Alexander died at thirty-three before he could fully execute his 'vision of a united world'.[140] In situating Alexander as Veidt's inspiration, Moore and Gibbons reference a motive that has long been attributed to Alexander the Great: the creation of a single world-system. But was such an ideology really the engine of the young man's vast undertaking or was the creation of a culturally unified Greek world merely the incidental result of his bottomless ambition?

Following the Peloponnesian War, Athens, Sparta, and Persia continued to intervene in one another's affairs. As the fourth century progressed, however, their rivalries were increasingly eclipsed by the rise of a new power to the north: Macedonia. Like its southern neighbour Thessaly, Macedonia had long been considered a backwater by the rest of Greece; the fact that it was ruled by a king, for one, made it antithetical to the way classical city-states like Athens had emphatically defined themselves. After ascending to the throne in 359 BCE, Philip II of Macedon sought both to fortify and extend Macedonian hegemony. In Athens, the orators Isocrates and Demosthenes differed openly in their interpretations of Philip's aims, both turning to a concept that had been key to bolstering Athenian identity in the previous century: the barbarian. Railing against that age-old enemy – the Persian empire – in a series of speeches, Isocrates called for a united campaign in the east, a jingoistic cry that did not quite conceal what was presumably his main concern: the preservation of order and upper-class property rights by sending certain rootless populations abroad.[141] Eventually, Isocrates would settle on Philip of Macedon as the ideal leader for such a crusade. Demosthenes, on the other hand, less persuaded of the merits of a major campaign against Persia, branded Philip himself a 'barbarian', suggesting that he was essentially 'other' to the Greeks in both strategic and conceptual terms.[142]

Although Philip, who defeated combined forces led by Thebes and Athens in 338, did not hesitate to exert his authority over the Greeks, whether Demosthenes' premise was correct, i.e. that the Macedonians were at the same time racially 'other' to the Greeks, remains a burning question to this day. Eugene Borza has demonstrated that ancient writers persistently referred to Greeks and Macedonians during Alexander's period as two distinct groups,[143] and Arrian (c. 86–160 CE) calls the Greeks and Macedonians two different races.[144] On the other hand, Herodotus reports that in the early fifth century, a member of the Macedonian royal family, claiming Argive descent, had been allowed to compete in the Olympic games, games pointedly restricted to 'Hellenes'.[145] Isocrates likewise assigns Greek descent to the Macedonian ruling family, and other traditions inserted the Macedonians as a collective group into the Hellenic genealogy via Hellen's son Aeolus.[146]

During the fourth century, as we have seen, cultural criteria had become increasingly pivotal in the constitution of 'Greekness', and in this realm there is evidence both that the Macedonians actively adopted Greek culture – Alexander the Great was famously tutored by Aristotle – and that they preserved other practices that marked them as distinct, including use of a separate linguistic form. Accounts of Alexander's life strikingly reveal that the young man usually spoke what registered as 'Greek' (or *koine*) by recording that once in a moment of great anger, he blurted out 'Macedonian', an indication, Plutarch says, of his extreme emotional duress.[147] Such an anecdote strongly suggests that 'Greekness' was in many ways a conscious performance for Alexander, one we can only fully apprehend today in its momentary failure (although the gap of almost 400 years between Alexander's life and Plutarch's reminds us of the frequent difficulty of working with ancient sources on such intricate issues). In the modern era, bloodline and culture continue to compete for authority in the Macedonian question, stirring passionate debate between Greece and the Republic of Macedonia, formerly part of Yugoslavia, over which national entity can legitimately assert identification as 'Macedonian', not to mention lay claim to Alexander himself.[148]

Despite the contested meaning of Macedonian, Philip strategically adopted the mantle of a unified Greece ('panhellenism') and began planning for a campaign against Persia, plans that were cut short by his assassination in 336. Succeeding to his father's throne, Alexander recognized the rhetorical power of prevailing Greek narratives and treated his subsequent campaigns not merely as recompense for Persian atrocities in the previous century, but as a kind of second Trojan War, casting himself as the new Achilles.[149] Following two earlier battles with the Persians (as well as the capture of various cities and territories along his route, including Egypt), Alexander defeated the Persians at Gaugamela in 331.[150] From there, he continued east into central Asia, destroying Persepolis and eliminating his last rival, Bessus, in Bactria. In 327, Alexander undertook a lengthy expedition to India, turning back only when his troops refused to go further. By 324, Alexander had arrived back at Susa, where he conducted a mass marriage ceremony joining nearly one hundred of his officers to Persian wives, while taking two Persian brides of his own. A year later, on June 10, 323 BCE, Alexander died unexpectedly, already by some accounts dreaming rival campaigns in the west.

In 1933, the British historian W. W. Tarn notoriously proposed that behind Alexander's territorial aspirations lay the desire to create a unified world, a 'brotherhood of mankind' in which all racial difference would presumably be eradicated.[151] This image of Alexander as an enlightened visionary – what Ernst Badian calls 'Alexander the Dreamer'[152] – has proven both seductive and remarkably persistent.[153] Indeed, long before Tarn, a number of ancient writers seemed to assign similar broadmindedness to Alexander. Strabo, for example, reports that Eratosthenes had praised Alexander for dividing people according to their actual merit, rather than adhering to a crude binary of Greeks versus barbarians.[154] Later, Plutarch portrayed Alexander as an aggressive promoter of unity, using the image of a great mixing-bowl and proclaiming that Alexander had openly rejected the views of Aristotle, who had allegedly recommended treating barbarians as animals or plants, meaning categorically different from – and obviously lower than – Greeks.[155]

In the absence of any reliable record of his own opinions on the matter,[156] attempts to determine Alexander's racial motives invariably rely on the public actions attributed to him. Borza has argued that the young general surrounded himself with a primarily Macedonian court throughout his campaigns.[157] Yet ancient sources testify that Alexander, in addition to his elaborate marriage ceremony, also adopted styles of Persian royal dress, as well as a range of Persian practices – including, controversially, *proskynesis*, i.e. obeisance. Ernst Fredricksmeyer finds multiple messages in these appropriations, noting that ancient sources credit it to 'Alexander's desire to emulate the extravagance and luxury of the Persian court, to impress the Persians and secure their allegiance, and to gain greater ascendancy over the Macedonians'.[158] A few weeks after the mass marriage, tensions provoked by such practices were openly apparent when Alexander was forced to settle a mutiny by his troops, who accused him of granting too many privileges to the now-defeated Persians.

Alexander likewise took on displays of power that would be culturally legible to his Egyptian audience during his brief sojourn in Egypt, including a dramatic detour to the oracle of Ammon at Siwah. After his visit to that remote locale, Alexander claimed to be the son of the god Ammon (connected to Zeus in Greek thought), and contemporary coinage often shows him with horns alluding to that relationship, although his Macedonian soldiers apparently mocked such pretensions. In the course of restoring the great Egyptian temple at Luxor, Alexander commissioned a new 'Shrine of the Bark' which prominently displayed his own image replete with pharaonic iconography; significantly, its 'fifty two images of Alexander are the largest corpus of his portraits in existence.'[159] Today most historians read such public displays and dramatic cultural appropriations less in terms of Alexander's liberal attitude toward racial diversity and more in terms of his own personal aggrandizement. Peter Green has called it Alexander's 'increasing need, as his career of conquest advanced, to be all things to all men,'[160] while others phrase it more bluntly, calling Alexander's vision and diverse range of cultural performances not enlightened racial policy but rather growing megalomania.

After Alexander's unexpected demise, some of the populations he had previously subdued were able to break away, and the remaining territory – still vast in area – was divided into the three Greek kingdoms, which would continue to war with one another until, in the words of one Agelaus, 'a looming cloud' started to appear in the west: Rome.[161] As the Romans went on to consolidate their own power in the Mediterranean, they both adapted earlier Greek racial formations, and created new modes of differentiation. Greg Woolf writes: 'Roman power in fact created new kinds of difference, between social classes, between regions and between individuals ... Rather than the expansion of one national or ethnic culture at the expense of others, we are dealing with the emergence of a new, highly differentiated social formation incorporating a new cultural logic and a new configuration of power'.[162] But just how did this 'looming cloud' first gather?

Becoming Roman

Archaeological evidence suggests that Rome had its first permanent settlement around 1000 BCE. By the later seventh century it had developed into a recognizably urban centre, and '(b)y around 500 BC Rome must have been one of the showplaces of the western Mediterranean'.[163] While the early period of Roman history is difficult to reconstruct, the Romans traced their own roots back to the Trojan leader Aeneas, who, according to the myth, had fled the burning city of Troy during the Greeks' final murderous assault. Arriving as an exile on Italian shores, Aeneas ostensibly settled at Lavinium, and the later establishment of the city of Rome – dated by the Romans to around 754 BCE – was credited to Romulus, from the royal dynasty of Alba Longa, whose act of civic foundation was premised on the murder of his own twin brother, Remus. Beginning with Romulus, Rome would be governed by a legendary sequence of kings, some of decidedly foreign origin. Romulus himself was associated with varied efforts to build the fledgling city's population, opening the city gates to fugitives of all kinds, including criminals and runaway slaves. Most notoriously, in order to introduce women into the exclusively male community, Romulus initiated the violent rape of the Sabine women, who forcibly became the first Roman wives.[164] Such stories connected with Roman origin – characterized by the incorporation of foreign kings, criminals, slaves, and Sabine wives – situated the boundaries of Rome, and Roman identity itself, as strikingly porous to outsiders from the very beginning.

Central to the formation of early Roman identity in practice, as opposed to mythic narrative, was the gradual incorporation of all the other populations in the Italian peninsula, a group whose heterogeneity prior to Roman conquest is suggested by the identification of forty distinct languages or dialects.[165] Florus, a second century CE Roman historian, later named three specific groups as central to this early process, having, as he phrases it, 'mixed' from 'one blood' with the Romans to make 'one body', 'one people': the Etruscans, Latins, and Sabines.[166] Rome itself was part of Latium, and the Latins were clearly the most 'proximate other' to the Romans, since 'although the majority of Romans were ethnically Latin, they were still capable of regarding some Latins as an "other" group'.[167] Actual expression of Latin identity is most evident in the so-called Latin League, an alliance that formed in opposition to growing Roman power. The Romans first defeated the Latin League in 499 BCE at Lake Regillus, and in 341 BCE, after suppressing a Latin revolt, the Romans dictated a settlement that would provide the blueprint for Roman expansion in the years to follow, specifically distinguishing a range of status levels that could be granted to those they had defeated: full citizen, citizen *sine suffragio* (without the vote), 'Latin', and ally. In this formula, 'Latin status ceased to have a distinct ethnic or linguistic significance, and came instead to depend on possession of legally defined rights and privileges that could be exercised in dealing with Roman citizens'.[168]

As such precise demarcation of civic status suggests, Roman citizenship played an integral role in the Roman incorporation of other groups. As Ray Laurence phrases it, '"Roman" does not refer to a person's ethnicity, nation, linguistic group, or common descent, but refers directly to a common citizenship'[169]. The Roman historian Velleius Paterculus (c. 19 BCE to sometime after 30 CE) made 'the extension of citizenship and the growth of the Roman name by the sharing of law' a key component in his account of Roman history from 390 BCE – 100 BCE.[170] Ancient sources suggest that regulation of the boundary between citizens and non-citizens was taken very seriously; while Cicero, for example, at one point argued against the practice of expelling foreigners from one's city, he nonetheless advocated punishment for non-citizens trying to exercise the rights of citizens.[171] Likewise, the *lex Licinia Mucia* had been passed in 95 BCE allowing one's citizenship status to be challenged by others, and later in the empire a number of people falsely pretending to be citizens were executed.[172] Providing an expansive view of what the bonds of citizenship provided, Cicero insisted that citizens shared 'the forum, shrines, porticoes, streets, laws, legal rights, courts, the vote, and in addition communal habits and friendships and business relations undertaken with many'.[173]

Given this heightened emphasis on citizenship, many scholars have argued that it eventually outweighed all other distinctions under the Romans, including race and ethnicity. Yet Cicero in the same work recognized that the bonds of race, nation and language were broader than citizenship,[174] and racial formations continued to hold meaning alongside citizenship throughout the Roman period. Suggestive of the intricate ways citizenship might be weighed against other sources of identity, Quintilian (born c. 30 CE) noted in his *Institutio Oratoria* ('*Institutes of Oratory*') that the Roman historian Livy had often been accused of retaining certain idioms from his hometown Padua. Quintilian advocated instead speaking in a style that seemed to come from a 'native of the city', that is, speech that displayed innate 'Romanness' (*Romana*) and not merely one acquired with citizenship (*donata civitate*).[175] Quintilian's insistence on drawing a line between 'Roman by birth' and 'Roman by citizenship' suggests some of the potential distinctions in Roman identity that are – like Alexander's alleged linguistic 'slip' – very revealing, if not routinely visible in our sources. And Quintilian's use of speech in weighing 'Romanness' is even more intriguing given that he himself was from Spain (even among the Roman emperors Hadrian evidently had to rid himself of a Spanish accent, while Septimius Severus allegedly never managed to shed his African one[176]). Eventually, in 212 CE, the emperor Caracalla granted citizenship to all free residents of the empire, an act that diminished its potency as a mode of differentiation and gave even greater substance to other struc-tures of identity, such as race.[177]

With his inclusion of social networks and business connections in the bonds joining citizens, Cicero's vision underlines the extreme importance of social class in Roman thought. Suggestive of their assimilation into Roman society, Latin families from throughout Latium can be identified in the Roman aristocracy, as can Sabine families, the group most closely associ-ated with the Romans after the Latins.[178] Although the Romans had expe-rienced various military challenges from the Sabines over the centuries, Sabine claims to inclusion in the Roman community were derived not only from the successive opening of political enfranchisement – they were granted citizenship *sine suffragio* in 290 and full citizenship in 268 – but also from their ostensible incorporation into the Roman population via the legendary rape of the Sabine women. The Sabines thereafter remained distinct enough as a group to have their own image (or stereotype) as austere, rustic, disci-plined, and pious, qualities some Roman writers explained by situating the Sabines as descendants of the Spartans.[179]

Of Florus' three groups, the Etruscans have long been the most intriguing to modern scholars. Since their 'rediscovery' in the eighteenth century, the Etruscans, a 'people who were civilised and literate long before Rome became important', have been the source of many intellectual and political projects, not least in Italy, where some have 'found in the civilisations of pre-Roman Italy a focus for their feelings of local and national patriotism';[180] in effect, the Etruscans have provided an attractive means for tracing an alternate history in ancient Italy, one that was – in the eyes of many scholars – emphatically less-militaristic than the Roman one.[181] The Etruscans (called Tyrrhenians by the Greeks) inhabited individual city-states on the west coast of Italy between the Tiber and Arno; their power was presumably at its peak from about the eighth to fifth centuries BCE. Suffering their first major defeat by the Romans with the capture of Veii in 396 BCE, the Etruscans were also on the losing side of the Roman victory at the Battle of Sentinum in 295, an event that 'decided the fate of peninsular Italy'.[182] Etruria itself, however, was not completely subdued until 264, and even then most of its cities were probably not awarded Roman citizenship until after the Social War (91–88 BCE), a conflict that broke out when the Romans' Italian allies demanded full citizenship.

Like the Sabines, the Etruscan connection to Rome was not just a matter of political and military engagement, but deeply grounded in perceptions of Rome's early history. The Etruscans were associated with the final dynasty of Roman kings, the Tarquins, and, most noteworthy among them was Tarquinus Superbus (Tarquin the Proud), whose violent rape of Lucretia was said to have brought about the end of monarchism and the beginning of the Roman Republic in 509 BCE. The presence of Etruscan rulers in the line of Rome's legendary kings has often been seen as a record of actual Etruscan domination in the late seventh and sixth centuries, perhaps even Etruscan occupation of the city, although other scholars contend that Etruscan influence on early Roman history and the development of Roman culture has been greatly overstated.[183] In any event, the Romans themselves perceived the Etruscans as having been overtaken by Roman advancement, 'old-fashioned' as it were,[184] and they were primarily associated with the introduction of particular religious rites at Rome.

Given this steady consolidation of Roman power in Italy, the concept of Italy or 'Italia' as a distinct entity became more and more pronounced, as did a sense of shared kinship among its residents.[185] Complaining of the Roman handling of its Italian allies, Velleius Paterculus underlined the inequity by insisting that Italians, although they were being treated as foreigners and strangers, were actually of the same race and blood as the Romans.[186] Before turning to Roman encounters with groups outside the Italian peninsula, a distinction essential to Roman intra-group identification should be briefly reiterated: class. Social class played a vital role in Roman history from the earliest periods. In fact, the enunciation of the boundary separating plebs from patricians was so essential to the historical development of Roman state structure in the early Republic that some historians in the late nineteenth and early twentieth centuries – consistent with contemporary ideas about race and class – argued that Roman plebs and patricians were descended from different racial groups, with the patrician class in one form of the argument explicitly associated with Aryan invaders.[187]

Even as Rome was utilizing various strategies of incorporation, it would nonetheless have questions about its own setting of racial boundaries, and no group would do more to unsettle the boundary between inside and outside than the Greeks. Beginning in the eighth century, Greek colonies had been founded in Sicily and the southern part of Italy; by the fifth century the prosperous region was known as Magna Graecia. Such contact with the Greek world transformed Italy both culturally and economically, although it was not until the fourth century that the Romans themselves would become politically involved in Magna Graecia. During that same time, Greek writers first started to record their perceptions of Rome, seeking in variant ways to enfold the origins of the new upstart within their own literary traditions. Greek writers thus helped shape – perhaps even initiated – the idea that the Romans had originally descended from Aeneas following the legendary Trojan War.[188] In some Greek circles, there was even suggestion of actual consanguinity between the Romans and Greeks.[189]

Working their way east, Rome would eventually gain control over the Greek Hellenistic kingdoms, and in 146 BCE, the Romans defeated the

Achaean League, signalling their rule over Greece proper.[190] Although the Romans exercised clear political authority over the Greeks from then on, they continued to struggle in various ways to digest and contest the profound influence of Greek culture on their own. The Roman poet Horace's infamous claim that 'captured Greece subdued its fierce conqueror' by its arts conveys well the general disquiet.[191] In a tactic that parallels the strategies they applied to Egypt, the Romans sought at times to downplay Greece's enormous cultural influence by showing strong disdain for contemporary Greeks, thus driving 'an ideological wedge between the inventors of civilization and the Greeks of their own day'.[192] Such rivalry between Greece and Rome continued to be elaborated, at least from the Greek perspective, by a cultural movement lasting from approximately the mid-first to early third century CE known as the 'Second Sophistic', a movement that as Tim Whitmarsh phrases it, sought 'to construct Greek identity in relationship to the Greek past and Roman present.'[193]

Still, 'Greek' itself remained a prominent form of identification for both individuals and groups under the Romans, especially in the eastern part of the empire, and Greg Woolf has argued convincingly that it persisted precisely because it did not compete directly with structures of identity that mattered most to the Romans. In effect, Woolf proposes that 'Greek' and 'Roman' identities coexisted under Roman rule, because they operated in radically different ways: 'Greeks spoke Greek, worshipped the same gods, had certain customs and had a common descent that could be traced back to mythical times, but they were not characterized by a particular style. Romans, by contrast, valued common descent hardly at all, and regarded material culture and morality as much more central constituents of their sense of self'.[194] We will return to the role of Roman material culture in the next chapter; here it is worth noting that Cicero attests to the primacy of culture in Roman stereotypes attached to the Greeks when he records what he considers the best traits of a number of racial groups – the Spanish their numbers, Gauls their strength, Carthaginians their cunning, Greeks their culture, and the Latins and Italians their common sense, concluding that the Romans are superior because of their piety and reverence for the power of the gods.[195] Likewise showing the continuing respect he accorded Greece, Cicero in a different work divided the Roman world into three parts: 'Graecia', 'Italia', and 'barbaria'.[196] And in 'barbaria', or the barbarian territories in the west, the Romans would face a quite different set of challenges.

Racial formation and Roman empire

In expressing their attitudes towards race and racial difference, the Romans made extensive use of the Greek concept of the 'barbarian', translating it directly as *barbarus* in Latin. Yet, given their different political structure, one that progressively promoted the incorporation of others into their empire (rather than, say, the merits of democracy and self-rule), Roman writers shifted the connotations of the term dramatically. As Tina Saavedra writes, 'the Roman use of the barbarian as "other," while drawing on Greek traditions, was quite distinct in that themes of civilization and assimilation directed the definition of barbarian. Barbarism for the Romans implied an inferior condition, rather than an inferior nature.'[197] Thompson likewise argues that 'barbarianism' was not an absolute for the Romans, but was located along a scale: 'If the ideological system was one in which the term *barbarus* conjured up a whole universe of negativity and inferior ways of life, the degree of barbarianism of each "known" barbarian people was qualitatively evaluated in terms of distance from Roman values and qualities (including material development).'[198] Foremost in the rationale of Roman expansion was precisely the idea that different groups could be transformed by contact with the Romans – that 'barbarians', in effect, could (and therefore *should*) be 'civilized' by Roman rule.

In general terms, the Romans entertained hostile views of the presumed softness, luxury and decadence of eastern cultures, and in doing so, as Benjamin Isaac observes, they would apply Greek stereotypes of the east to the Greeks themselves, including many ideas once associated with the hated Persians.[199] Polybius (c. 200 BCE to sometime after 118) identifies three foreign combatants that were critical to Rome's rise in its early period – the Spanish, the Celts, and the Carthaginians – claiming that conquest of the latter, in particular, gave rise to Roman ambitions for world domination.[200] While all three groups occupied an important position in Rome's ongoing encounter with racial 'others' (Hannibal's feats, in particular, would haunt the Roman imaginary),[201] I would like to conclude this chapter with discussion of two groups whose prominent place in Roman racial thought testifies to the crucial intersection of racial formation and empire-building: the Gauls and Germans.[202]

Gauls and Germans

In 387 BCE the Gauls sacked Rome, an act that was 'in a sense, the start of modern Roman history for the authors of the late Republic';[203] Rome subsequently performed a kind of symbolic second foundation and from there it launched its progressive bid to expand its power and so never suffer similar defeat. The memory of this event would strongly resonate throughout later Roman depictions of the Gauls, and, in the third century, a group of Gauls invaded Greece and Asia Minor, forcefully entering the Hellenistic imaginary as well. These latter invasions are often assigned to the 'Celts' (derived from the Greek *Keltoi*), and J. H. C. Williams notes that the label 'Celt' has become especially popular in recent years, due in part to the current desire to 'posit the existence of a prehistoric European community under the name of "the Celts" as an encouragement to believe in the possibility of a future European unity'.[204] Regardless of motive, as Williams contends, the use of 'Celt' or 'Gaul' is only viable as an analytic tool if it is understood as designating a racial group or category defined externally (i.e. by the Romans), and not taken as connoting a collective racial identification from within,[205] a stipulation that is also necessary when talking about ancient 'Germans'. In fact, the so-called 'Gauls' and 'Germans' in antiquity generally identified themselves in terms of smaller groups or tribes, and the Romans themselves were frequently confused about how exactly to apply their own labels, i.e. where the spatial and conceptual boundaries between Gauls (or Celts) and Germans actually fell.[206]

Throughout the centuries, the Gauls gave the Romans endless headaches; yet, as Woolf points out, Roman accounts often obscure such difficulty:

'The point is not that the Gauls were not conquered and pacified – they were repeatedly – but rather that the establishment of a Roman order (*pax*) in Gaul was a longer process than Romans liked to admit'.[207] Testifying to some of the complexity of the Roman encounter with Gauls, the Gauls south of the Alps (i.e. in Cisalpine Gaul) had actually been subdued in the 190s, and just as 'Cicero was stirring up atavistic hatred between Romans and Gauls in support of Caesar's command in 56 BC',[208] these Gauls located in northern Italy were actually on the verge of Roman citizenship. Roughly a hundred years later, in 48 CE, the Roman senate deliberated whether to allow Gauls from across the Alps (from 'Gallia Comata' or 'long-haired Gaul') into the Senate, an occasion that allowed the Romans to reflect back on their prior treatment of foreign groups and their earlier encounters with the Gauls more specifically. The emperor Claudius' appeal for their admission, in which he referenced his own Sabine origins and the foreign roots of other prominent Roman families, evidently won the day.[209]

The Roman province Transalpine Gaul (often simply called 'Province' by the Romans or later Gallia Narbonensis) had been acquired in 121 BCE, and covered the southern part of Gaul from roughly the Alps to the Pyrenees. From 58–51 BCE, Julius Caesar led a series of campaigns in the remaining parts of Gaul, ostensibly to prevent the Helvetii tribe and Germans led by Ariovistus from gaining traction in territories closer to Rome. During those years, Caesar would not only achieve his immediate goals by brutally pacifying Gallia Comata – a territory which included, in today's terms, central and northern France, Belgium, the southern part of Holland, and the Rhineland – but also extend his mandate to cross the Rhine briefly, to cross the English Channel twice for short campaigns in Britain, and finally to put down a revolt led by the young upstart Vercingetorix at Alesia in 52 BCE. To keep his Roman audience engaged in his efforts, Caesar provided a written account of his campaigns, *The Gallic Wars*, describing not just the events of each year, but also the customs and characters of the various groups he encountered, in effect providing 'a justification, at an ethnographic level, both for subjugating the three Gauls and for renouncing any conquest of the lands beyond the Rhine'.[210]

In his discussion of the differences between the Gauls and Germans, Caesar adopted a more moderate tone about the Gauls than many of his contemporaries, although he noted that, just as the Gauls were themselves divided into two factions, factions and divisions occurred in every level of their society.[211] Caesar then explained that the Gauls lived in a strictly stratified society (with the plebs nearly the equivalent of slaves), a hierarchy dominated by the Druids and knights, the former clearly of greatest interest to Caesar.[212] He remarked that because of their religious beliefs they engaged in human sacrifice, although they ostensibly worshipped gods with Roman names like Mercury and Minerva and conducted lavish funerals for the dead. Finally, Caesar mentioned their dowry practice, in which husbands seemed to pay an equal portion, and also their practice of keeping children out of sight in public until they reached military age.[213]

The Germans, Caesar observed, differed greatly from the Gauls; lacking the same level of religious organization, for one, they believed only in divine elements they could see. According to Caesar, the Germans pursued a lifestyle defined by hunting and military pursuits, with no private property. Lacking agriculture, their diet consisted of milk, cheese, and meat. The Germans delayed sexual contact until after twenty (although appeared naked in public), and sought to maintain an uninhabited boundary between their territory and that of other people, undertaking armed raids in territory beyond their borders, although they respected the rights of guests.[214] Comparing the two groups, Caesar found that most of the Gauls, because of their greater contact with Roman provinces, had actually become 'softer' than the Germans, becoming accustomed, as he phrased it, to both luxury and defeat.[215] By framing his contrast of the Gauls and Germans in this way, Caesar importantly raised the prospect of the negative side of Rome's imperial mission, that is, its capacity to 'soften' character through its provision of both greater ease and greater luxury – a suspicion that Roman writers would find harder and harder to shake over time.

The character and customs of the Germans was an even greater theme for the Roman author Tacitus (c. 56–117 CE), and by Tacitus' time the Germans were a more immediate concern than they had been in Caesar's day, for in 9 CE, in what is today known as the *Varusschlacht* in German, the Germans led by Arminius had massacred Publius Quintilius Varus and his Roman forces, including three elite legions, in the Teutoburg Forest.[216] So traumatic was this event to the Roman consciousness that the numbers of the legions were apparently never used again, and the Roman historian Suetonius (born c. 70 CE) recounts a dishevelled emperor Augustus crying out at night for Varus to give him back his legions.[217] As Adrian Murdoch describes the impact: 'The loss of their presumed military infallibility affected the Roman psyche deeply. At a geopolitical level, Rome gave up any thoughts of the Elbe as the imperial boundary and retreated to the Rhine'.[218] Even as the defeat would force the Romans to readjust their strategic goals, Murdoch argues that it also transformed visions of Europe's landscape for centuries, making woodland spaces suddenly seem ominous and threatening and not merely pastoral or mystical. Later, the event would reemerge with gusto in narratives of German nationalism.[219]

In his *Annals,* Tacitus describes Germanicus' later indecisive campaigns in Germany, during which he and his men allegedly came upon the horrific scene of a battlefield from the previous slaughter.[220] Tacitus' most significant contribution to Roman views of the Germans, however, was his extensive ethnographic treatise, the *Germania*, in which he evinced both wariness toward the Germans and a certain admiration for them, constructing them as a kind of 'noble savage' in order to call attention to the dangers of the Romans' own increasing susceptibility to the softness and luxury of their empire. Tacitus' account follows the general structure of themes established by Caesar, although treating many at greater depth, e.g., the structuring of German society around war, their simple housing and lack of both cities and monetary systems, their marriage customs, and lifestyle and diet (in the latter case he notes their predilection for overindulging in beer).[221] Having given a general description of the Germans in the first half, Tacitus attempts in the second part to distinguish individual tribes, moving progressively to more remote areas.[222] Without question, the most notorious part of Tacitus' account is his insistence in the opening chapters on the autochthony and purity of the German race, expressing his belief that they have never intermarried with other groups and proposing that this practice allows all of them to share the same physical traits: 'fierce blue eyes, ruddy hair, and massive bodies fit for forceful action'.[223]

In assessing the Romans' attitudes towards the Germans, Benjamin Isaac suggests that the Germans provided the most pristine embodiment of the ancient environmental theory, serving as the archetypal 'northern' population. Isaac then links this potent position in the Roman racial imaginary to the Romans' unwillingness to engage the Germans in any final decisive confrontation.[224] Such an interpretation forges a powerful connection between racial theory and imperial practice, and it is tempting to assume that racial theory always informed Greek and Roman treatment of other groups. But there are many racial theories from antiquity that would be misleading if we treated them as manuals of actual practice. The Stoics, for example, had introduced the idea of the unity of humankind, advocating the necessity of recognizing such a bond by showing compassion for everyone.[225] Despite its influence on many Roman intellectuals, such a theory was clearly not able to offset the demands of Rome's growing empire,[226] reminding us that racial theory and racial practice do not always fully or coherently align: what we say or think – or say we think – about race is not always what we 'do' about it.

At a very different historical moment, Martin Luther King, Jr. pointed to the 'promissory note' that America had signed in its 'magnificent words of the Constitution and Declaration of Independence', with 'the promise that all men . . . would be guaranteed the unalienable rights of life, liberty, and the pursuit of happiness'. Yet King avowed that such ideals had failed to take shape in American practice, insisting that America 'has given the Negro people a bad check: a check which has come back marked "insufficient funds"'.[227] So it is time now to examine, on their own terms, some of the racial performances, and perhaps 'insufficient funds', that recurred in the conduct of everyday life in antiquity. By turning to race as a mode of social performance, we can shift from discussion of the ways the Greeks and Romans formulated racial categories in theory and ethnography to the infinite and intricate ways such categories were endorsed, subverted, and at times transformed by individual subjects themselves.

CHAPTER II

RACE AS
SOCIAL PRACTICE

So if anyone asks you what Her Britannic Majesty Queen Victoria had in common with Chinua Achebe, the answer is: they both lost their Albert![1]

Chinua Achebe

Reflecting on his upbringing in colonial Nigeria, author Chinua Achebe described the factors that governed his passage between two languages, Igbo and English, as well as his decision to drop the first part of his given name, Albert Chinualumogu – a decision that was not always recognized by friends and family; his mother stuck determinedly to 'Albert' 'to the bitter end'.[2] In this chapter, I want to examine the ways in which racial identities were formed and performed in the course of everyday life in antiquity, that is, within the variegated, and at times deeply intimate, nexus of personal decisions and practices that Achebe gives voice to. As Achebe's wry reference to Queen Victoria above illustrates, the seeming banality of everyday life does not correlate with its dearth of meaning in our understanding of race. Rather everyday acts situate race as a dynamic and perpetually negotiated field of engagement, one that takes place not merely in philosophical or ethnographic treatises, but also in more routine-seeming activities, such as filling out forms or the adoption and rejection of particular names. I want to treat social practice, then, as another distinct locus of ancient racial formation, looking not only at the habitual procedures of daily life, but also, by the end of the chapter, those practices and identifications undertaken *in extremis*.

As he looked back on the remarkable political transformations that had taken place during the reign of Augustus, the historian Cassius Dio (c. 163–235 CE) imagined one of Augustus' advisors advocating the virtues of a Roman monarchy by warning that '(o)ur population embraces every variety of mankind in terms of both race and character; hence both their tempers and their desires are infinitely diverse, and these evils have gone so far that they can only be controlled with great difficulty'[3]. Such sentiment reveals well that racial diversity could be perceived as a purveyor of great instability, an 'evil', requiring the Roman state to attend not only to the expansion of its power, but also the 'control' of the many populations it had absorbed. Michel de Certeau has drawn a distinction that helps open the operation of such governmental 'control' to further analysis. To begin, de Certeau associates the 'strategy' with those entities 'with will and power (a business, an army, a city, a scientific institution)', who – in their exercise of authority – employ place, i.e. that which 'can be delimited as its *own* and serve as the base from which relations with an *exteriority* composed of targets or threats (customers or competitors, enemies, the country surrounding the city, objectives and objects of research, etc) can be managed'.[4] A 'tactic', on the other hand, is the 'art of the weak', relying on the absence of power but partaking of the 'clever *utilization of time*, of the opportunities it presents and also of the play that it introduces into the foundations of power (*sic*)'.[5] My examination of race as social practice, then, seeks to highlight the daily negotiations that take place between institutional strategies and individual tactics, between the hegemonic procedures set down in space by those in power and the ephemeral acts that 'the weak' use to affirm or destabilize such structures at any one moment.

More specifically, this chapter concentrates on life in Ptolemaic Egypt and the Roman empire, and explores some of the particular sites and institutions in which racial formations were both produced and contested during these periods. In her study of the intersections of race, gender and sexuality within more modern colonial contexts, Anne McClintock lists well some of the institutions that help distribute power in such settings. McClintock writes:

I am deeply interested in the myriad forms of both imperial and anti-imperial agency. I am less interested, however, in agency as a purely formal or philosophical question than I am in the host of difficult ways in which people's actions and desires are mediated through institutions of power: the family, the media, the law, armies, nationalist movements and so on. From the outset, people's experiences of desire and rage, memory and power, community and revolt are inflected and mediated by the institutions through which they find their meaning – and which they, in turn, transform.[6]

As we shall see, institutions like language, law, army, government bureaucracy, family, and city were profoundly implicated in racial formations under the Ptolemies and Romans; so, too, the demands placed on individuals and groups in these environments led to a range of responses, including armed revolt. While I will examine more fully the role of such institutions in regard to racial formation and social practice, including the 'strategies' and 'tactics' that animated them, I want to turn first to a topic that has attracted considerable attention in recent years: where we might actually find the trace of ancient racial performances, a question that has circulated with special frequency around archaeology and the study of material remains from the past.

Material culture and racial formation

In distinguishing Greek and Roman modes of identification, Greg Woolf, as we have seen in the last chapter, attributes greater reliance on material culture to the Romans. While acknowledging that Greek material culture is of enormous interest to modern audiences, Woolf contrasts the meaning we make of it with its lack of centrality to the Greeks: 'But the fact that Hellenic culture, in all its various and loosely articulated forms, has left material traces through which *we* might characterize "the culture of the Greeks" does not imply that those who thought of themselves as Greeks regarded material culture as a particularly important mark of their identity.'[7]

In effect, Woolf calls attention to the fact that although every culture uses material practices (e.g., builds housing structures, wears clothing, eats food, creates art), not all cultures invest the same meaning in those practices; in short, how material goods are perceived by the groups producing and using them needs to be historicized every bit as much as the objects themselves.[8]

Seeking to interpret the dramatic spread of Roman material culture throughout the space of the Roman empire, classical historians once posited a forceful corollary to Hellenization: Romanization.[9] David Mattingly, identifying what he calls the '-ization problem' astutely notes that 'what makes Romanization and Hellenization particularly unhelpful constructs is that the terms are used to describe both *process* and *outcome*, so that the terms have become their own explanation.'[10] As an historical model, Romanization thus presumes that the infiltration of Roman material culture invariably entails broader social outcomes, i.e. that in the course of building and maintaining their empire the Romans also transformed 'non-Romans' in fundamental ways. In other words, the theory posits that the appearance of Roman pottery in the archaeological record in Britain indicates not just new consumer practices or the availability of new consumer goods, but more deep-seated changes in the meaning of British identity itself vis-à-vis the Romans.[11]

Theories of Romanization were closely linked to the rise of archaeology as a professional discipline in Britain in the early twentieth century, as we shall see in Chapter IV. This timing strongly suggests its foundations in modern imperial thought, and early proponents of Romanization often employed Rome as an explicit model for the modern British empire, placing '(a)t its core . . . imperial images that presented the idea of empire as divinely sanctioned.'[12] In addition to being a concept that openly took the side of empire, Romanization also showed its vulnerabilities when applied to actual evidence since, on the one hand, it presupposed the 'creation of imperial unity', while, on the other, '(e)ven a superficial knowledge of the archaeological material indicates that the culture of empire varied from location to location.'[13] Reinforcing the significance of local variation, post-colonial perspectives have encouraged a major reassessment of Romanization, and not least its implicit assumption that cultural change only travels from the top down. Ray Laurence proposes instead that '(w)hat we find in the Roman Empire is a situation of greater complexity, in which individual agents have far greater choice over how they construct or present their identity within the context of Roman colonization'.[14] In recent years, then, discussions of Roman material culture have aimed less at asserting Rome's 'civilizing' benefits (including assumptions about, say, how wonderful it might be to get Roman aqueducts) and more at identifying the wide array of users and uses of Roman culture as it spread.

The proposition that material culture can grant modern audiences access to 'a more complete lived experience in the past' is an appealing one,[15] although assumptions that frame archaeology and the study of material culture can often be deceptive. For one, as many scholars have observed, traditional terminology like 'archaeological culture' can itself imply a level of cohesion among surviving artefacts that is more apparent to the modern archaeologist than the original group.[16] Some archaeologists have also argued that archaeology's traditional reliance on material artefacts and their concomitant spatial arrangement yields dangerous conclusions about the testimony such patterning provides. For example, there is often a presumption that the sheer quantity of a certain object or style in the archaeological record correlates with its original significance. Yet most people carry keys today, and would their recurring appearance in a future archaeological record give witness to a meaningful aspect of our lives, i.e. do we invest the kind of meaning in keys that might be suggested by their number alone? Any attempt to link the common use of material goods specifically to the formation and articulation of group identity is even more precarious.[17] To cite just one example: although the buying of American cars has acquired connotations of nationalism for some consumers in the US, any sense that the purchase of American cars makes a uniform statement about national identity – and could be taken as such one hundred years from now – is clearly mitigated by many factors, not least that American consumers face increasing confusion over just how to define an 'American' car given that many 'foreign' brands are currently manufactured in the United States.

Financial concerns are perhaps even more pressing to most consumers. So to what extent could we distinguish choices based on slogans like 'drive American' from choices based on the actual costs of individual cars, not to mention their perceived reliability? In short, how can we reconstruct the varied motives of consumption from the surviving objects alone? Given the economic basis of many material practices, some scholars have argued that material culture is invariably a more reliable indicator of social class than race or ethnicity, and such distinctions are especially salient to the study of classical antiquity since the widespread adoption of Greek and Roman material culture – often most apparent in the distribution of so-called 'luxury goods' (e.g., jewellery and painted vases) – has traditionally been attributed to elite groups.[18] Indeed, a related bias recurs throughout other forms of ancient evidence, not least classical literature, making detailed reconstruction of the lives of lower-class groups a continuing challenge for classical historians.

Despite such convolutions, it is clear that material practice *can* provide insight into racial formation – at times people clearly *do* adopt material practices to assert a form of group identification, such as the use of pink triangles to signify gay pride – but that does not mean every act or material object, even when unique to a group, invariably *does*, e.g., that every ancient practice, such as burial custom or language use, gave a group or its individual members a salient sense of their collective bond and was being actively employed in affirming that bond. In calling for greater precision when applying archaeological evidence specifically to questions of what he calls ancient ethnic identity, Jonathan Hall has thus argued that 'while material symbols can certainly be selected as active emblems of a consciously proclaimed ethnic identity, it is a mistake to assume that material culture patterning can serve as an objective or passive indication of ethnic groups'.[19] In other words, when reconstructing ancient identity from the evidence of certain cultural practices, it is not enough to show that a certain group used a distinctive style of dress or a particular type of pottery without also demonstrating that the group used such practice in part to express its status *as* a group.

Given such caveats, Hall has strongly maintained that the reconstruction of ancient ethnic identity must ultimately rely on a very specific kind of evidence; Hall writes:

Ethnic identity is not a 'natural' fact of life; it is something that needs to be actively proclaimed, reclaimed and disclaimed through discursive channels. For this reason, it is the literary evidence which must constitute the first and final frame of analysis in the study of ancient ethnicity. In saying this, I am certainly not advocating a general principle of granting to literary evidence a primacy in *all* approaches to antiquity; it is simply that the very nature of ethnic identity demands this.[20]

Hall's conclusions have provoked considerable debate,[21] and I do not intend to resolve the matter here; I merely want to underline that while material evidence presents compelling ways of 'knowing' ancient people, inviting us into their lives in ways that differ markedly from other kinds of evidence, it also creates significant interpretive dilemmas, especially when it comes to reconstructing racial formations among past populations. It may finally only be possible – as Carla Antonaccio proposes when looking at group identification during Greek colonization of Sicily – to discern 'the *ethnic resonance* of certain cultural categories',[22] that is, to infer the influence of race or ethnicity in certain material remains without necessarily pinpointing the precise content, meaning or even boundary of the various racial identities themselves.

I will turn to literature's role in racial formations in the next chapter; for now, while continuing to utilize the language of race rather than ethnicity, I want to broaden Hall's notion of what 'discursive channels' might entail to include documentary papyri from Egypt, textual evidence that testifies to a range of racial strategies and tactics undertaken in the course of successive Greek and Roman rule.

Egypt under the Ptolemies

While modern perceptions of Egypt after Alexander the Great's conquest had been based for centuries on art and literature that survived from Alexandria (a major Greek city founded on Egypt's Mediterranean coast by Alexander himself, as its name suggests[23]), from the 1880s on the study of Ptolemaic and Roman Egypt was transformed by the dramatic discovery of hoards of ancient papyri.[24] Papyrus, a form of paper produced from a reed native to Egypt, was an important writing material in antiquity and was used in the recording of both public and private documents. While papyrus was a major Ptolemaic export, its unprecedented rate of survival in Egypt itself can be traced both to the dry climate and its reuse during the Ptolemaic period in the mummification process. With the exception of cities like Memphis, the most significant papyrological finds have come from the Fayum, a basin area to the west of the Nile that developed rapidly under the Ptolemies.

The vast majority of documents recorded on papyri in Egypt are written in Greek, although some have also been found in Demotic, the form of Egyptian used throughout the Ptolemaic and early Roman period; Coptic, a form of Egyptian written in Greek letters that emerges alongside the development of Christianity; and Latin, a language that was restricted to very limited communities in Roman Egypt, such as the army. The unearthing of ancient papyri has contributed in exciting ways to our corpus of classical literature. Victorian interest in the poetry of Sappho reached even greater fervour when Bernard Grenfell and Arthur Hunt discovered new fragments of her poetry in excavations at Oxyrhynchus.[25] But it is the remains of documentary papyri – the legal appeals, contracts, census and tax forms, school exercises, and personal letters – that have changed ancient studies by giving historians a more detailed picture of everyday life in Egypt than in any other part of the former Greco-Roman world.[26]

Papyrological evidence is unique because of the sheer plurality of voices and experiences it records, but consideration of its limits should precede any discussion.[27] First and foremost, given its paper-like properties, most papyri survive only in pieces or fragments, making many documents only partially legible at best. Even then, the information gleaned from papyri is necessarily restricted to what was recorded in writing, whether a reflection of personal preference, social convention or legal stipulation; in this way, certain kinds of racial performances remain out of reach, unless explicitly recorded by first-hand observers. The majority of surviving papyri also adheres closely to bureaucratic contexts, creating a bias toward formal and tightly regulated discursive expressions, i.e. texts bound by legal and other conventions. While literacy was certainly a factor in the production of ancient documents, potentially creating another serious bias – levels of literacy can be witnessed in both the actual form of writing and the signatories of many documents – scribes could be hired to help with the process, a profession interesting in its own right.

Stores of excavated papyri also differ greatly in the kinds of information they offer; in some cases, excavations reveal what seem to be personal document troves, while in others, more official collections – the difference akin to recovering something like a person's home filing cabinet (or now, perhaps, home computer) versus the archive of a government office like HM Revenue and Customs. Because of such varied sources, most documents frustratingly present themselves in total isolation, with limited possibility of determining how matters raised in them were ultimately responded to, or resolved by, their writers or recipients. Finally, interpretation of Greek versus Roman rule in Egypt is restricted to the kinds of documents recovered from each period, which evolve over time. Certain types of petitions, for example, become much more prominent in the Roman period, consonant with the growing political and social unrest,[28] but the prominence of these documents potentially drowns out other kinds of information.

Despite these limitations, papyri has provided an invaluable resource for ancient historians, one far outweighing any drawbacks, and as new details of everyday life began to emerge from the papyri, historians frequently applied perceptions of state power in the twentieth century to their interpretations of the material. Michael Rostovtzeff's harsh view of Roman economic policy in Egypt, for one, drew implicit parallels from his own experience of Marxist Russia.[29] Historians of Ptolemaic Egypt especially began to mull over the advantages of using modern experiences of colonialism, and postcolonial theory, in their studies. Praising the insights granted by modern anti-colonial movements, Edouard Will, for example, used comparative models from anthropology to propose a four-part typology he believed could be used to locate with greater nuance the potential range of Egyptian responses to Greek rule: active acceptance, passive acceptance, passive opposition, or active opposition.[30]

While later Roman rule in Egypt took a form familiar to audiences today (i.e. the Romans annexed Egypt as part of a larger empire), Ptolemaic Egypt was not entirely consistent with modern types of colonialism.[31] Following Alexander's death, the Ptolemaic dynasty established its roots firmly in Egypt so that even though they might be considered 'foreign' rulers, it would be impossible to link them to any state structure outside of Egypt. In other words, while it might be possible to imagine or even demand the departure of the Ptolemies, it would not be possible to adopt a slogan insisting that they 'go home' (as any viewer of Monty Python's *Life of Brian* knows is possible of the Romans, provided proper Latin forms are used). The papyrologist Roger Bagnall has therefore urged greater caution in applying certain kinds of modern comparisons to Ptolemaic Egypt. Of Will's typology itself, Bagnall highlights the potential confusion inherent in its simplistic classification of complex power relations, arguing: 'From the point of view of the indigenous population, acceptance and rejection may not be the real choices; even some types of rejection may be types of acceptance.'[32] How would we draw the line, for example, between persons refusing to fill out colonial paperwork and persons who, although they complete the requisite forms, do so with false information?

Bagnall also identified what he thought were key differences between ancient and modern versions of colonialism, including the dominant role of racism and religion in modern colonial projects. The function of ancient religion is undeniably a complex topic. Generally speaking, in antiquity, religion formed part of a set of cultural practices that, depending on the group, could help demarcate racial boundaries. Although there were occasions when members of certain religions were persecuted, the Greeks and Romans were not uniformly opposed to other religions, and the ancient Greeks certainly did not place religion, or religious conversion, at the heart of their colonial endeavours. Whether racism was also more negligible in antiquity is a difficult question, for even if racism was not the explicit engine of Greek conquest (we have seen the difficulties inherent in recon-structing Alexander's motives), perceptions of racial difference patently shaped Greek views of the world and their conduct within it.

Advocating additional points of contrast between Ptolemaic Egypt and modern forms of colonialism, Bagnall pointed out that the Ptolemies them-selves resided in Alexandria, not in some metropolitan capital outside the 'colony'.[33] Yet, as some historians have pointed out, Alexandria – where the Ptolemies and a large population of Greeks resided – was not exactly 'inside' Egypt conceptually, but remained in many ways exceptional from the time of its legendary founding.[34] Unseating Memphis, the traditional capital of Lower Egypt, Alexandria was a supremely Greek colonial inven-tion, one that stood primarily as – or in – surplus to the rest of Egypt. Its ambivalent relationship to Egypt in ancient thought is well encapsulated by the later Roman linguistic treatment of it as a separate entity: 'Alexandria by Egypt' (*Alexandria ad Aegyptum*).[35] While Bagnall ultimately concluded that comparative approaches threatened to distort our understanding of Egypt under Greek domination rather than enhance it, he did allow at least one promising vehicle of comparison, namely the 'imaginative literature growing out of the colonial experience'.[36] Offering the novels of Pramoedya Ananta Toer as an example, Bagnall proposed that such literature could attest to the private achievements and humiliations experienced under colonial rule, an emotional terrain mostly missing from, or suppressed deep within, the often-dry papyrological documents that survive.

Beyond these continuing debates about the 'colonial' nature of Ptolemaic Egypt, scholars have sought to define the precise modes of interaction between its various populations. Suggestive of the many diverse racial groups residing in Egypt, Dorothy Thompson has found evidence for the pres-ence of Phoenicians, Caromemphites, Jews, and Idumaeans in Memphis

during the Ptolemaic period.[37] Still, there, as elsewhere, the largest populations were always the native Egyptians and Greek colonizers, and the
points and tenor of contact between these two groups fashioned Ptolemaic
rule more than any other.

Greeks and Egyptians

Waves of Greek immigrants followed Alexander's campaigns,[38] and, after
the Greek conquest, Greek soldiers were also encouraged by land grants to
settle permanently in Egypt. This system of land distribution spread Greek
land-holders (or 'cleruchs') throughout the countryside, meaning that
arriving Greeks were not confined to cities or Greek settlements, but lived
alongside native Egyptians in many parts of Egypt.[39] What, then, was the
nature of their contact with one another? Was racial difference a palpable
part of the daily experience of Ptolemaic rule? Bagnall articulates concisely
the evolving scholarly opinion about this burning question:

> For more than half a century, the interaction of Greeks and Egyptians,
> and of Greek and Egyptian cultures, has provided the central inter-
> pretive motif for studies of Hellenistic Egypt. From the belief in a
> mixed society and culture which dominated scholarly thinking for
> more than a century until the Second World War, scholars have moved
> to something approaching consensus that by and large Greeks and
> Egyptians led parallel rather than converging lives, that their cultures
> coexisted rather than blended.[40]

The terms of Bagnall's account are revealing, as is the clear shift over time
from emphasis on the 'mixing' of the two groups to their fundamental
partition, a shift that relies less on the discovery of new papyri and more
on the ways racial practices and boundaries have been perceived over time
by different scholars.[41]

In its treatment of 'Greeks and Egyptians' and 'Greek and Egyptian
cultures' as corresponding terms of analysis, Bagnall's formulation also points

to a noteworthy slippage between racial identity (or 'society') and culture. Given the frequent reliance on cultural factors in ancient racial formations, linkage of the two initially seems quite valid; indeed, many ancient historians have turned completely to the notion of 'cultural identity' in labelling ancient modes of differentiation. But scholars in other disciplines have expressed concern about the prevailing tendency for simply replacing 'race' with 'culture' in many contexts when talking about collective identity. Katya Gibel Azoulay, for example, avers that the shift is made simply to avoid the frequent discomfort generated by race; in her words, '(t)he culture concept never quite replaced race thinking – it merely provided a new terminology that was less blatantly offensive'.[42] Walter Benn Michaels similarly declares that race's frequent recourse to essentialist ideologies, one of its most disturbing features, is merely re-inscribed in less obvious ways when using 'culture' instead. Michaels writes:

> Our sense of culture is characteristically meant to replace race, but ... culture has turned out to be a way of continuing rather than repudiating racial thought. It is only the appeal to race that makes culture an object of affect and that gives notions like losing our culture, preserving it, stealing someone else's culture, restoring people's culture to them, and so on, their pathos.[43]

Such caveats do not negate the significant heuristic value of a term like 'cultural identity' (indeed, many historians have applied it to the ancient world with great insight), but they do suggest unsettling reasons for the term's rapid rise in popularity in recent years, calling attention to some of the connotations 'culture' relies on for its meaning yet, at the same time, suppresses and evades.[44]

Michaels' conviction that 'it is only the appeal to race that makes culture an object of affect' or gives it 'pathos', moreover, seems born out by the treatment of culture in many discussions of classical antiquity. When characterizing the cultural practices of Greeks in Ptolemaic Egypt, for example, Bagnall suggests that '(t)he ability of the Greeks to adapt to new circumstances without fundamental cultural alteration, along with their position of power in Egypt, enabled them to take whatever they wished from Egypt *without ceasing to be Greeks*. It is not obvious that the Egyptians could do the same (my emphasis).'[45] Such an assertion helpfully underlines the role of power in cultural exchange (those in power surely can and often do 'take whatever they wish'), but does it overvalue the ostensible power and permanence of the category 'Greek', especially in completely denying any possibility of 'fundamental' change? (Not to mention the difficulty we might encounter in trying to distinguish between 'fundamental cultural alteration' and, say, 'minimal' much less 'partial' alteration in our sources.)

It is not hard to trace the underlying premise of this view back to Herodotus himself, who believed that the Greeks were skilled consumers of *nomoi*, able to retain the integrity of their own group even as they 'improved' it by borrowing strategically from others. But such a blanket statement about Greek cultural 'strength' here not only discounts any parallel agency on the part of Egyptians (i.e. failing to conceive that the Egyptians might have developed their own cultural tactics in this colonial environment), but also imposes equal and absolute results – not to mention desires – onto every cultural exchange, not to mention every 'Greek'. And what if a Greek borrowed Egyptian cultural practices without regard for her or his standing as 'Greek' or even intentionally to transform it?[46] Nor does the argument allow for the emergence of culturally hybrid practices (i.e. cultural forms that were neither 'Greek' nor 'Egyptian' exclusively), including those that may have permitted or even consciously promoted a range of racial identifications. The god Serapis was a divinity derived from the amalgamation of both religious systems, and was presumably popular among both Greeks and Egyptians.[47] How might we reconstruct the 'changes' his worship wrought in cultural or racial terms across this prospective audience? So, too, Egyptian gods of the dead appear comfortably alongside Greek and, later, Roman iconography in the catacombs of Alexandria,[48] including an intriguing representation of an Anubis wearing Roman armour – and who is to say the subjectivity of these users did not alter fundamentally with the deployment of such hybrid cultural forms?[49]

Setting aside the question of culture *per se*, we can identify many social and political structures that helped the Greeks uphold their 'position of power in Egypt'. Land, for one, was an important source of power and revenue under the Ptolemies. Most land was considered a crown possession, although cleruch land eventually became hereditary, meaning it could be passed down within the families of Greek soldiers, creating a class that saw itself 'more and more as a kind of landed aristocracy, and less and less as soldiers'.[50] Other land was granted to the Egyptian temples from which the class of Egyptian priests – a group instrumental to the Ptolemies – derived much of its wealth and privilege. The majority of Egyptians, however, laboured on the land as tenant farmers, taking leases either from the crown or from the Greek cleruchs. As such, they were responsible for taxes on the land, but were given little opportunity to amass economic advantages from it.

Education also helped buttress Ptolemaic rule in significant ways. Given the progressive reliance on Greek as the official language, Greek education was essential for producing a steady supply of civil servants. Knowledge of Greek, in turn, provided tangible benefits to the individuals who were able to attain it, allowing them to work within or negotiate the state bureaucracy more skilfully. While it served the state's needs, education in Ptolemaic Egypt was a private concern, funded by students and their families, linking it primarily to the upper class.[51] The ability to read and write Demotic, on the other hand, was evidently transmitted through temple schools in Egypt, and there is some evidence that Greek was also taught at those sites.[52] In this way, Greek and Greek education were not the sole possession of Greeks, but also became important tools of social mobility for the Egyptian upper class as well. To what extent the acquisition of Greek education brought personal crisis to individual students is another story. One Demotic school text preserves the poignant outburst: 'I will not write Greek letters; I am stubborn.'[53]

As we shall see, although they were financed privately, teachers eventually received a tax break from the Ptolemies, suggesting some of the economic strategies the Ptolemaic government developed to promote its social goals.

The concept of governmentality, a concept first introduced by Michel Foucault, helps further unveil the operation of Ptolemaic state power, what I have loosely been calling state 'strategies'. In noting that governmentality places primary emphasis on *how* rule is conducted rather than who rules or why, Mitchell Dean suggests that one axis of governmental conduct pertains specifically to identity formation, allowing us to query: 'what forms of person, self and identity are presupposed by different practices of government, and what sort of transformations . . . these practices seek'.[54] In real terms, then, we might ask how governmental actions serve to set boundaries between groups, rewarding some and placing others at a disadvantage, and with what consequences or in aim of what sorts of changes among its population. To give just one example, many recent debates in the United States have openly deliberated whether it is in the interest of the US government to require that everyone conform to a range of 'American' practices in public, such as use of the English language – debates that, on one side, clearly see the assimilation of immigrant groups as essential to national interests.

David Theo Goldberg further highlights some of the mundane bureaucratic practices that aid governmental conduct with regard to race: 'Racial governmentality is defined and administered by means of forms (pieces of administrative paper). Bureaucratic forms reproduce as they reflect racial identities, distributing them both throughout the culture.'[55] – meaning that by checking a box under 'race' when we fill out certain government forms, we endorse and perpetuate a logic that sees such categories, and the production of knowledge around such categories, as fundamental to good governmental policy. In their attempts to sort their populations racially, as well as monitor the racial boundaries they have created, many governments have turned to a very specific kind of form and practice: the census.

Racial governmentality

The American census began in 1790, as mandated by the US Constitution. Although US census data can be used to determine the distribution of public resources – allowing local governments to estimate, for example, the number of hospitals or level of public services needed in any area – it has only one official purpose: to determine representation in Congress. From its origins, the US census has employed racial categories in counting its population, initially distinguishing 'between "free white males," "free white females," "all other free persons" (by sex and colour), "untaxed Indians," and "slaves,"'[56] the latter whose count as 'three fifths' a person as stipulated by the Constitution was factored into the calculation of congressional representation, while 'Indians not taxed' were excluded altogether (Article 1, Section 2, Paragraph 3). Over time, even as they no longer directly influenced congressional representation, racial categories were retained on the census, albeit using evolving categories that sought to track changing social and historical factors; thus the option 'Chinese' was added in 1870 due to the extensive importation of Chinese labour in the west.[57]

Given its continuing commitment to tracking certain aspects of identity among the American population, the US Census has attempted, often inadequately, to keep pace with the changing views and terminology of American race. As Goldberg observes, '(t)he form . . . like those employed in the census that speak to identity, always lags behind the complex negotiation of identities and (self-)identifications in everyday experience, even as it serves in part to shape and to fix those identities and identifications.'[58] Through its attempts to 'describe' the American population, in other words, the census both fails to capture the range of lived experiences among the population and, at the same time, advances racial attitudes and racial terminology that may take root in some of those filling out the forms, whether consciously or not. Central to the American census has always been its reliance on self-declaration, meaning that individuals are asked to fill out their own forms and their answers are not subject to 'validation' by external observers or government officials. While the census remains anonymous by design, President Obama openly announced that he had checked 'Black, African-Am or Negro' on his 2010 census form – refusing the option to mark more than one category or to write in his own[59] – an announcement that caused considerable comment given his own widely-publicized interracial background, not to mention calling attention to the fact that the census itself still employed the term 'Negro', a term many considered outdated.

Many ancient governments conducted a census, albeit for very different motives. In pharaonic Egypt, the census was used to determine the availability of labour,[60] while in Rome the census initially tracked available military resources, but later become firmly linked to public declaration of wealth and so formal determination of one's class rank.[61] In Ptolemaic Egypt, the census – which apparently utilized both personal declaration and records maintained by government officials – was explicitly linked to taxation: a population count was desired precisely so taxes could be assessed.[62] As with the census, close examination of tax policy reveals the ideology and priorities of state systems in unique ways. The differential treatment of married couples and non-married individuals has long been a subject of contention in the US tax code. So, too, US tax policies have traditionally rewarded property ownership and other types of wealth accumulation, thus treating as a federal priority the shoring up of a specific economic class. Tax systems likewise give revealing insight into the ideologies of ancient states, as well as their discriminatory impulses. Perhaps the most dramatic example is the special tax levied on Jewish residents of the empire by the Romans following the Jewish wars (66–73 CE), a tax (the *fiscus Iudaicus*) that demanded recompense for the costs of the war and, not inconsequentially, required formal state identification of Jews.

Under the Ptolemies, as later Romans, both people and land were taxed, and taxes levied on individuals illustrate the explicit economic privilege awarded to certain groups. While the obol tax, equivalent to approximately one day's wage, would later be dissolved into something called the salt-tax, Ptolemaic tax records suggest that exemptions were given during its use to those who classified as 'Greeks' ('Hellenes') and 'Persians', the latter group accounting for only about one percent of the population.[63] Willy Clarysse has called this obol tax 'clear proof of official discrimination against the Egyptian part of the population.' He continues: 'Such a discrimination, even if the payment involved was very small, necessitated separate registers of Greeks and Egyptians. Thus, being a Greek or an Egyptian was not just a matter of personal and community feeling ("ethnicity"), but also an official policy.[64]

In assessing the approximate size of the privileged 'Greek' group, Dorothy Thompson estimates that only sixteen percent of the adult population in one region of Egypt claimed the designation 'Greek'. She further insists that this status of 'Greek' did not rely on claims of Greek origin alone:

> (s)ome of these tax-Hellenes were certainly ethnic Greeks, . . . the category also included those from Egyptian families who worked within the administration and came to form part of the privileged group. Greek origins were clearly not necessary for the acquisition of an Hellenic designation; Jews too might count as Hellenes. 'Greeks' were no longer Greeks . . .[65]

As Thompson's terminology of 'tax-Hellenes' suggests, then, taxation provided one context in which racial identity could be formed and expressed in Ptolemaic Egypt, and such a context set boundaries in ways perhaps different from our expectations: Jews and Egyptians were also able in some cases to claim 'Greek' tax-status, and so receive its financial benefits.

Accounts of the salt-tax, the more enduring form of poll-tax, indicate that its rate went down over time, but that exemptions were now granted to 'schoolteachers, athletic coaches, (most probably) artists of Dionysus, and victors in the games of the various Alexandrian festivals'.[66] Over time, Ptolemaic tax policy thus explicitly turned to cultural criteria rather than 'Hellenes' *per se* when granting exemptions. As Thompson sees it, these exemptions couched in 'cultural' terms now gave clear 'dispensation to those prepared to "go Greek."'[67] This transition in tax code from privileges for 'Hellenes' to privileges for those who supported key Greek cultural practices reinforces conclusions discussed elsewhere (e.g., Chapter I), namely that during the Hellenistic period, cultural practice was acquiring greater and greater authority in defining Greek identity. But we might stop to consider further this state investment in getting certain non-Greeks to 'go

Greek' – was assimilation a major Ptolemaic state strategy? What was the impact of such policies on those governed? Even more, was the opportunity to 'go Greek' available to everyone or monitored strictly by other criteria? In trying to capture the actual tone of such policies, modern scholars have used very different characterizations, dividing over whether Ptolemaic rule operated with a carrot or stick; thus, while some scholars underline the possibility of reward and positive incentives, others emphasize the punishment for those not meeting the criteria. One scholar has even used the word 'apartheid' of Ptolemaic Egypt.[68]

As Dean insists, it is nonetheless critical to distinguish the identities produced by various kinds of governmental practices from the actual range of identifications and actions undertaken by the people themselves:

> Regimes of government do not *determine* forms of subjectivity. They elicit, promote, facilitate, foster and attribute various capacities, qualities and statuses to particular agents. They are successful to the extent that these agents come to experience themselves through such capacities (e.g., of rational decision-making), qualities (e.g., as having a sexuality), and statuses (e.g., as being an active citizen).[69]

And when looking more closely at the surviving documents, the racial practices of individuals undertaken in response to Ptolemaic rule seem more fluid than we might anticipate, so also more varied.

Racial subjectivity

Although Greek functioned as the official language of Ptolemaic rule, the use of Demotic persisted in certain administrative contexts.[70] So, too, a separate Egyptian legal system existed alongside the newer Greek one for a long time. In 146 BCE, it was mandated that every Egyptian contract (i.e. one executed in the native Demotic language) be recorded also in a Greek registry office,[71] presumably in order to make the Egyptian court obsolete. Nearly thirty years later, however, Ptolemy VIII issued an edict that, among other provisions, sought to clarify the jurisdiction of both the Greek and Egyptian court systems, testifying to the continuing survival of both.[72] Even more, the language of the edict suggested that users of each court system were not following what might seem like racially predictable patterns, that is, 'Egyptians and Greeks were making contracts with one another both in Greek and Demotic Egyptian, and . . . Greeks might even make contracts with Greeks in Demotic'.[73]

We can witness more personal responses to Ptolemaic racial governmentality in the cases of individuals whose extant documents testify to the ways identity was perceived and mobilized in everyday encounters. Many of these documents shed light on the meaning, and often seeming privilege, attached to the category of 'Greek', but we will also see that it was a privilege at times challenged by others. Among the papers of Zenon, an estate manager who lived in Philadelphia (near modern Cairo) in the mid-third century BCE, is an intriguing request from an unnamed person, perhaps originally from Syria, for Zenon's help in getting a payment due to him. Claiming poor treatment from two of Zenon's subordinates, who, he insists, are trying to force him to accept wine in lieu of his salary, the petitioner bemoans the fact that he is being mistreated because he is a 'barbarian' and, even more suggestively, because he 'does not know how to act like a Hellene'.[74] Crediting his discrimination to the fact that he is not Greek, the petitioner, through such loaded phrasing, gives apparent support to two of the racial theories we encountered in the last chapter, that is, the use of 'barbarian' in categorizing all non-Greeks and the increasing reliance on practice, on 'acting the Hellene', in establishing the boundary between 'Greeks' and others.

While the petition to Zenon attributes economic abuse to racial discrimination, many papyri seek redress for other forms of misconduct, including open acts of violence. Among the recovered files of a certain Diophanes, a *strategos* (i.e. district governor) of the Arsinoite nome from 222–218 BCE, there are twenty-five papyri showing Greeks and Egyptians in direct conflict with one another, one-fifth of the documents surviving in the collection. Eighteen of these complaints come from Greeks, and half of the documents alleging physical violence are brought by Greeks against Egyptians, with only one complaint from an Egyptian against a Greek.[75] In perhaps the most striking case, a man named Herakleides, who identifies himself explicitly as a 'Greek and a visitor', demands that the Egyptian woman Psenobastis be punished for dumping a full chamber pot on him, then physically assaulting him.[76] Although Herakleides places considerable emphasis on his own status as 'Greek', we have no way of knowing whether Herakleides' 'Greekness' motivated Psenobastis' acts in the first place (or, if so, how exactly she would have recognized him as Greek, perhaps through the tone of superiority he dons in his petition), nor even if she was eventually punished. Even more, we can discern the complementary role of gender in Herakleides' outrage, for he makes it abundantly clear that it is not just an Egyptian, but an Egyptian *woman* who has so publicly demeaned him.

Similar indignation infuses a later series of texts that come from a large sanctuary complex dedicated to the god Serapis outside Memphis. In one appeal dated to 163 BCE, Ptolemaios, a so-called 'recluse' living in the sanctuary, complains that temple bakers have attempted to drive him out of the temple, as they did previously 'when the revolt was on'; he then expands that they attempted such action 'despite the fact that I am a Greek!'[77] Two years later, he repeats the same phrasing – 'despite the fact that I am a Greek!' – when he complains of another attack by the same group, presumably Egyptians, whom he first calls 'temple cleaners', but later identifies by a broader range of occupations, including clothing seller and baker.[78] While we lack any record of why the alleged attacks were made, (not to mention any 'defence' offered by those committing them), the phrasing of Ptolemaios' appeal itself reveals important perceptions about the role of identity in such encounters, at least from Ptolemaios' vantage point.

For one, even as Ptolemaios claims emphatic identification as Greek in the body of each complaint, he also asserts a more specific identity as Macedonian, initially calling himself 'Ptolemaios, son of Glaukias, Macedonian'. Such a tactic establishes his identity within the category 'Greek' (or among Greeks, for whom 'Macedonian' presumably retained a certain amount of prestige through its historical associations with Alexander) even as his petition itself relies on setting 'Greek' against 'Egyptian' in encapsulating the degree of his maltreatment. This dual identification signals the continuing relevance of both external and internal modes of Greek identification, at least according to Ptolemaios, well into the Ptolemaic period. Finally, although Ptolemaios explicitly labels himself 'Greek', he uses economic class or occupation instead to classify his attackers, presumably reinforcing the gap opened by his 'Greekness'. Such a strategy finds revealing parallel in the many intersections of race and class in more modern eras, and occupation or profession may correlate with another important marker of racial identity in Ptolemaic Egypt: names.

When historians seek to determine the racial identities of various individuals in the papyri, a considerable problem arises – how exactly can Greeks and Egyptians be distinguished in the surviving texts given that the explicit use of such terminology is far from universal? In other words, although Ptolemaios and others at times openly label themselves 'Greek' and others 'Egyptian', such identities are far more often implicit in the texts and need to be inferred by modern scholars. Papyrologists have conventionally identified those with Greek-sounding names as Greek and those with Egyptian-sounding names as Egyptian. But as Achebe's experience denotes, any reliance on names alone is endangered by the intricacy of their operation, involving potential concerns about who has assigned the name, when it is being used, and why. Heightening this complexity is the differential use of names, as well as differential economic advantages, existing within individual families in Ptolemaic Egypt. In looking at tax records, Thompson has thus found 'in two cases . . . Egyptian named brothers . . . (who) pay the full rate of both the salt-tax and the obol tax, while the brothers with Greek names pay only the salt tax',[79] a situation that raises all sorts of questions for a modern audience, not least how such a dynamic came about, what distinguishes the brothers on each side, and what role such difference might have played in interactions among family members.

Perhaps even more unexpectedly, scholars have discovered the use of double names in Ptolemaic Egypt, that is, individuals employing a Greek name in one context and an Egyptian name in another. In one case, public documents from the village of Kerkeosiris in the latter part of the first century BCE (c. 120–110 BCE) attest to the activities of a village scribe named Menkhes, but private documents show him also using the Greek name Asklepiades. In the latter context, Asklepiades defines himself openly as a 'Greek born in Egypt', phrasing that notably asserts a 'Greek' essence distinct from his geographic origin.[80] Given such divergent names, some scholars have opened Menkhes' interstitial position in the colonial bureaucracy to greater examination, wondering what his personal background, including this private allegiance to 'Greekness', might have meant when conducting his official duties. For, although the general function of the village scribe was to keep agricultural records, Menkhes received five different complaints on a single day from Egyptian farmers complaining about the outrageous behaviour of a Greek cleruch in his village[81] – what personal biases or social networks, if any, might Menkhes have brought to the mediation of such encounters?[82]

From examples like these, Willy Clarysse has proposed that, while names might be fairly reliable indicators of racial identification early in the Ptolemaic era, by the second century BCE, names could correlate more closely with occupation in some cases, meaning that the racialization of certain occupations outweighed the personal sensibility of its holder, i.e. the person's own racial identification. Clarysse expands:

> I do not want to suggest that there was any legal obligation to change one's name or to use a Greek or Egyptian name upon becoming *epistates* or village scribe respectively . . . But one job was felt to be Egyptian in character, the other was felt to be Greek, and since the people involved seem quite often to have had double names, the corresponding name was used more frequently than the other.[83]

Since our evidence for such a phenomenon seems to fall primarily within the Ptolemaic bureaucracy, the use of double names might, of course, be related to the possession of other distinct privileges, and Clarysse notes that a broader social phenomenon apparently facilitated such practices, i.e. that the people in these positions presumably already had double names when they assumed their jobs, placing them within another prominent colonial institution: Greek and Egyptian intermarriage.

Family in the colonial contest

In addition to furnishing structures for economic accumulation and distribution through features like the dowry, marriage has historically provided an important social and legal framework for both regulating the relations between men and women and for setting boundaries between communities. The energy expended on the latter function can be witnessed in the way marriage customs are established by particular groups, most notably whether marriage is practiced *within* a particular community (endogamy) or conducted *between* different communities (exogamy). The role of exogamous marriage is apparent in the Roman myth of the Sabines, which enshrines the fundamental 'outsider' status of Roman wives at the very origins of Roman self-definition.[84] At the other end of the scale, an extreme version of endogamy can be witnessed in Egyptian brother-sister marriages, although the actual rate of such marriages has been widely debated in the Greek and Roman periods – public image of the Ptolemies aside.[85] McClintock considers family a key institution marked by colonial power relations: in what ways did family and marriage practice help organize racial formation in the context of Ptolemaic Egypt?

Using tax and census documents from the early Greek period, Dorothy Thompson has identified potentially striking differences between Greek and Egyptian household structures, with Greek households generally incorporating more people, including non-kin, and Greek cleruchs having the largest households overall, confirming the economic privilege they routinely show in other types of records.[86] Two other differences of note also appear: slaves are mostly confined to Greek households and Greek households show proportionately fewer women, suggesting either the conscious under-reporting of women – who paid taxes in this period – or differing attitudes about female children across Greek and Egyptian culture, with the exposure of female children possibly practiced by Greek families.[87] There is obviously a genuine risk in looking at family structure through the lens of race, hence heated debates in the US over the infamous 1965 'Moynihan report' on the 'Negro family'.[88] Yet Thompson's analysis raises important questions about the family as a racialized institution, including the respective attitudes towards slaves and women in each group.

The earliest Greek document from Egypt is a marriage contract between a couple named Demetria and Heracleides, dated to 311 BCE;[89] such names, especially at this time, suggest they both belonged to the newly arriving population of Greeks, and some Greeks surely continued to follow consciously endogamous patterns in this colonial setting. The earliest document attesting to marriage between Greeks and Egyptians dates to 250 BCE, however, and other documents affirm that such marriages later became common in the Ptolemaic period.[90] Thompson found that nine percent of 'Greek' households in her sample featured wives with Egyptian names, while there were no examples of the reverse: Egyptian named heads of household with Greek named wives. Such disparity may, of course, reflect contemporary social mores, but it also presumably reflects the military roots of the Greek population, as well as the disturbing paucity of women in Greek households,[91] placing greater pressure on Greek men to seek marriage partners outside their racial group.

By the end of the third century, children of these marriages, who regularly bear both Greek and Egyptian names, appear throughout the documentary record,[92] and there is little evidence in surviving Ptolemaic evidence for the kind of anxiety about miscegenation or 'race-mixing' that appears in other historical contexts. In fact, the opening of the racial category 'Greek' to such children suggests the opposite. Still, the general pairing of race and gender – Egyptian and female, Greek and male – within such interracial families seems to establish clear patterns in subsequent generations with daughters in those families more likely to retain Egyptian names than sons. Such practices might reflect the limited entry of women into public life, where Greek names and knowledge of Greek would clearly have been advantageous, but there is a provocative example of a woman holding dual names that allows closer examination of the potential choices of Egyptian women within such marriages, as well as the difficulties with which this entire class of so-called 'Greco-Egyptians' is approached by modern scholars.

One of the most well-attested cases of intermarriage from the Ptolemaic period involves a man named Dryton, an active member of a Greek cavalry unit, who was transferred to the town of Pathyris around the year 152 BCE. While there, he married a young girl, perhaps as much as thirty years younger than himself. This new wife – either his second or third – was from a family whose members already possessed double names, and she herself went by both the Greek name Apollonia and an Egyptian one, Senmonthis. Displaying conspicuous economic power, Senmonthis appears in a range of financial documents after her marriage and her willing use of her Egyptian name in such contexts, as well as employment of Demotic in some, seems to defy general scholarly assumptions about privilege and upward mobility in this era, namely that anyone who *could* claim access to 'Greekness' in Ptolemaic Egypt invariably *would*. Criticizing those who deny Senmouthis a primary identity as Greek – and arguing that 'she explicitly styles herself a "Greek" in both Demotic and Greek legal documents' – Robert Ritner proposes that these scholars have insisted on her essential 'Egyptianness' precisely because they are uncomfortable with the possibility of a Greek woman choosing to 'act' Egyptian on occasion, apparently seeing it akin to a kind of 'slumming'.[93] More broadly, Senmonthis' own patent failure to show absolute preference for one identity over the other continually frustrates modern scholars' attempts to pinpoint her 'true' identity, i.e. to discern whether she was 'really' Greek or 'really' Egyptian beyond such legal procedures. Indicative of the stalemate, at one point 'four scholars – two Demoticists and two Hellenists – divide(d) evenly in print on this point, with one Demoticist and one Hellenist on each side.'[94]

Given the bias of surviving papyri toward bureaucratic paperwork, such controversy illustrates well the problems we encounter in seeking to weigh public expressions of racial identity against the more private or intimate identifications that might have worked differently behind closed doors in such a colonial environment – who Senmonthis thought she 'really' was, if indeed she looked at it that way. Lewis notes that over time, especially after the death of Dryton, Senmonthis and Dryton's daughters increasingly used their Egyptian names, which might be suggestive of greater personal allegiance to the Egyptian identification. He further proposes that these were 'the names by which they were generally known and addressed locally, the names which they and their neighbours used in an area where nearly all the population were of Egyptian descent'.[95] Eventually, the daughters were even able to use their Egyptian names in Greek tax receipts, presumably without jeopardizing their 'non-Egyptian' tax status.[96] Still, three of the sisters used Demotic documents for their respective divorces, and their tactics (as well as Senmonthis') might also emanate from the greater power of women in the Egyptian legal system, which allowed women to conduct business without a male guardian unlike the Greek system. (Underscoring the divergent ways gender is inflected within colonial and imperial structures, economic opportunities for women apparently increased even more during the Roman period. Two separate studies have now shown that some women in Roman Egypt were able to exercise greater autonomy during times of economic duress,[97] a phenomenon that finds intriguing parallel in American women's economic gains during World War II, a growing power well-captured in the iconic image of Rosie the Riveter.)

The modern urge to pigeonhole Senmonthis racially in one category or another, as fundamentally Greek or Egyptian (one being her essence, the other presumably only ephemeral performance), might call to mind our impulses toward an even more prominent woman of hybrid identifications in Ptolemaic Egypt: Cleopatra. Gerry Smyth has helpfully called out scholarly tendencies that treat the concept of hybridity as 'a permanent oppositional force, a panacea for the ills of colonialism that emerges always and everywhere within designated "colonial" formations', claiming that it is dangerous to romanticize or project our own notions of resistance onto people experiencing colonial situations in the past, especially when their solutions seem so intriguingly post-modern.[98] Even so, it seems possible to conclude that during the Ptolemaic period racially hybrid identities were possible for both men and women – at least among a certain social class –

even if men and women did not employ them, or even have access to them, at the same rate.

In the world of Ptolemaic Egypt, then, 'Greekness' was not an identification defined solely by essentialism; entry into the racial category of Greek could be opened to 'others' under certain conditions, especially as the era progressed. At the same time, the procedures of Ptolemaic governmentality suggest that the categories themselves retained their usefulness, that a conceptual and ideological boundary separating 'Greek' and 'Egyptian' remained intact despite its crossings, as well as an accompanying value system that placed 'Greek' over 'Egyptian.'[99] Given the persistence of such hierarchies – hierarchies that, as the documents demonstrate, filtered from government conduct into less formal or everyday encounters – for the vast majority of Egyptians such crossings were presumably unattainable under any circumstances. By the Roman period, the door would be even more firmly shut.

Egypt under Roman rule

From the time Augustus took possession of Egypt in 30 BCE, he treated it as his own personal possession, designating it as a special kind of province that would be ruled by a prefect not the standard proconsul, a designation that allowed him to appoint members of the equestrian order to the high office, as well as control the movement of Roman senators, his main rivals, into and out of Egypt. Charged with providing grain in large quantities to Rome, Roman prefects over the centuries exploited Egypt's resources mercilessly, imposing burdens on individuals through both substantial liturgies, i.e. compulsory public services, and increasingly oppressive methods of taxation.[100] Illustrating the Romans' own awareness of their extreme levels of coercion, the emperor Tiberius, when receiving larger revenues than expected from Egypt, once infamously 'reminded' one prefect, 'I want you to shear my sheep not flay them'[101] – a demeaning statement far more explicit in the pleasure it takes from imperial power than anything that survives from the Ptolemies.

Under the Romans, Egyptians paid the highest rate of the poll-tax, and although individual Roman officials would occasionally show leniency, by the early third century CE, the Roman administration had sought to exact such exorbitant taxes from the residents of Egypt that a growing class of 'tax fugitives' was created, i.e. those who had fled from their homes because they were unable to pay. The strain on local communities by such losses was further exacerbated when the Romans, for a time, made the rest of the community collectively responsible for the taxes of those who had disappeared.[102] There is widespread evidence for dramatic population decline in many Egyptian villages in these later eras, and some scholars have argued that natural disasters like drought must have been at least partially to blame. Rostovtzeff, however, forcefully counters such theories, maintaining that any ongoing crisis in crop production was attributable solely to overreaching Roman greed.[103] One of the most explicit documents of Roman racial governmentality in Egypt, a document dating almost two hundred and fifty years after the death of Cleopatra, illustrates well the Roman antipathy toward 'tax-fugitives', as well as providing a fascinating set of instructions for identifying those fugitives who were presumably using the cover of the city to 'pass' as something else.

In 215 CE, as the Roman emperor Caracalla was planning war with Parthia, certain residents of Alexandria evidently ridiculed him openly. When Caracalla subsequently arrived in Egypt, a number of Alexandrians came out to meet him, and he brutally ordered them to be executed on the spot. After allowing his soldiers to wreak havoc in the city, Caracalla next issued a series of edicts, including one that is often loosely described as an attempt to expel all Egyptians from the city. The edict reads in part:

All Egyptians who are in Alexandria, and particularly country folk who have fled thither from elsewhere and can easily be identified, are absolutely by every means to be expelled, not, however dealers in pigs and river-boat men and those who bring in reeds for heating the baths. But expel all the rest, who disturb the city by their very numbers and their lack of occupation. I am informed that at the festival of Serapis and on certain festal days – and even on other days as well

– Egyptians observe the custom of bringing in bulls and some other animals for sacrifice. They are not to be prevented from coming in for that. The ones to be prevented are those who flee the countryside where they belong in order to avoid farmwork, not those who converge upon Alexandria out of a desire to view the glorious city or come here in pursuit of a more cultured existence or on occasional business.[104]

Caracalla's edict is unprecedented among surviving Roman imperial documents in not only demanding specific actions against a racial group, but also explicitly detailing the methods by which that group's members are to be identified. Thus, the edict further spells out: 'Amongst the linen weavers the true Egyptians can easily be recognized by their speech, which reveals that they are affecting the appearance and dress of others. What is more, in the way they live their manners, the opposite of urbane behaviour, reveal them to be Egyptian rustics.'[105]

When working with racial governmentality the devil is at times in the details, and the first point to notice when reading Caracalla's edict is that while it begins with what seems a categorical instruction ('all Egyptians'), it soon becomes evident that not every Egyptian is to be removed, rather those contributing to the economic life of Alexandria are exempted. The real target of the expulsion is that group of Egyptians who are fleeing from their responsibilities in the countryside, presumably meaning tax fugitives, and once again we find a powerful link between race and economic class. In seeking to define the precise Egyptians for expulsion, moreover, the document emphatically adopts the language of essentialism ('true Egyptians'), yet when it actually clarifies how to identify 'true Egyptians,' the document leans on social performance, not the physical body or some other marker of 'essence', naming both the performances that it believes conceal such essence (appearance and dress) and also the performances that conversely give it away (speech and manners).

In all, through the document's attempts to expunge certain 'undeserving' groups from Alexandria, we apprehend once again a clear tension between seeing and being, performance and essence, but now from the perspective of Roman governmentality as it attempts to regulate vigorously and violently both the limits of the city and the identities of its subjects. Roman rule in Egypt would likewise seek to dictate the boundaries of family, especially in regard to another key imperial institution: the Roman army.

Marriage and army in Roman Egypt

When the Romans arrived in Egypt, they forcefully reconfigured prior Ptolemaic racial categories, most notably collapsing the previous boundary between Greek and Egyptian, a boundary that, as we have seen, held enduring significance under the Ptolemies despite its many crossings. Now, as Naphtali Lewis summarizes:

> If you were an inhabitant of Egypt, but not Roman, a citizen of one of the four *poleis* [i.e. Greek cities], or a Jew, to the Roman government you were an Egyptian. No matter that you were descended from six or seven generations of military reservists, that class of hereditary privilege settled on the land under the Ptolemies. That privileged status was now gone, and with it those ethnic designations by which you used proudly to proclaim your family's origin in the Greek or Macedonian homeland – Coan, Cretan, Thessalian, and so forth. In the government records you were all now Egyptians, nothing more.[106]

Erasing a longstanding distinction between 'Greek' and 'Egyptian' (not to mention differences within the category 'Greek' itself), the Romans, as Lewis suggests, imposed new structures of identity and difference on Egypt, and Roman attempts to monitor the boundaries of their categories, as well as those circumscribing Roman citizenship, were greatly facilitated by their recognition of marriage as a key institution in such regulation.

Following his dramatic victory over Cleopatra and Antony, Augustus introduced greater restrictions on marriage in Rome as part of a much-heralded attempt to restore traditional values. The precise form and purpose of such legislation is not entirely clear, but it seems to have been aimed at enforcing class boundaries rather than strictly racial ones.[107] A papyrus from around the same time, the *Gnomon of the Idios Logos* (or the 'Special Account') dictates a series of economic rules and penalties imposed by the new Roman occupiers in Egypt, shedding light on the presumably far more extensive set of rules pertaining to marriage in that provincial space. As Naphtali Lewis remarks, 'A perusal of the stringent regulations leaves no doubt that a prime objective set by Augustus and maintained by his successors for two hundred years was to impede social mobility and keep the several population strata as discrete and immutable as possible.'[108]

Throughout its detailed list of policies, the 'Special Account' carefully demarcates individual and economic rights by a range of status categories, focusing in particular on the distribution of property after death, a persistent Roman obsession. Openly enforcing rigid boundaries between groups, one rule maintains that '(t)hose who style themselves improperly . . .and those who knowingly concur therein are fined a fourth of their estates'. Thus, while the document seems to express confidence in its administrative procedures on one level, like the Caracalla edict, it reveals simultaneous anxiety about 'passing', i.e. the potential for people to use certain kinds of performances to create the impression that they are something they are not, at least from the perspective of the state.[109] Some of the other dictates prohibit specific kinds of marriages, including those between freedmen of Alexandria and Egyptian women, and also between Romans and Egyptians more generally. On a number of occasions, revealing its concern with those illegitimately 'passing' as Roman citizens, the document prescribes explicit penalties for those who illegally 'style themselves Romans', including 'Egyptian women married to discharged soldiers' and soldiers themselves 'who have not received a legal discharge'.[110]

As such dictates in the 'Special Account' demonstrate, soldiers and the army – the latter, another of the institutions that McClintock identifies as mediating colonial power – presented occasional concern for the Romans; as Benjamin Isaac points out, given the army's position on the 'frontlines' of the expanding empire, its capacity to be itself corrupted by foreign influences was frequently raised by ancient writers.[111] The Roman army was one of the most visible communities of Romans in Egypt, especially since Roman soldiers were generally housed together in military installations rather than resident among the broader population as the Greek cleruchs had been. During the Roman period, the occupying army consisted of two legions of Roman citizens with various auxiliary units of non-citizens. Native Egyptians were forbidden from entering the auxiliary units until late in the second century CE, and these units seemed to draw instead from the new Roman social category of 'metropolites', i.e. residents of the capitals of the districts or nomes of Egypt, who were presumably descended from members of the prior Greco-Egyptian class.[112] Upon finishing their active service, Roman soldiers were awarded Roman citizenship, if not citizens already, and in some cases they were also given land grants, frequently settling thereafter in colonies with other Roman veterans.

Seeking to place the operation of 'Romanness' in broader Egyptian social contexts, Richard Alston has examined the lives of Roman veterans and their descendants in a study of the village of Karanis in the Egyptian Fayum. Calculating the size of the group associated with the Roman army, Alston found that they composed approximately fourteen percent of the total population and were disproportionately among the wealthier residents, although the overall economic differentiation was relatively small in the modest village.[113] While the legal documents emanating from these Romans often emphasized social connections with other Romans (one document even presumably featuring a sly attempt by one individual to pass as a citizen), private documents show a broader range of relationships between the Roman group and others in the village, including Egyptians.[114] Observing that '(t)he army has traditionally been seen as one of the main ways in which imperial culture was disseminated among the provincials', i.e. that the Roman army is often seen as a primary force behind 'Romanization,' Alston finds such processes absent at Karanis. Implying a conjunction of race and culture that may require some caution (as we have seen), he nonetheless concludes that 'the cultural impact of the soldiers on the town is not archaeologically detectable and the papyri do not suggest that the soldiers differed in cultural terms from their Graeco-Egyptian neighbours'.[115] Does this suggest that the barriers built by Roman governmentality were, in fact, far less evident in the practice of everyday life in such villages?

Active-duty soldiers were not allowed to marry, yet documents at Karanis and elsewhere show they regularly entered into a range of domestic arrangements, causing some difficulty in legal status later on, 'since the children of a marriage between a Roman citizen and a person of different status normally adopted the lower status'.[116] In one surviving document a woman named Sempronia Gemella records the birth of illegitimate twins, whose father may have been a soldier.[117] We do not have much evidence for the more transient sex trade that presumably took place around Roman military bases, although there are certainly hints of more coercive forms of sexual practice in the letter of a soldier named Claudius Terentianus requesting permission to buy a slave as his wife.[118] In another document from 189 CE, a fleet veteran, C. Longinus Castor, leaves the bulk of his property to two freedwomen, Marcella and Cleopatra, as well as a legacy to the daughter of one of them, Serapia – a document that is difficult to read without speculating about Castor's paternity of Serapia, as well as the nature of his relations with both freedwomen.[119]

Some Roman sources do admit the consequences of, or display hostility toward, Roman soldiers becoming permanently involved with local women in the territories they served. Following the Second Punic War, for example, some of Scipio Africanus' soldiers had remained in Spain, eventually leading to the foundation of a colony in 171 BCE for the children produced by the union of these soldiers with native Spanish women – the first Latin colony outside of Italy.[120] Much later, in his *Odes*, Horace asks scornfully whether Crassus' soldiers have taken 'barbarian' wives, following the Roman defeat at Carrhae in 53 BCE, and so forgotten their loyalties to Rome.[121] While such marriages caused a certain legal and perhaps even conceptual crisis, the children of such unions do not seem to be the focus of major anxiety, at least in racial terms. Robert Young characterizes modern colonial racial theory as being really 'about people having sex – interminably adulterating, aleatory, illicit, interracial sex,'[122] and the Earl of Cromer included a whole appendix on intermarriage in his 1910 study *Ancient and Modern Imperialism.*[123] But although Augustus had Cleopatra's son by Caesar, Caesarion, and Antony's eldest son by his Roman wife Fulvia brutally executed to prevent any threats they might make to his position, he actually spared the children Cleopatra and Antony bore together, apparently giving them to his own sister (and Antony's former wife!) Octavia to raise.[124] Antony and Cleopatra's own daughter, Cleopatra Selene, was even later given in marriage to Juba II of Mauretania. In effect, having demonized Cleopatra throughout her life by her sexual appetites, the actual 'products' of those activities do not seem to present a dilemma for Augustus beyond his own political expediencies; there is nothing to suggest a taboo against 'racial mixing' and its progeny *per se.*

On the other hand, a number of texts from the Roman imperial period – not linked to Egypt – convey an interest specifically in the birth of black children from 'unlikely' mothers, a theme that perhaps calls attention, at least on the surface, to a form of interracial sex.[125] Whether the primary interest of these authors derives from racialized fantasies about the sexual coupling itself or the fact that such a birth could provide irrefutable evidence of female transgression in an age before DNA testing, however, is actually difficult to determine. In addition to its appearance in Roman invective (a genre generally involving the ridicule of others), the scenario was evidently a standard 'problem' assigned for rhetorical performance, thus, 'in the course of their fantastic rhetorical training the young were sometimes called on to debate the case of a married woman who gave birth to an Ethiopian baby, the defence being that an Ethiopian-looking child need not necessarily be the son of a black parent'.[126] As George Orwell famously professed, 'To see what is in front of one's nose is a constant struggle', and I do not want to disregard out of hand the priority of blackness in such scenarios. Yet, such stock formulas seem to me more indicative of misogyny and fantasies about female sexuality (given their special emphasis on the behaviour of Roman wives) than race *per se.* But with such scenarios, Roman authors invite us to visit a very vibrant and multifaceted site of racial formation: the multicultural city.

Racial formation and the ancient city

Central to Roman administration of Egypt was the priority given to citizenship, a status that relied in large part on residency in one of the limited number of Greek cities, especially Alexandria. Indeed, Alexandrian citizenship was presumably a requisite stage on the path to Roman citizenship, as demonstrated by a revealing exchange between Pliny the Younger and the emperor Trajan. In one letter to the emperor, having earlier requested Roman citizenship for his 'therapist', an Egyptian named Harpocras, Pliny is forced to confess that he erred in not asking for Alexandrian citizenship first for Harpocras 'because he is Egyptian'. In his response granting Alexandrian citizenship retroactively, Trajan seems distinctly unimpressed by the oversight.[127] Placing similar weight on Greek urban structures when distributing privilege, the Romans, as we have seen, created the 'metropolite' status in the nome capitals as distinct, and above, that of the Egyptian villagers.[128]

Under the Romans, Alexandria itself continued to be one of the most impressive cities of the ancient world, rivalling even Rome. Ancient observers often remarked upon the cosmopolitan aura of both Rome and Alexandria, an impression reinforced by their respective geographic and economic power. Thus, Dio Chrysostom (c. 40 CE to c. 120), in a speech to the Alexandrians, applauds Alexandria for its impressive shipping and trade, noting the diversity of population such commerce yields.[129] Aelius Aristides (c. 117 CE to 181) likewise depicts Rome as the commercial capital of the world, powerfully drawing its resources from every corner of the globe.[130] Martial (c. 40 CE to c. 104), on the other hand, presents a bawdier image of Rome's magnetism when he criticizes a Roman girl for drawing men from all over the world, as if, he blusters, a Roman penis was not good enough for her.[131] Alongside such passages that paint the ancient city as a lively multicultural emporium, we might place Michel de Certeau's statement that '(l)inking the city to the concept never makes them identical, but it plays on their progressive symbiosis: to plan a city is both to *think the very plurality* of the real and to make that way of thinking the plural *effective*; it is to know how to articulate it and be able to do it.'[132] So, if economic power and the 'successful' incorporation of difference gird the image of ancient cities like Rome and Alexandria, what about the actual experiences, the plurality of the real, of their diverse users?[133]

The size of Rome's population – which included upper-class senators and 'knights' (*equites*), lower-class *plebs*, slaves and resident foreigners (called *peregrini*) – is difficult to calculate, but David Noy accepts one million at the time of Augustus as a fairly safe estimate.[134] Slaves were often of foreign origin,[135] and 'foreigners' themselves might also be Roman citizens. The Romans marked the civic significance of the category of free, non-Roman residential foreigners in Rome when they created an office directly charged with handling their concerns, called the *praetor peregrinus*. Immigrants arrived in Rome from throughout the empire,[136] and, perhaps helping anchor their experience of the city, they seemingly collected in the equivalent of ethnic neighbourhoods. There is evidence for Jewish neighbourhoods in Trastevere, for example, and (although less clear) Syrians living on the Aventine and Janiculum and Egyptians in the Campus Martius.[137] Reflecting on what it meant to leave one's homeland, the Roman author Seneca the Younger (born between 4 BCE and 1 CE) once described the arrival of all sorts of populations in Rome. Noting that Rome was scarcely able to house all the teeming masses, he proclaimed the Roman state (*civitas*) one 'shared by all', and credited such immigrants with a wide range of motivations for coming to a city 'not their own'.[138] Seneca's careful phrasing here is telling, especially in its delineation of the status of immigrants in the city. For his language establishes a bifurcated sense of both inclusion, their sharing of *civitas*, and exclusion, 'not their own'. Such a distinction evokes once again a presumed (if at times imperceptible in our sources) line between 'real' Romans who 'own' the city and those made Roman by citizenship, who merely share its *civitas* – a distinction, even if primarily a social rather than legal one, worth placing alongside frequent characterizations of Roman citizenship as providing a completely level playing field for all who attained it.

In defining the space of the city, the Romans employed the concept of the *pomerium*, a symbolic boundary that separated the conceptual 'inside' of the city from its 'outside'. Trastevere – where Cleopatra stayed during her time in Rome – was, in fact, located outside the *pomerium*, seemingly contributing to its appeal to foreigners, who were able to construct temples for foreign cults there, along with Jewish synagogues. Although the Egyptian cult of Isis remained popular at Rome, Augustus forbade her worship within the *pomerium* sometime before 28 BCE, later pushing that limit to the first milestone of the city.[139] As such injunctions suggest, the Romans carefully regulated the inside of the *pomerium* by occasionally expelling certain groups or practices from its limits (so Caracalla's similar edict pertaining to Alexandria).[140] Astrologers were a group often targeted, but there are also disputed references to the expulsion of Jews from Rome in both 139 BCE and 19 CE, with the latter incident perhaps targeting religious rites, that is, practices rather than people *per se*, and including Egyptians as well.[141]

Testifying to the continuing complexity of ancient racial formations, especially in urban settings, Noy mentions a unique epitaph from Rome in which a woman identifies her homeland as Apamea, but her race as Greek.[142] Those identifying as Greek were not uncommon in Rome; it evidently had a distinct veneer of 'Greekness'.[143] The Roman satirist Juvenal (born sometime between 50 and 65 CE) states bluntly that he cannot tolerate the 'Greek city'.[144] Juvenal expands that few of the Greeks in Rome actually originate in Greece and even those that come as slaves hold more prestige and power in the city than he does. Juvenal's work presents one of the most extensive representations of the city of Rome as a lived space, but it is one that is relentlessly gloomy and full of petty resentments. In fact, one of Juvenal's main critiques bears remarkable resemblance to modern laments about immigration, namely that Rome was being overrun by foreigners, 'transplanted metropolitan Others ... who symbolically violate, engulf, and cannibalize the beleaguered native male every day in the city of his birth'.[145]

Juvenal is remarkably even-handed when doling out his acid abuse, including a scathing attack on women of all backgrounds in *Satire* 6. The Jews of Rome come in for their share of vilification as well: in *Satire* 3, Juvenal disparages a Jewish neighbourhood in Rome, a once-holy district now 'rented to Jews'.[146] Elsewhere he paints a harsh picture of a Jewish beggar woman, selling fortunes for pennies, one of many foreign groups he accuses of performing such practices.[147] Finally, in *Satire* 14, Juvenal scornfully lists certain Jewish religious customs passed from fathers to sons, accusing Jews of preserving the laws of Moses, while 'despising the laws of Rome'.[148] The Jewish community in Rome, estimated at around 40–50,000, was characterized by a certain level of poverty[149], although, as Juvenal's attacks show, Jewish difference wrought occasional fear and hostility nonetheless from its Roman observers. Suggesting a visibility and perhaps political will of the Roman Jewish community, Cicero references Jewish unrest outside the courtroom in his defence of Lucius Valerius Flaccus in 59 BCE, presumably a response to Flaccus' seizure of the annual payment the Jews of Asia had collected to send to the Temple in Jerusalem.[150]

The multivalence of Jewish identity in the Greek and Roman world makes it a rich site for thinking about many dimensions of ancient racial formation; in particular, ancient Jewish identity opens questions about the precise relationship between racial categories and racial identifications, that is, between an external labelling of 'Jews' and internal claims within the group itself to that identity. So it is useful to consider Jewish identity briefly on its own terms before placing it once again in the context of the ancient city.

Ancient Jewish identity

Much like the label 'Ethiopian', the term 'Jew' could hold a range of connotations in antiquity, alternately denoting geographic origin, formal membership in the Jewish state, or a religious identity.[151] Recognizing their ongoing status as a distinct group, Jews were alternately called an *ethnos*, *natio*, and *gens* by Greek and Roman writers.[152] As the evidence from Ptolemaic Egypt suggests, Jews could be counted as 'Hellenes', and they could also be considered 'Roman' if they possessed Roman citizenship. In fact, when Paul was arrested, his statement that he was a Roman citizen presumably prevented the use of further violence against him, underlining the fact that Roman citizenship dictated not just a concrete set of legal rights, but also the inviolability of the male citizen body.[153]

In more recent historical periods, potent stereotypes have been developed that claim Jews can be identified by physical appearance alone. In the modern nineteenth century, for example, Jews became associated with 'blackness' – a proposition certain writers suggested had its source in the alleged Jewish 'interbreeding' with 'Africans' in ancient Alexandria.[154] As Shaye Cohen notes, however, ancient writers did not take an unequivocal stand on how one could 'recognize' Jews: '(n)ot a single ancient author says that Jews are distinctive because of their looks, clothing, speech, names, or occupations'.[155] Greek and Roman writers often listed particular practices associated with Jews, such as isolationism, monotheism, abstention from the eating of pork, observation of the Sabbath, circumcision, and proselytism,[156] but although one might draw 'plausible inferences' about a person from these acts or certain other behaviours like residence in a Jewish neighbourhood or association with Jews, none of these on its own, according to Cohen, was conclusive.[157] Instead, Cohen argues that self-identification was the only reliable indicator of Jewish identity in antiquity, that '(i)n antiquity you did not know a Jew when you saw one, but if someone said he or she was a Jew, that statement alone apparently sufficed to establish the fact . . . In this respect as in so many others antiquity anticipates modernity'.[158]

While it may be difficult to discern precisely how the Greeks or Romans identified individual Jews in their midst (as opposed to the targeting of a Jewish community more broadly[159]), it is clear that some kind of procedure was required on occasion, such as during Roman expulsion efforts. Likewise, the institution of a Jewish tax necessitated some kind of state strategy for identification of Jews beyond their own self-declarations. Claiming that at an earlier time 'the Jewish tax was aggressively levied, including on those who were conducting their lives as Jews without declaring it and on those who avoided the Jewish tax by concealing their origin', Suetonius remembers as a young man seeing a ninety-year old man publicly inspected for circumcision to determine if he was Jewish.[160] Still, circumcision was banned for a while beginning with Hadrian, and its role as a marker of Jewish identity clearly only ever served for men and even then, other men were also thought to practice circumcision, including Egyptian priests.[161] Moreover, the Roman insistence on identifying Jews within a punitive context (e.g., to exact a tax) generated numerous acts of resistance; as Suetonius' phrasing makes clear, some Jews presumably sought to 'pass' as non-Jews precisely to avoid the tax.[162] Attempts to establish the clear boundary between Jews and others also intersect with concerns we have witnessed elsewhere, namely the tensions between essence and practice. In certain contexts, ancient writers thus sought meticulously to parse the line between '"truly being a Jew" and "acting the part of a Jew", or between "truly being a Jew" and "being called a Jew"'[163] – a distinction made even more complicated by the openness of Judaism to conversion.[164]

For Jews themselves, as Cohen argues, Jewish identity depended greatly on the space in which it was expressed: 'In the Judaean homeland (at least until the fourth century CE) Jewishness ... for Jews was natural, perhaps inevitable, but in the diaspora Jewishness was a conscious choice, easily avoided or hidden, sometimes welcomed by society at large, sometimes tolerated, and sometimes harassed.'[165] Jews had begun dwelling in large numbers outside of Palestine beginning in 587 BCE with the Babylonian capture of Jerusalem. Population movement of all sorts was greatly accelerated by Alexander's conquests, and by the end of the second century BCE, 'Jews had found their way not only to Egypt, Syria, Mesopotamia, and the Iranian plateau, but also to the cities and principalities of Asia Minor, to the islands of the Aegean, to Greece itself, to Crete, Cyprus, and Cyrene'.[166] In the diaspora, Jewish identity had a kind of double consciousness; as Erich Gruen explains, Jews 'represent a different culture, background, tradition, and history, but in the Hellenistic era, and indeed in the Greek East of the Roman period, they were part and parcel of a Greek cultural community.'[167] Significantly, Jewish literature in the diaspora was composed primarily in Greek.

There is evidence for a Jewish military community in Egypt at Elephantine as far back as the sixth century BCE, and, among other later settlements, a Jewish temple at Leontopolis. The Ptolemies encouraged the development of a sizeable Jewish population in nearby Cyrene,[168] and Jews evidently settled as well in the Egyptian countryside, including Menkhes' small village[169]. By far the most influential population of Jews in Egypt was in Alexandria, however, which served as a centre of Jewish cultural life for much of the diaspora. The *Letter of Aristeas* describes the translation of Jewish scripture into Greek under the patronage of Ptolemy Philadelphus (283–246 BCE), the so-called Septuagint, portraying a dynamic interaction of Greek and Jewish culture in the city.[170] While Jewish theology and religious practice, as with later Christians, would play a contributing role in the articulation of racial boundaries,[171] I want to focus next on the violence experienced by the Jewish community in Egypt, which shows serious fissures in Roman racial governmentality.

The multicultural city boils over

In his lengthy account of Egypt, the Roman geographer Strabo (born c. 64 BCE), records that Polybius had once characterized the population of Alexandria as consisting of three groups: Egyptians, 'mercenaries', and Alexandrians, the latter a 'mixed' group, but Greek in origin.[172] Finding it impossible to believe that Polybius would call the Egyptians 'civilized' ('*politikon*' as the manuscript reads), modern editors have often quietly reworked this important passage, proposing a different reading of the adjective ('litigous', '*poludikon*') or simply inserting a 'not' or 'un-' before the word[173] – a phenomenon that reminds us how thoroughly the modern processes of textual criticism and editing filter our unsuspecting engagement with ancient texts. In any event, Polybius' omission of the Jews from his list has also generated debates about the status of Jews in Alexandria, who apparently occupied a separate neighbourhood in the city:[174] were Jews simply included in the 'Alexandrian' category?

Scholars often confront similar problems of terminology when attempting to determine the broader place of Jews in the Greek and Roman world. At times, for example, ancient writers called the Jewish community a *politeuma*, which suggests a form of civic structure, but did this designation function within the ancient city or was it indicative of a structure point-edly separate from, and outside, the *polis*?[175] In Alexandria, Jews seem generally to have held rights that placed them higher than Egyptians, but they apparently did not necessarily hold Alexandrian citizenship as Greek residents of the city did. The label 'Alexandrian' itself can therefore be diffi-cult to construe in ancient texts, denoting at times only Greek citizens (i.e. Alexandrian citizens) and at others the broader resident population. Such confusion may have afflicted ancient people as well, for in one provocative document 'the designation "Alexandrian" has been crossed out from the petition of the Jew Helenos, son of Tryphon, and replaced by "a Jew from Alexandria"'.[176]

In negotiating Roman rule, Jewish writers often evoked Augustus' alleged tolerance as a model for later emperors (any conclusions we might draw about the nature of his own personal views might be moderated, however, by Augustus' alleged quip on hearing that Herod had killed his own child that 'it is better to be Herod's pig than his son'[177]). Yet, beginning in 38 CE, violent events rocked the city of Alexandria, events that challenged the tenuous balance of the city's diverse groups. According to Philo (c. 15 BCE–45 CE), trouble began when the Greeks in Alexandria urged the Roman governor of Egypt, Avillius Flaccus, to curtail Jewish rights in the city; shortly after, when the Jewish leader Agrippa I visited, full-scale riots ensued resulting in extreme violence and wide-scale destruction of Jewish property, as well as the forcible regulation of the Jews to a single part of the city.[178] Among the revealing criticisms Philo levies against Flaccus himself in describing the brutal persecution of the Jewish population is Flaccus' alleged proclamation calling Jews 'foreigners and aliens' and also his will-ingness to let Jewish magistrates be publicly whipped with the kind of lash normally reserved for Egyptians.[179] The Roman emperor Caligula eventu-ally had Flaccus arrested,[180] but the unrest continued and soon two sets of embassies were sent to Rome to seek a more definitive resolution. Following Caligula's death, violence was renewed, leading the new emperor Claudius to issue his 'Letter to the Alexandrians' dictating the rights of each group, and dampening the hostilities, at least temporarily.

Claudius' 'Letter' has many revealing features, including an opening that suggests an ominous, from the Jewish perspective, intimacy with the Greek population of Alexandria. Still, when Claudius reiterates the rights awarded to the Greeks by Augustus and other previous emperors, he denies their request for an independent city council, a refusal that seems to remain a major sticking point for Alexandrians throughout the Roman period. Claudius then pronounces himself unwilling to determine the source of the violence in Alexandria, but warns both groups that if there is any renewal of enmity he 'shall be driven to show what a benevolent emperor can be when turned to righteous indignation'. Claudius urges the Greeks to respect the rights of the Jews, but when he turns to the Jews themselves he both chastises them for sending their own embassy 'as if they lived in two separate cities' and advises them to be satisfied with the rights they currently have in a 'city not their own' – statements that are either in bald contradiction with one another or suggestive of a fastidiously precise calibration of Jewish status, one perhaps reminiscent of Seneca's sense of Romans and foreigners unified by *civitas*, yet not quite equal possessors of Rome itself.[181] Finally, employing an expression that has caused considerable consternation, Claudius warns them not to admit Jews who are creating tensions outside the borders of Egypt, an act that would compel him to 'proceed against them as fomenters of what is a general plague of the whole world.'[182] Interpreters of this passage have disagreed over whether Claudius means to label Judaism itself a plague or the violence being stirred up elsewhere – a difficult question to resolve, but one that has obvious implications for measuring the degree of Roman anti-Semitism.[183]

In 70 CE, the Romans destroyed the Temple in Jerusalem, an act many have seen as 'the seminal event in the formation of both early Christianity and Rabbinic Judaism'.[184] From that point on, '(r)elations between Jews and the world of Greece and Rome took an irreversible turn', becoming substantially more hostile.[185] During the Jewish wars that sparked the Romans' devastating act, riots also took place in Alexandria, and following the Temple's destruction, Egyptian Jews – as Jews throughout the empire – would be subject to a special tax. Later, in 116–117 CE, Jews in Egypt took part in what is known as the 'Diaspora Revolt', a movement that made its way into most of the Egyptian countryside until it was brutally suppressed;[186] eerily, annual commemoration of the Jewish defeat was celebrated in Egypt long afterwards.[187] Cumulatively, these events seem to have decimated the Jewish population in Alexandria and throughout Egypt, henceforth making Rome the most important urban centre of diaspora Jews.[188] Such precipitous decline is evident in literary terms in the *Acts of the Alexandrian Martyrs*, a collection of dramatic scenarios featuring various Alexandrian Greeks acting defiantly towards the Roman emperors; although many early scenes present the Jews as equal adversaries to the Greeks, they are conspicuously absent from later scenes.[189]

As the *Acts* suggest, the Alexandrian Greeks themselves continued to have fraught relations with Rome.[190] Egyptians, on the other hand, are notably missing from ancient accounts of the events originating under Flaccus, and it is impossible to know how, or even if, they took part as a group. Jewish sources present an importunate hostility towards native Egyptians, including deep animosity towards Egyptian religion, and some scholars have used this literary evidence in arguing that the Egyptians, given such mutual antagonism, would invariably have sided against the Jews.[191] The use of literary evidence in this context seems potentially hazardous (would Jewish attitudes about Egyptians likely be formed by literary representations of the Exodus as opposed to Egyptian families actually living near them?[192]), but one particular form of literature from this period does invite speculation about the variant political aspirations produced within such colonial settings: apocalyptic literature.

Apocalyptic literature by convention adopts a style of expression so obscure that it is difficult to connect to a concrete time and place; in defying the status quo, it promotes not dramatic uprising but rather a kind of moralizing patience, suggesting that foreign rulers will get their comeuppance at some unspecified point of time. Scholars once viewed apocalyptic literature as Jewish in origin, but there is good reason to place it within a more expansive cultural horizon.[193] Three surviving works of apocalyptic literature predict the overthrow of foreign rulers in Egypt itself: the

'Oracle of the Potter'[194] and *The Demotic Chronicle*[195] presumably written by Egyptians in the Ptolemaic era,[196] and Book Three and Five of the Sibylline oracles produced by Jewish authors, possibly active in Alexandria, during the Roman period.[197] Because of its opacity, some scholars have queried the actual efficacy of apocalyptic literature in fostering meaningful political dissent: what precise action might apocalyptic literature have encouraged or, alternately, what comfort might it have given its writers or readers? I will turn to literature's significant role in racial formations in the next chapter; for now, apocalyptic literature opens one further topic for examination: racial practice as political resistance.

Racial formation and its discontents

Given our general reliance on sources produced by the elite in antiquity, it can be difficult to apprehend the full range of individual and collective tactics used to defy state power. As James C. Scott states, 'domination . . . produces an official transcript that provides convincing evidence of willing, even enthusiastic complicity'.[198] Yet ruptures do appear in the historical record, and we can glimpse provocative acts of resistance in numerous ancient texts.[199] Strabo in his *Geography*, for example, claims that Pyrrhus of Epirus was prevented from entering the city of Argos when an old woman dropped a tile on his head.[200] Later Strabo records that in Corinth some individuals threw mud at Roman ambassadors, one of many acts, he adds, for which the city was severely punished.[201] Ancient Egyptian sources record a range of subversive practices related specifically to labour issues. In pharanoic times, for example, workers would often take refuge in religious sanctuaries when they had labour grievances,[202] while, in Ptolemaic Egypt, similar acts surely intersected in complex ways with racial structures of thought. Thus, Bagnall identifies an episode under the Ptolemies when Egyptian farmers, told that the revenue they had to return from land they were farming was going to be calculated ahead of time, took refuge in a nearby temple, thereby refusing to accept the new terms.[203] Menkhes likewise records a strike by farmers working crown land.[204]

We have seen that accounts of violence in Ptolemaic Egypt often hinged on perceptions of racial difference, and there is also evidence for a series of open revolts beginning in the mid-third century BCE.[205] Some of these efforts were able to establish rival governments in other parts of Egypt; one rival pharaoh even ruled in Thebes for two decades beginning in 206 BCE. Given the sparse nature of our evidence, it is not always clear what precipitated each revolt, although Polybius suggests that certain Egyptians had first been emboldened – not to mention armed – in 217 BCE when they were admitted to the Ptolemaic army to assist the beleaguered Ptolemaic forces at the battle of Raphia. From there, Polybius explains, the Egyptians 'were no longer able to endure what was prescribed for them, but began to seek a leader and a personality, regarding themselves as capable of looking after themselves'.[206]

Smyth rightly proposes that 'the postcolonial critic must always historicize, or at least learn to historicize, the theories through which a discourse of resistance might be conceptualized'[207], and one of the most persistent debates about the Roman empire, in particular, is whether large-scale resistance emerged from feelings of race or 'nationalism' (i.e. collective identity among a conquered group)[208] or was merely a backlash against specific Roman governmental practices (e.g., excessive tax rates or especially coercive collection procedures). Under the Romans, rebellions took place in many parts of the empire; as Stephen L. Dyson states of such events: 'One of the most persistent phenomena related to the extension of Roman conquest and control in the Western empire was the sudden, widespread native revolt. This is not the initial resistance to the Roman advance, but an uprising among people who are regarded as basically conquered and in the process of Romanization.' Dyson further suggests that 'the similarity of these revolts is sufficiently striking to make one wonder whether they do not raise common problems on the nature and limitations of the Romanization process'.[209]

While 'Romanization' as a term of analysis has been subject to extensive scrutiny in recent years, as Dyson admits, any approach to 'native revolts' that focuses on the systematic vulnerabilities of Roman power contradicts the tendency in modern times to treat resistance to Roman hegemony 'in the individual context of particular provinces, which has often led to nationalistic or partially nationalistic interpretation'.[210] In other words, we tend to attribute such rebellions today to the discursive power of the 'nation', a term that seems obviously compelling from our modern perspective. Figures like Boadicea (or Boudica) in Britain and Vercingetorix in France – figures that, not without some irony, are known to us primarily through Roman sources – therefore remain popular icons of pre-national nationalism.[211] But, as we have seen, the Romans would have perceived most of the participants in such resistance movements as racially 'other' to themselves, and the question remains to what extent these groups' own racial identifications mattered, if at all, when raising armed response to Roman rule.

The revolts in Judea have long attracted special scholarly scrutiny, although even there the motives can be tough to isolate – were the Jewish wars religious, racial, or 'national' in origin? Some combination of all three?[212] Perhaps most captivating for modern audiences is the story of Masada, a mountain fortress located near the Red Sea, at which approximately one thousand Jews, known as the Sicarii, were said to have held out against a Roman siege for six months in 72–73 CE, eventually committing mass suicide rather than be taken prisoner. Despite continuing debate over the event's veracity, Masada entered the modern American consciousness through the broadcast of a lavish television mini-series in 1981. Still today, the meanings of Masada as a resistance narrative for Jewish audiences are compelling, if contested, due in part to a 'Masada mythical narrative' that emerged beginning in the 1940s, one reinforced by the site's widely publicized excavation under the auspices of the new Israeli state.[213]

As slave revolts show, resistance to Rome was not always connected to designated geographic spaces or specific racial populations *per se*.[214] But, taken together, the expressive power of these kinds of events demonstrates how much they still matter today, widening – even at times romanticizing – our view of the possibilities of opposition to Roman power. Still, any bona fide understanding of what was at stake in most resistance efforts 'can only be found by looking at the views of the provincials themselves,'[215] and these are severely lacking in our historical record. As Martin Goodman elaborates:

> (t)he boundaries may be unclear in the sources between a peasant protest at the extortion of taxes (when the main aim may simply have been pillage), a campaign of violent rampage by a group of brigands, and a full-scale war aimed at the recovery of liberty from Roman rule. An inscription referring to military action against provincials, or archaeological evidence of widespread urban destruction, or a regional programme of reconstruction, could refer to any or all of these phenomena.[216]

We seem, then, to have come full-circle: to be confronted once again with the difficulty of identifying racial identities or racial performances when only certain kinds of evidence survive.

While not quite the full or 'thick' explanation we might crave, we can nonetheless find glimpses of the fraught experiences of various individuals during such tumultuous events. A number of letters, for example, have been found showing the impact of the 'Diaspora Revolt' on the family of Apollonios, the *strategos* of Apollinopolis-Heptacomias. Mentioning particular military engagements, the letters record material shortages, land damage, and a mother's alarm, in a disputed text, that 'the Jews may "roast" her son.'[217] Similarly, Claudius Terentianus – the same man who wanted to buy a concubine as a wife – cites his involvement in suppressing riots in Alexandria, perhaps becoming injured in the process.[218] Perhaps the most poignant testimony of the human cost of such resistance to Roman rule, however, comes from the archive of personal documents found in a cave on the western shore of the Dead Sea,[219] where a Jewish woman named Babatha took refuge with her family during the Bar Kochba Revolt, a failed independence movement from 132–135 CE.[220] Babatha's documents do not record the events or motives of the war itself, but the reason for the collection's placement in the cave has been unbearably reinforced by the discovery of the remains of a small settlement of Roman soldiers on the cliff above, presumably there to wait out, or starve out, the hidden refugees. And ultimately it is the everyday nature of Babatha's documents, so incongruous when set against the terror and finality of Roman power, that makes her archive so compelling and heartrending.

By my inclusion of the experiences of individuals working both for and against oppressive structures of power, I certainly do not mean to suggest that all suffering is the same morally (that deep-seated racism against Jews, for example, does not contribute to fears of their cannibalism), but as McClintock asserts, both imperial *and* anti-imperial agencies mould colonial rule and its racial practices. In thinking about the status of someone like Ptolemaios at Memphis, moreover, Thompson has identified a provocative resource for Ptolemaios' own racial identifications: his library. Ptolemaios' personal collection of texts, which he shared with his brother Apollonios, included both Egyptian and Greek material,[221] but it is the copy of a passage from *Telephus* by the Greek author Euripides that underlines the relevance of the texts to the lives of the two men. For the *Telephus* records the experiences of a Greek king ruling outside of Greece and at the bottom of the passage, 'in a sentence almost illegible, Apollonios has added the outburst, "Apollonios the Macedonian . . . a Macedonian I say".[222] As insight into personal affiliations with colonial power, this marginalia is as revealing as a reader in colonial India owning and inserting himself into a work by Kipling.[223] Such marginalia, in other words, reveal that it is not merely his practice of everyday life, but also his reading habits that helped shape Apollonios' sense of self – that Euripides' play gave him a literary space in which to interpolate his own experiences and explore privately what it might mean to be Greek (or 'Macedonian') in the 'foreign' space of Egypt. So I want to turn now to more thorough investigation of racial representations, including the profound contributions to ancient racial formation made by literature and art.

CHAPTER III

RACIAL REPRESENTATIONS

Explicit or implicit, the Africanist presence informs in compelling and inescapable ways the texture of American literature. It is a dark and abiding presence, there for the literary imagination as both a visible and invisible mediating force. Even, and especially, when American texts are not 'about' Africanist presences or characters or narrative or idiom, the shadow hovers in implication, in sign, in line of demarcation.[1]

Toni Morrison

Greek cultural practices clearly helped articulate racial boundaries in Ptolemaic Egypt, even if they were not the only criteria at every point in time. Notably, Greek culture also provided an important symbol of power for the Ptolemies. One of the goals of the Ptolemaic dynasty was thus to establish Alexandria as the rightful heir to once-golden Athens. Such aspirations announced themselves in the Museum, a centre for scholarly study, and the Library of Alexandria, both situated within the royal district of the new capital. The Library, in particular, provided a means for not only producing definitive editions of classic Greek literature, but also acquiring a collection of material that would outrank any other in the world. By some accounts, the Ptolemies aspired to gain 'copies of all books ever written, although translated into Greek first',[2] and the Ptolemaic era would yield an important account of Egyptian history written in Greek by the Egyptian priest Manetho. So important was this literary collection to the Ptolemaic expression of superiority that the Ptolemies allegedly confiscated all the books that came into their harbours, returning only copies to the original owners[3] – much like Ptolemy Soter hijacked another important badge of authority, Alexander the Great's body itself, putting it on display in Alexandria to proclaim his status as the young general's most legitimate successor[4]. While the Ptolemies sought through such strategies to announce *that* they possessed the most authentic collection of Greek literature, I want to examine in this chapter *what* such texts themselves actually conveyed to their ancient audiences about the structure and meanings of ancient racial formation.

In *Playing in the Dark: Whiteness and the Literary Imagination,* Toni Morrison explores the ways in which conceptions of blackness were essential to the formulation of a white American identity in early American literature – a phenomenon Morrison believes can be found both in literary works that openly suggest such strategies and in the pregnant silences of others.[5] In pursuing her argument, Morrison insists on taking representation seriously, that is, she seeks to demonstrate the covert methods such cultural texts use to define potent concepts like nation, gender, race, and class for their audiences, concepts whose force resonates far beyond any 'entertainment' value the texts may provide. Moreover, in encouraging their audiences to envision the production of such entities – by imagining 'America' itself or what it means to be 'American' – such texts also display the people and ideas *against* which such ideas are formed, or, as Morrison terms it, the 'dark and abiding presences' that help shape those entities from the outside.

Morrison's dedication to finding meaning in the gaps in American literature, in uncovering the primacy of race even when it is left unnamed or unspoken, helps shed light on the ways art and literature speak through their omissions and suppressions. Indeed, although it is often taken for granted by classicists, the invisibility of Egypt and Egyptians in many forms of literature from Hellenistic Alexandria is striking. For literature of this period seems pointedly to conceal its colonial context through its nostalgia for, and dialogue with, earlier Greek literary traditions. While it may not be evident on the surface, however, Susan Stephens has argued that Alexandrian literature incorporates many Egyptian ideas and motifs through 'optical illusion', making its 'Egyptianness' visible only at specific angles – although, even then, it re-enacts its own domination by presenting the Egyptian element as emphatically 'contained within or domesticated by its imposing framework of Greekness'.[6] In one poem, dated to the early third century BCE, the Greek poet Theocritus gives a provocative glimpse into just such a dynamic.

Theocritus' *Idyll* 15 depicts the experiences of two pompous Greek women ('*Syracusan*', as they insist), who are planning to attend the festival of Adonis in Alexandria's royal district. As the women walk along the bustling streets of the city, one of them raises the spectre of the native Egyptian population. Excoriating Egyptians as thieves and pickpockets, she laments: 'Ye gods, what a crowd! How and when will we ever get through this mob? Ants without number or measure! You've done many commendable things, Ptolemy, since your father has been among the immortals. No villain creeps up upon one in the street, Egyptian-wise, bent on mischief, as in the past – a trick that pack of rogues used to play, one as bad as the other, all of them scoundrels'.[7] Taken as literary evidence of the interaction between colonizers and colonized in Ptolemaic Alexandria, this outburst is depressingly brief and one-sided. The attitudes of the Egyptian population towards the snobbish Greek women, not to mention their reactions to the lavish displays of the Greek monarchy, remain unspoken. Indeed, just as any Egyptian menace has allegedly been eliminated by Ptolemy, Egyptians themselves are expelled from the rest of poem. But it is precisely because of its placement within a poem centred on the elaborate staging of a Greek festival that the moment is instructive, for by prefacing Greek cultural performance on a suppressed Egyptian threat, this scene illustrates well some of the colonial fantasies and anxieties upon which Greek identity in Egypt was founded.[8]

While such suppressions reveal the immense uncertainty and anxiety plaguing many racial formations – the Parthians, for example, rarely appear in Roman literature[9] – it is, of course, easier to grapple with what is manifestly present, so in this chapter, I want to explore some of the discernible contributions public art and culture made to ancient racial formations. Given the incredible range of both ancient art and literature, not to mention the long tradition of their interpretation, I aim here not to present any conclusive reading of all the intersections of public culture and racial formation in antiquity, but rather to suggest the breadth of their collaboration by sampling a range of genres, such as epic, vase painting, tragedy, and the Roman triumph. In looking at such racial representations, a number of themes will recur, including the difficulty in correlating early Greek myth with later racial formations, the central role of the Persians in shaping Greek racial thought, and the role of racial imagery in justifying the Roman imperial project.

The richness of art and literature from any period stems from its reliance on the ways diverse viewers or readers engage and make meaning from it, a slippery process that produces the potential for multiple, even contradictory interpretations. Robert Stam and Ella Shohat have noted, for example, the complex identifications a movie character like Tarzan demands from non-white audiences, urging them, to 'root against' the menacing African peoples that threaten Tarzan's survival.[10] While my discussion here focuses on the overt manufacture of racial formations in art and literature, I therefore also try in places to point to the simultaneous phenomenon by which such texts open the possibility of multiple, even opposing readings or even call into question the very viability of such formations.[11] I begin, though, by looking at ancient epic, the earliest and most imposing literary genre in antiquity, one that seems especially devoted to composing the Greek and Roman 'self'.

Mapping the self

Greek and Roman epic poetry contributed greatly to ancient racial formations, even when racial strategies seem notable by their absence. Homer's *Iliad*, as we have seen, generally avoids drawing a fundamental distinction between the Greek and Trojan sides, although one will be retrojected back by later writers. Homer's *Odyssey*, on the other hand, an elaborate account of the Greek hero Odysseus' return home from Troy, has been read as a voyage of Greek self-discovery, one played out in relation to the expanding geography of Greek colonization. As Carol Dougherty phrases it, 'Homer's *Odyssey* is a poem about travel, cross-cultural contact, and narrative, and in it, New World accounts of trade and overseas exploration intersect with familiar tales of epic poetry to produce a rich and complex picture of a world in transition'.[12]

Combining the Homeric themes of war and sea voyage, the Roman poet Vergil began writing his epic *Aeneid* shortly after Augustus' victory over Antony and Cleopatra. Recounting the story of Rome's origins, the *Aeneid* uses the mythic past to both help the Romans digest the civil wars that had beleaguered their society for decades and encourage their belief in the possibility of a future 'empire without end'[13]. Key to this endeavour was the poem's vibrant engagement with Roman self-definition, a project conceived in both distant and proximate modes.[14] During the Trojans' laborious struggle to reach Italy, for example, they land at Carthage where the Trojan leader Aeneas becomes embroiled in a love affair with the Phoenician queen Dido. The disastrous ending of this affair ultimately serves to foreshadow the Romans' brutal wars with Carthage, as well as call to mind the recent suicide of that other foreign queen, Cleopatra.

Dido herself signifies as 'Phoenician' throughout the literary episode,[15] yet Vergil acknowledges her broader African milieu through the character of Iarbas, a local king whose marriage offer Dido has rejected prior to Aeneas' arrival. Iarbas, the son of Jupiter Ammon to whom he appeals for help (Jupiter being the Roman version of Zeus), is not described in terms that mark him as dramatically different from the Trojans; if anything, Iarbas employs his own racializing gaze when he makes use of stereotypes of eastern effeminacy against the Trojan Aeneas.[16] The Roman poet Lucan (c. 70–160 CE) took his later epic about the Roman civil wars also to North Africa, but while he briefly describes the exploits of local leaders like Juba, king of Numidia, he devotes greatest attention to the oddities and barrenness of Africa's landscape, most notably when Cato leads his troops on a miserable snake-laden march through the desert in Book 9.[17]

While Aeneas' sea voyage allows the *Aeneid* to engage with foreign sites like Carthage, Katharine Toll has argued that the more proximate space of Italy provides a pivotal backdrop for constructing 'Roman-ness' once the Trojans land there in the second half of the poem. In Toll's words: '(Vergil) a man to whom his own identities as Roman and Italian had arrived separately and who thus had conducted his own reconsideration and scrutiny of them, was peculiarly suited to contribute to his people's already ongoing processes of review and adjustment, helping Romans and Italians to think about who they had become, in their new conjunction.'[18] Recognizing the formation of a growing empire beyond Italy, the *Aeneid* thus also deliberates the meaning of the Romans' consolidation of the more proximate peninsula. It is in Italy, after all, that Aeneas marries to solidify his political standing and conducts war to affirm his territorial claims, signalling the dual processes of acquisition and incorporation.

The *Moretum*, an intriguing poem once falsely attributed to Vergil, presents a rare attempt to map the Roman 'self' in terms of a lower-class subjectivity, consisting of the account of a poor labourer, Simulus, whose sole actions involve waking up and preparing his lunch, his *moretum* – a dish made from garlic, cheese, and herbs that gives the poem its name. The 'relation between the poem's elaborately decorous style . . . and banal subject matter' has been difficult for contemporary scholars to interpret[19]: does the epic tone give dignity to Simulus and his pained efforts or hold him and his labour up for ridicule? In addition to Simulus, the poem features Scybale, Simulus' servant, who is pointedly said to be of African origin.[20] A play on the Greek word 'rubbish' or 'dung', Scybale's name itself encapsulates well the narrative's underlying hostility towards her, and the detailed account the text provides of Scybale's body, in particular, raises serious questions.

The poem proffers a rationale for its voyeurism by claiming that Scybale's appearance 'testifies to her homeland', and the description then moves from the top of her head down, commenting on her hair, face, chest, breasts, stomach, legs and feet.[21] In doing so, the narrative treats her body as if it were completely nude, showing no regard for any clothing covering her.

This passage presents the most extensive physical description of an African character in Greek and Roman literature; in fact, Snowden relies heavily on Scybale when compiling the physical characteristics of his ancient Ethiopian 'type'.[22] Yet such dispassionate scholarly usage of her body uncomfortably reinforces Scybale's objectification without calling attention to its disturbing role in the original narrative, and it remains difficult to determine the extent to which Scybale's status as 'African' is responsible for the textual treatment she receives. In other words, is '*Afra*' the primary basis for our unprecedented access to her body or is that designation only one part of a much larger set of power relationships – including male and female, master and servant, viewer and object – that expose her to our gaze?[23] We might go even further by contrasting the absolute exposure of Scybale's form to a similar scan of the female body presented by the Roman poet Ovid (43 BCE–17 CE). After describing how he has forcibly disrobed his lover, Corinna, in one of his erotic poems, Ovid proceeds to describe her naked body, but even as he builds the reader's anticipation Ovid suddenly stops halfway down, jokingly protesting 'why describe each part? Everything was praiseworthy'.[24]

Calling attention to the *Moretum*'s disquieting undercurrents for audiences today – especially given the combination of Scybale's servile role and her African origin – William Fitzgerald observes that it is from this poem that the United States took the phrase '*e pluribus unum*' for its Great Seal and dollar bill. In appropriating the slogan from the description of Simulus' act of mixing his *moretum*, however, American usage avoided adding a key ingredient: '*color*'. For the original reads: *color est e pluribus unus* or 'there is one *colour* from many' (my emphasis).[25] Such striking omission of '*color*' surely enacts the very type of racial suppression that Morrison finds throughout early American thought, and Fitzgerald proposes that '(t)o return the word *color* to the Great Seal's motto is to allow the motto's subconscious to float to the surface'.[26]

The attention given to Scybale's body in the *Moretum* stands out even more given that physical description is not generally a major part of characterization in ancient literature. In his article 'What does Aeneas look like?', Mark Griffith captures well the normal limits of our vision: 'Vergil's Aeneas is big, strong, and handsome, a proper epic hero. But we are not told whether he is dark or fair, youthful or grizzled, bearded or clean-shaven, long or short-haired, burly or slim'.[27] Physical appearance remains a regular feature of ancient art, however, and ancient art at times openly portrays figures with black skin colour. Snowden made such images central to his study of ancient attitudes towards 'blacks', so how might ancient art contribute to our understanding of racial formations, including any of their visual dimensions?[28]

Viewing the 'other'

Greek vase painting, one of our best sources for the workings of the Greek visual imaginary, demonstrates well the necessity of taking artistic conventions into account when seeking to track racial formations in art, since it is clear that skin colour is salient in some ways but a (pardon the expression) complete red herring in others. While the Greek city of Corinth dominated early production of pottery, Athenian or Attic pottery soon came to dominate the market, and by 600 BCE, Athenian pottery was routinely employing a 'black figure' technique, one that was gradually replaced by 'red figure' during the fifth century.[29] In seeking to interpret the scenes – and peoples – painted on Greek vases, perhaps the first point to underline is that transition from black to red figure signals a change in mode of production not racial ideology. Moreover, skin colour differences on Greek vases serve primarily to delineate sexual not racial difference: where the skin of male figures is black on black figure vases, women and goddesses are routinely portrayed with white skin. Pale skin was evidently a sign of female beauty in antiquity, and there is evidence – dreadful to contemplate – that Greek women applied lead to their skin to achieve a lighter effect.[30] While this standard may seem at first glance laden with racial connotations, it presumably began as a class marker, deriving from an aristocratic ideal that sought to confine Greek women inside the house and away from manual labour outdoors.

Greek vases depict many episodes from Greek mythology, as well as styl-ized scenes of everyday life, and the appearance on surviving vases of Memnon, one of the most prominent Ethiopian characters in Greek myth, raises important questions about his actual visual representation *as* Ethiopian. Accounts of Memnon are generally very positive in myth; he was part of the Trojan myth cycle, fighting courageously at Troy until he was killed by the Greek Achilles. Memnon was occasionally linked to Asia or Africa in myth, although he was increasingly associated with Africa,[31] presumably in accordance with evolving ideas about Ethiopians more generally. In Greek art, Memnon was often portrayed with skin colour and physical features mirroring other heroes, a fundamental 'sameness' affirmed by his standard armour. Thus, one black figure vase depicts Memnon accompanied by two Ethiopian attendants, and, unlike his attendants whose physical features identify them as black African, Memnon is shown in generically heroic terms, with no apparent racial markers.[32]

Claude Bérard insists that the visual contrast between Memnon and his Ethiopian companions on the vase is significant, arguing that 'Memnon has . . . never been portrayed as Black, although, as we have seen, there were no technical obstacles to doing so; the artists were not able to conceive of a prestigious heroic figure as bearing the mark of negritude'. Positing a fundamental colour prejudice in Greek thought, Bérard continues: '(r)acism thus raises its head: Once the Ethiopians have been assimilated to Negroes, they can no longer be directly confronted. Negroes are not hoplites; Negroes are not heroes. In mythological imagery, whites are superior to Blacks'.[33] But another explanation might simply be that Memnon's representation has been caught between two discursive modes: the mythic and the ethno-graphic. Edith Hall has asserted that 'ethnicity was scarcely an issue in the archaic literary world of heroes',[34] and this suggests that Greek artists might have had difficulty reconciling the longstanding 'sameness' of Memnon in relation to other heroes with the growing ethnographic awareness of Ethiopian difference. In other words, while 'hero' was once Memnon's main identifier, the significance of his 'Ethiopianness' gained greater currency over time in relation to expanding worldviews. Thus, the artist of this vase may simply have been experimenting with new methods for conveying this feature of Memnon's; indeed, it may be precisely the job of Memnon's Ethiopian servants – and not Memnon's body itself – to signal his 'Ethiopianness' on the vase.

Even as Memnon's representations may present a conundrum for modern audiences, other Greek vases provide a more explicit rendering of black Africans. Among surviving vases, there are a number of drinking cups adorned with moulded heads at the base, and some of these heads are portrayed with clearly identifiable African features, including black skin colour. Even more, these so-called Janiform vessels at times directly contrast the head of a dark-skinned person on one side with a light-skinned person on the other.[35] Such stark visual juxtaposition is potentially the most compelling evidence for arguing that the opposition of black and white remained a fundamental contrast in ancient racial formations. Scholars moreover argue that some of these vases portray their black subjects in grossly exaggerated ways meant to provoke ridicule (many characteristics, such as prominent lips, are indeed uncomfortable for a modern viewer, especially when placed against our own distorted history of black visual stereotypes). Yet Snowden has cautioned those who bring modern preconceptions to such value judgments, pointing to their inherently subjective nature.[36] And what about the presumed use or audience of such cups? Can they help us better understand the message?

François Lissarrague points out that these vessels 'belong in the context of a particular use, well known in its time – that of the symposium – where the images they carry intermingle with the customs of wine-drinking and conviviality among men, among citizens'.[37] Even more, the Janiform vases are far more likely to involve female figures than male ones, with a range of pairings featured – women and satyrs, white women with one another, women and men (often Hercules), and white women and black women.[38] Placing these images alongside the range of vases featuring animal types, Lissarrague argues that '(b)y using these vessels . . . the Greek drinker came face to face with forms of the animal world or otherness that took him outside his masculine universe'; specifically, such vases 'by evoking various categories, favouring the image of the "other" – barbarian, woman, or animal – enable him to reaffirm his own identity.'[39] In other words, the Greek male drinker is able to encounter and perhaps 'tame' a range of outsiders in the safe company of other men when using the cups.

Centuries later, a similar contrast between black and white women, one likewise constructed around the male gaze, appears in a pair of Latin poems by Ovid.[40] Explicitly defining the black woman as the slave of the Roman woman, these poems testify to the complexity of the erotic web Ovid weaves when he denies in the first poem that he has had sex with a slave (what free man would? he asks), while in the second attempts to seduce 'dark' Cypassis. Snowden argues from this that black women could be seen as objects of desire by ancient writers, and so finds Ovid's attraction to the slave an encouraging sign,[41] but such positive assessment evades the asymmetry in Ovid's blunt attempts to coerce the unwilling slave woman into sex, including his threat to reveal everything to her mistress if she does not comply.[42] This pair of poems – as also the Janiform vases – clearly focus on the private contours of male desire by offering up a range of differences against which it could be articulated: male/female, black/white, slave/master, etc. And in both contexts, skin colour carries discursive weight – but how much? By drinking from the cups, the Greek male citizen presumably derived pleasure and a sense of self-standing from the visual alterity of blackness; indeed, there is a drinking vessel that shows a pygmy being mauled by a crocodile, suggestive of an even more degrading view of the potentially exotic black 'other'.[43] But can blackness be a trope of difference without acquiring exclusive racial force – a way of viewing an – not *the* – 'other'?

What does it mean, moreover, when in Ovid and the *Moretum* blackness is paired with slavery, given that slavery was not defined by skin colour distinctions in antiquity? In the American context so well outlined by Toni Morrison, the blackness of American slaves – the most proximate 'other' not just to, but rooted deeply within, the American 'self' – is fundamentally that against which white American identity was written. Greek and Roman artists likewise were invested in the representations of those populations with whom contact was most immediate and threatening, and for most of antiquity that was not Ethiopians or black Africans. While representations of black skin colour certainly demand interpretation (and may be disturbing at times in their objectifications), it is necessary to weigh them against classical art that represents other racial groups. So we turn, as our evidence so often invites, to the world of fifth-century Athens and its monumental encounter with the Persian empire.

Persians and pseudo-Persians

The changing depiction of Amazons helps track the ideological shifts of the Athenian fifth century, including the growing treatment of Persian difference as a kind of umbrella for all differences that threatened Greek order. In early versions of their myth, the Amazons were presented as warriors first and foremost, the allies of some men and the enemies of others. Beginning in the sixth century, Amazons thus frequently appear on Attic black figure vases in scenes that emphasize their militaristic pursuits, including combat with individual heroes and more generic battle scenes known as Amazonomachies. Significantly, Amazon dress on these early vases is not yet standardized, and they are often represented wearing the uniform of hoplites, the typical Greek foot soldier.[44] In the fifth century, however, following closely on the heels of the hostilities stirring between Greece and Persia, Athenian artists began to employ the legendary wars with the Amazons as a parallel to their current struggles. In this context, depictions of Amazons started to reflect eastern stereotypes, and rather than the armour of Greek men, they wore flamboyant pantsuits – with frenetic patterns signifying they were made from animal hide or leather – and distinctive pointed caps. Now insisting adamantly on their difference from Greek hoplites, such uniforms firmly cast Amazons as archers, drawing close visual parallels to both the Scythians and the Persians themselves.[45]

While racial differences were often portrayed in Greek art via clothing and physical features, as the transformation in Amazon iconography indicates, Greek artists and writers also utilized what we might call a 'semiotics of weaponry' to encapsulate the fundamental differences between various combatants. In particular, the contrast between hoplite and archer was crucial, creating a conceptual distance between 'a cuirassed warrior, protected for fighting face to face, body to body, and the archer who fights at a distance and hits the target without getting near it.'[46] Slightly less negative was the peltast, 'who has not yet attained hoplite status'[47], a more lightly armed soldier who used a spear and distinctive half-moon shield, and was generally shown wearing patterned garments rather than hoplite armour. The Thracians were traditionally portrayed as peltasts – either on horseback or on foot – in Greek art,[48] while Scythians were conventionally shown as archers, the latter a designation that would eventually be applied to the Persians as well.

Just as the Persians were placed within a broader discourse of armament, Greek conflict with Persia was often compared to other archetypal battles in Athenian art, including Centauromachies and Amazonomachies – both of which tested the boundaries of Greek male power by setting it against groups defined as the complete opposite, non-humans on one hand, women on the other.[49] Even more, the Trojan War was now viewed as both a precursor and a mirror for the Persian Wars, demanding a new accentuation of the putative racial difference between the two sides.[50] Combining all these iconographic strategies, the Stoa Poikile in the Athenian agora (dated to around 460 BCE) displayed a painted scene of the historical battle of Marathon, then reinforced the anti-Persian message with accompanying images of the Athenians fighting the Amazons and the capture of Troy.[51] Nor was Persian defeat relegated primarily to subtext in Athenian art; one Attic vase shows a Greek man moving forward holding his erect penis as a Persian man leans over on the other side of the vessel, preparing for the rape. Its inscription 'I am Eurymedon; I stand bent over' indicates that the vase commemorates a very specific moment of Persian submission: the Greek victory at the Eurymedon river in 465 BCE.[52]

In subsequent centuries, visual representations of the Persians continued to reflect the conventions established by Athenian art and ideology, although artists could also bend such strategies or show greater nuance and even sympathy. In a famous mosaic from the late second century BCE in Pompeii, for example, Alexander the Great is depicted fighting the Persian king Darius, presumably at the battle of Issos in 333 BCE.[53] Prominent visual cues distinguish the two leaders: Alexander rushing forward on his horse Boukephalas is bare-headed and bare-faced, wearing a shining cuirass and brandishing a spear that is already piercing a dying Persian; the hat-wearing and bearded Darius, on the other hand, looks back from a chariot, his body seemingly exposed without armour and his arm outstretched in a gesture of supplication. As Andrew Stewart maintains, consonant with lingering stereotypes, the Persians are 'portrayed as hierarchical, luxurious (many wear jewellery), and emotional', but he argues nonetheless that there are enough counter-messages in the mosaic to assure that Alexander's victory is in part glorious because of the noble resistance offered by his Persian enemy.[54]

To return to the fifth century, a recent article has examined Greek representations of the Lydians and Phrygians – the former, a group bordering the Greek cities in Asia Minor, and the latter residing just beyond that – concluding that, in the case of the Phrygians, a consistent visual link to representations of Persians had developed by the second half of the fifth century.[55] Such imposition of Persian difference onto other groups, as with the Amazons, helps explain the changing representations of two other important African figures in Greek myth: Busiris, the mythical king of Egypt, and Andromeda, a legendary Ethiopian princess.[56] Busiris was a patently threatening figure in Greek myth given his practice of sacrificing foreigners on the altar of Zeus. As the myth goes, when Hercules entered Egypt, he was taken captive and broke free just as he was being prepared for sacrifice. The image of Hercules' escape and subsequent punishment of his captors is a popular theme in Greek art, 'emphasizing contrasts in number and race: one against many, Greek versus Egyptian'.[57]

Margaret Miller argues that '(t)he consistency with which Attic vase-painters through the second quarter of the fifth century highlighted the Egyptian nationality of Bousiris and his priests is striking. Alone of Archaic royal figures, Bousiris was presented as a foreigner by means of clothing and physiognomy'.[58] Noting that in early Greek myth, as we saw with Memnon, a perception of heroic sameness seems to outweigh differences suggested by geographic origin, Miller proposes that it was Busiris' specific practice of human sacrifice that necessitated such visual iteration of his difference: 'that Bousiris is ethnically alien because he is ethically alien'.[59] Over time, Busiris' representations on Greek vases intersected with broader narratives about tyranny, a term that became increasingly loaded during the era of the Persian Wars. Even as depictions of the scene become much rarer after 460 BCE, Miller argues that Persia and stereotypes of its kings became a more prevailing point of reference than Egypt in portraying Busiris, linking such strategies to the general 'Persianization' of myth, which encouraged Greek artists 'to recast the royal figures of their mythical world – whether Phyrgian, Ethiopian, or Egyptian – as Persians', in effect subsuming all other forms of difference into one paramount distinction.[60]

This practice of 'Persianization' also apparently affected representations of Andromeda, another popular subject in ancient art. As the story goes, Andromeda, daughter of the Ethiopian king Cepheus and his wife Cassiopeia, was chained to a rock as punishment for her mother's boasts until the Greek hero Perseus, flying by with the head of Medusa, saw the princess and rescued her from an approaching sea monster. A black figure vase from around 460 BCE shows a white-skinned Andromeda in distinctly eastern dress surrounded by Ethiopian attendants – identifiable by a range of features – who are preparing her for the sacrifice.[61] Like Memnon, Andromeda was initially linked to both Asia and Africa before becoming regularly associated with Africa[62], and the decision to present her as visually different from other Ethiopians is potentially bound by some of the same dynamics we encountered with Memnon (i.e. a tension between the 'sameness' of characters in myth and the 'difference' of Ethiopian ethnographic discourse). But Andromeda's white skin colour presumably also reflects Greek notions of beauty, and her representations on Athenian vases likewise bear the additional burden of her mythic connection to the Persians, one allegedly created by her marriage to Perseus and the birth of their son Perses, from whom, according to Herodotus, the Persians got their name.[63]

That Andromeda's representation as Persian (or 'proto-Persian') – meaning not just light-skinned, but also 'eastern' – was especially relevant to fifth-century Athenians seems reinforced by the later re-emergence of images that portray her with light skin without Persian connotations or that explicitly attribute a more recognizable 'Ethiopianness' to her. A vase from the mid-fourth century found in southern Italy represents Andromeda with noticeably black features,[64] and, in the Roman period, Ovid uses the same term to describe Andromeda that he used of Cypassis, his lover's slave in the *Amores*: '*fusca*' or 'dark'.[65] On the other hand, a tradition of portraying Andromeda with white skin seems to persist in classical painting, presumably employing her whiteness as a convention of female beauty since her pale skin often provides strong visual contrast to the darker tones of the male hero, Perseus.[66] Still, given that skin colour could hold more than one function in Andromeda's myth – remaining subject to the conflicting demands of her Ethiopian origin and ancient ideals of beauty – it does not mean that the two were happily resolved by choosing one over the other, and Heliodorus, a Greek writer from Emesa in Syria, eventually tackled the dilemma of a white Andromeda head-on.

In his novel *The Ethiopian Story* (a text difficult to date, but most likely from the third century CE), Heliodorus tells the story of a white Ethiopian princess, Chariklea, who was sent away at birth by her mother, the black queen, fearing accusations of adultery – the inverse of scenarios we saw in the last chapter, which were premised on the 'problem' of black children born from Roman mothers. Later, discovering her true origin, Chariklea is presented with an arresting explanation of the source of her whiteness: she was born with light skin because at the moment of her conception, her mother was looking at a painting of Andromeda.[67] Tracing the novel's influence on modern African–American thought, Daniel Selden explains that Chariklea's 'skin functions as a mark, a sign, which precipitates the child willy-nilly into the realm of the symbolic'. Although Heliodorus makes skin colour central to his narrative, however, Selden argues that he intentionally keeps its meaning elusive, treating it as 'an *aporia*' that demonstrates the 'impossibility of correlating skin colour with ethnicity or race in any meaningful way at all'.[68] In effect, we might say that Heliodorus calls attention to, and perhaps even pokes fun at, a representational dilemma that remained hidden in plain sight in ancient art: how could an Ethiopian princess possibly be light-skinned? By avoiding a scientific explanation of her skin colour, moreover, Heliodorus calls attention to the generative force of representation itself – it is representations of whiteness that beget further whiteness. It would surely be a mistake to read Heliodorus's coy novel as offering clear opinions about racial identity and its 'actual' source in either geography or skin colour, but it is clear that his treatment invites his ancient audience to confront Andromeda's whiteness as a representational crisis, perhaps for the very first time.

In assessing Andromeda's visual impact, including her prospective 'Persianness', for a specifically fifth-century Athenian audience, it would be invaluable to compare her representation on Attic vases with her appearance on stage given that she was the subject of plays by both Euripides (born c. 480 BCE) and Sophocles (born c. 490 BCE). Unfortunately, little of either work survives – although a Persian gown is mentioned in the fragments from Sophocles' play and at least one scholar has argued its staging is shown on a vase in the British Museum, which depicts the royal family in Persian garb, producing a clear visual contrast with both the Ethiopian attendants and Perseus.[69] The connection of vase paintings to actual theatrical productions suggests an exciting synergy between two very different Athenian genres; and, while much of tragedy's visual effect is lost for us today, we can discern its fundamental commitment to putting the 'other' on public display in the texts of the plays that survive.

Staging the 'other'

Greek tragedy provides a rich record of Athenian views of 'self' and 'other' throughout the fifth century. We can witness in its development across the century both the supreme self-assurance of Athens following the Persian Wars and Athens' eroding vision of itself as it became progressively embroiled in devastating conflict with Sparta. In providing the Athenians with an opportunity to deliberate both the meaning of their city and their status as 'Athenians', tragedy was intimately involved in what Edith Hall has termed the 'invention of the barbarian'. As part of such processes, Hall forcefully contends that tragedy was central to the 'racialization' of Greek myth (I am paraphrasing slightly given Hall's preference for 'ethnicity'),[70] that is, for the imposition of racial identities onto the generic heroes of Greek myth, for whom – as we saw with Memnon – geographic origin previously seemed to function in fairly hazy terms. Greek tragedy, in short, enabled the transformation of Trojan *Hector* into *Trojan* Hector.

First performed in 472 BCE, Aeschylus' *Persians* is the oldest extant Athenian tragedy, a play Hall calls 'the first unmistakable file in the archive of Orientalism'.[71] The *Persians* is unique among surviving tragedies in depicting historical figures and events rather than episodes from Greek mythology. Set at Susa shortly after the Persian defeat at Salamis, the play focuses on the Persian Queen Atossa, the widow of Darius and Xerxes' mother.[72] Although no Greeks are ever shown onstage, a contrast is drawn throughout between the victorious Greeks and the conquered Persians. The structure of the play – in which Atossa first wonders what Athens is like before hearing news of the Persians' crushing defeat – allows explicit articulation of a series of oppositions that define the two groups: the Persians are characterized by gold, the Greeks by silver (a reference to Athenian silver mines); the Persians use bows, the Greeks spears and shields; and the Persians fight for kings, while the Greeks are slave to no one.[73] This binary relation of Persians to Greeks is even more directly expressed in a dream Atossa relates in which two women, one representing Greece, the other Persia, have varying responses when Xerxes attempts to yoke them to his chariot – the Persian woman eagerly yielding to the harness, while the Greek one refuses violently, dislodging Xerxes from his perch in the process.[74] By adamantly insisting on such opposing features, the play, in effect, is able to posit a racial rationale for the stunning Greek victory, maintaining that the Greeks ultimately defeated the Persians *because* they were Greek.

Another play by Aeschylus, *Suppliant Women* (463 BCE), has occupied a central place in debates about early Greek origin (see Chapters I and IV). The play depicts the plight of Danaus and his daughters, the Danaids, who have fled from Danaus' brother Aegyptus and his sons, the latter who want to make the Danaids their wives. Arriving in Greece, Danaus and the Danaids appeal to the king Pelasgus for protection, an appeal that commands rescue by Greek men, while casting Egyptian male desire as violently anti-social.[75] The play itself contains a number of provocative and potentially racialized elements, including its reference to skin colour in describing the Danaids, the Egyptian sailors, and Aegyptus' sons.[76] Noting that the meaning of colour terminology reaches beyond race, however, Vasunia has argued that such 'blackness' might serve in part to symbolize death,[77] and the expansive interpretation of such language is important, not least because the actual racial identification of the Danaids intentionally eludes precise definition in the play.

For one, when the Danaids appeal to the myth of Io, they remind the audience that their mother, Io, was herself Greek, even though she was impregnated by Zeus alongside the Nile.[78] When the Danaids claim descent from Zeus and Io, they thus insinuate their own Greek origin, despite other features (like skin colour and birth in Egypt) that might point to their difference – underlining a kind of 'dual claim', as Vasunia calls it.[79] Nor is Aeschylus' play the only version of the myth to ponder the meaning of 'blackness' to the tale. In a fragment from Sophocles' *Inachus* Zeus is seemingly described as 'black' as he appears to Io, and the force of the designation there – not to mention the actual staging – is disputed; perhaps it is meant to 'explain' their Egyptian offspring by attributing a darker skin colour back to the father, a kind of reverse inheritance. Or is colour simply part of a larger set of ideas attached to Zeus' arrival?[80] The question remains, then, what weight we place on skin colour when reading ancient texts and whether, profoundly influenced by our own modern experiences, we are simply bringing too many assumptions about its density and 'inherent' meaning. There is no doubt that Egyptian men are negatively portrayed in *Suppliant Women*, but what does skin colour contribute to such characterization for an ancient audience as opposed to the connotations of Egypt itself, a densely wrought signifier on its own terms?

While *Suppliant Women* posits the dangers of Egyptian male sexual desire, as well as the symbolic connection of Egypt to death – both further elaborated by the playwright Euripides in his *Helen* (412 BCE)[81] – Greek tragedy also explored the specific practice of marriage with foreign women, a continuing site of anxiety for the Athenians. Euripides' *Medea*, produced in 431 BCE graphically invokes the dangers of such pairings when Medea, who comes from Colchis near the Black Sea, takes revenge on her Greek husband Jason by killing the Greek bride he intends to abandon her for along with her own children with Jason – acts a shocked Jason renounces with a bitter speech. Lamenting that he ever, in madness, brought Medea from her 'home among barbarians' to a Greek one, Jason insists that 'no Greek woman' would ever have done what she did.[82] Medea's murder of her own children remains a very troubling aspect of the play, yet many scholars suggest Euripides' treatment of her elicits a certain sympathy nonetheless, perhaps most prominently in the speech where she laments both her plight as a woman and her additional vulnerability because of her foreignness in the Greek city.[83]

Given such openings, as Thomas and others have argued, Euripides seems to be one of a number of Greek writers who were finding it harder and harder to credit the stark dichotomy of Greek and barbarian as the century wore on, and who sought instead to expose its limits and weaknesses.[84] Euripides' *Trojan Women* (415 BCE) depicts the Greeks' callous treatment of the Trojan royal women following the sack of Troy, and another of Euripides' plays, *Iphigenia at Tauris* (dated around 414), also interrogates the behaviour and moral standing of Greeks in relation to the barbarian 'other'. *Iphigenia at Tauris* focuses on the young woman Iphigenia, who, just as her father Agamemnon was about to sacrifice her, was snatched up by Artemis and taken to Tauris, near the Black Sea. As the play opens, Iphigenia decries the custom that Artemis forces her to uphold among the barbarians at Tauris: the execution of all foreigners.[85] Her brother Orestes and his companion Pylades soon arrive, and once the siblings are reunited they hatch a plan for escape. Hesitant to kill the local king Thoas, whom she professes has been kind to her, Iphigenia proposes that she reveal Orestes' murder of their mother and claim that the statue of Artemis has been polluted by him, requiring her to take it to the shore for cleansing. At the seaside, the three young Greeks then make a failed attempt at escape, and it is only the arrival of the goddess Athena that allows their departure.

Throughout the play, Euripides makes use of many conventional elements in distinguishing the Greeks from barbarians – not only the ritual sacrifice of foreigners undertaken by barbarians, but also the advanced fighting methods of the Greeks and their greater intelligence in deriving a plan for escape – but the play also continually undermines its own opposition. The Greeks' plot requires Athena for successful completion, after all, and although Orestes and Pylades are first described as using swords, the Greeks turn in the end to weapons far less noble: first their fists, then bows and arrows.[86] Even more, Iphigenia's plan relies on the innate piousness of the barbarians, their concern over Orestes' pollution of their cult statue. Horrified at hearing of Orestes' matricide, Thoas even poignantly asks what barbarian would ever do such a thing,[87] effectively turning on its head Jason's lament in the *Medea*. In the economy of the play, then, the barbarian sacrifice of foreigners is openly set against the homicidal urges of Greek myth, which, as Thoas sees it, patterns the more outrageous killing of kin.

Even as Greek playwrights were exploring – and at times unravelling – the meaning of the barbarian in mythic terms on the tragic stage, barbarian characters also appeared in Greek comedy. Employing prominent stereotypes about groups like the Thracians or Scythians, such plays were more domestic in nature and often struck directly at the closest point of Greek contact with the barbarian: the slave. As Timothy Long argues, '(i)n comedy the appearance of a foreigner in Athens or a Greek's travelling to another country usually ends in undermining the confidence with which an Athenian could ordinarily approach the barbarian slaves of his own household'.[88] Later Roman comedy would adopt some of these same concerns, while also adding a sly and self-conscious dialogue with 'Greekness' itself.[89] While ancient comedy collaborates in significant ways with contemporary racial ideology, I would like to turn to a slightly different genre of racial representation, one that conjures the barbarian not for laughter on the stage, but for rhetorical effect in the courtroom. In doing so, we turn now to the world of Rome and the imperial roots of many racial formations.

Voicing the 'other'

Noting the frequent reliance on stereotype in Roman oratory, Ann Vasaly wryly states: 'To paraphrase a cynical maxim of our day, no Roman orator ever came to grief overestimating his audience's prejudices towards ethnic minorities'.[90] Such ethnic or racial strategies were especially prominent in legal proceedings involving the prosecution of Roman officials for misconduct in the provinces, allowing a Roman audience to witness the work of empire and its exploitation of the foreign 'other' from the comfort of home as it were.[91] When seeking to defend Marcus Fonteius against charges of abuse of power in Gaul in 69 BCE, Cicero thus openly employed stereotypes of the Gauls as 'a wild and threatening race . . . consumed with a desire for revenge against their conquerors'.[92] Cicero's strategy operated on two fronts: both attacking the present credibility of the Gallic witnesses and reminding the Roman jury of the intrinsic danger of the Gauls, evoking specifically their alleged custom of human sacrifice and their historical sack of Rome. Similarly, Cicero's defence of Flaccus in 59 BCE levied a range of stereotypes against Greek prosecution witnesses, although Cicero had to tread carefully since he needed to simultaneously encourage trust in those Greeks who were testifying on Flaccus' behalf, leading him to draw an insistent (if dubious) line between mainland Greeks and Greeks residing in Asia.[93]

We can see in another of Cicero's speeches the use of Greek stereotypes against Greeks in Egypt, affirming clear Roman awareness of the 'Greekness' of Alexandria and its ruling dynasty. In 54 BCE, Cicero was charged with defending Rabirius Postumus, who was strongly implicated in the shady financial dealings involving Cleopatra's own father, Ptolemy XII Neos Dionysus, known as 'Auletes'. Beginning in 59 BCE, when trying to stabilize his shaky position in Egypt, Auletes had apparently both taken extensive loans from different Roman groups of 'investors' and also promised other Romans enormous bribes. Anxious to protect their financial interests, certain Romans helped Auletes regain his throne in 55 BCE, making Rabirius *dioiketes,* i.e. the treasury secretary of Egypt, in the process. While serving in this role, Rabirius was able to extract some repayment for those Romans with financial interests in Egypt, although not without building enough bad feeling that he was forced to flee the country. More critically, from the Roman perspective, Rabirius presumably only recovered funds for some of Auletes' creditors.[94]

In his defence of Rabirius Postumus, which he states is strictly a matter of 'missing' money, Cicero seeks first to disentangle Rabirius' case from an earlier (and seemingly successful) prosecution of another figure involved in the matter. His speech then alludes to evident public distaste in Rome for Rabirius' acceptance of an office in Egypt, and hence service to a foreign king. In seeking to contextualize Rabirius' actions, however, Cicero places little weight on Egypt itself as a signifier, instead playing up the 'Greekness' of Auletes, whose *'libido'* or 'appetite', Cicero claims, forced Rabirius to endure many things.[95] Cicero further casts doubt on the testimony of the Alexandrian witnesses by claiming that from Alexandria 'comes all deceit and falsehood', as well as the plots of mime-shows (a putdown perhaps equivalent in modern terms to calling it the home of all reality television).[96] Forced to defend Rabirius against the accusation that he wore Greek clothing in Alexandria, Cicero highlights the similar practice of other Romans past and present, arguing, in effect, that Rabirius may have been foolish, but such 'going Greek' was not exactly unprecedented.[97]

While negative images of the Alexandrians would persist, especially in times of crisis,[98] widespread recognition of Egypt's putative 'Greekness' seems to evaporate following Augustus' defeat of Cleopatra. From that point on, Roman representations would return to stock stereotypes about Egyptians and frozen images of Egypt's past, a process already evident in, and perhaps accelerated by, the treatment of Cleopatra herself. Tacitus in his *Histories* suspends Egypt in just such a bubble, calling it a province that continued to need close supervision given that it was so 'difficult to access, fertile in grain, unsettled and influenced by superstition and vice, and unknowing of laws and unfamiliar with civic rule'.[99] Ancient Greek and Latin novels from the imperial period similarly employ Egypt and Egyptians as part of their dense symbolic landscape, although their fantastical – and often emphatically timeless – narrative conventions make them difficult to place securely in any context of production or consumption, not to mention the fact that Greek novels generally evade any explicit reference to the Romans themselves.[100] Such emphasis on an Egypt isolated in time and place usually entailed focus on either the earlier pharaonic era or life in the Egyptian countryside, with little acknowledgement of the Greek urban structures that were so essential to actual Roman administration of Egypt. The visual corollary of such practices can be found in the elaborate Nile mosaic at Palestrina, which displays 'a spirited and decidedly panoramic, scene of the Nile in flood', replete with all sorts of exotic plants and animals, images that become even more fantastic as one 'follows' the Nile south.[101]

In *Satire* 15, Juvenal presents a dramatic account of the Egyptian countryside, one perfectly designed to provoke Roman disgust. Focusing on alleged events in Egypt, Juvenal adopts a viewpoint very different from his representations of racial difference within his own city. Nancy Shumate conveys the contrast in mindset: 'In Juvenal, the speaker's scorn for Egyptians is colonialist when they are still restricted to the safely distant space of the subdued province, but they become a challenge to national identity when they begin to infiltrate the metropolitan centre of empire'.[102] We have seen that Greek tragedy involved an elaborate engagement with the 'barbarian', but Juvenal announces near the beginning that his narrative culminates with a crime worse than anything found in tragedy, for tragedy, he notes, does not feature deeds committed by an entire people.[103] Turning to the Egyptians themselves, Juvenal mocks their animal worship, a common target of Roman ridicule. He then accuses the Egyptians of cannibalism, citing a brawl that broke out between two country towns when they were celebrating rival festivals.

Describing the festivals initially in terms of their excess, the scene eventually turns to all-out violence and leads to one group consuming – raw – a fallen member of the opposing side. Juxtaposing this horrible act with those of other groups foreign to the Romans, Juvenal claims: 'no dreadful Cimbrians or Britons, nor savage Scythians or monstrous Agathyrsians ever raged with such madness as this unwarlike and useless mob'.[104] In naming these northern groups, Juvenal implicitly draws on the traditional northern and southern opposition producing, in effect, a hierarchy of racial difference in which '(t)he emasculated and entirely contemptible Egyptians are opposed to the manly barbarians to the north and west'.[105] While Juvenal admits that stories of cannibalism have attached to other barbarian groups, he immediately assures his reader that those acts were done out of strict necessity, and – even more – that such groups have since been transformed by contact with Rome.[106] But not even Rome, it seems, can make a dent when it comes to the Egyptians, a perverse group 'in whose mind anger and hunger are the same thing',[107] and such 'fusion of "primitive" and "degenerate"' remained integral to the representation of Egyptians throughout Roman textuality.[108]

Later, Athenaeus, from the Greek city of Naucratis (active c. 200 CE), would show noteworthy deviations from the standard Roman vision of Egypt, focusing not on the exotic wonders of the earlier pharaonic period, but rather the 'here and now' in his writings.[109] Still, negative stereotypes about the Egyptians themselves were too powerful to resist, and Athenaeus' running comments 'add up to a critical view, to a scorn and disdain of Egyptians familiar in the Roman period.'[110] Such disdain, while it continued to reverberate throughout Roman texts, can also be traced in visual display of Egyptian subjugation, including the parading of Cleopatra's children and her own body in effigy as part of Augustus' triumph in 29 BCE.[111] Nor was this the first such extravaganza, since from its inceptions, the Roman triumph had situated exhibition of the racial 'other' within a constellation of symbols dramatically announcing Roman conquest to an eager Roman public.

Displaying the defeated 'other'

The Roman triumph consisted of an elaborate public procession in which the achievements of a specific military leader were abundantly celebrated. Central to the triumph was not only the appearance of the leader himself, but also the flaunting of the copious wealth and defeated peoples taken in battle. Marking the conceptual movement that brought foreign wars from outside Rome into its very streets, triumphs started beyond the *pomerium* and ended at the Capitoline, the heart of Rome's civic and religious life.[112] While objects could be used to symbolize foreign conquest – the triumph depicted on the Arch of Titus commemorating Roman victory in the Jewish wars showed prominent display of the menorah taken from the demolished Temple – the presence of human captives was essential to the triumph's message. As Mary Beard states, '(t)he most obvious point is that the triumph and its captives amounted to a physical realization of empire and imperialism'.[113]

Ancient accounts of triumphs suggest that the visual effect at times relied on including captives from as wide a range of groups as possible, illustrating the extent of Roman reach in human terms.[114] Yet, the display of foreign royals and their families was perhaps even more crucial; Jugurtha of Numidia and his sons were part of a triumph in 104, and Caesar's multiple triumphs in 46 would give the Roman public an opportunity to see Cleopatra's older sister Arsinoe, Juba king of Mauretania and Vercingetorix in the flesh.[115] So potent was this human degradation in communicating Roman conquest to the public that, whether accurate or not, Roman writers record a series of stories in which foreign leaders – including Cleopatra – took their lives precisely so that they would not have to endure the Roman triumph.[116] Aware of the centrality of the practice to Roman self-esteem, the Parthians, in turn, apparently staged a mock triumph when they defeated Crassus, 'with a prisoner dressed in women's clothes taking the part of the triumphing Crassus.'[117]

While there is evidence that prisoners were put to death as part of the triumph on occasion, it is not clear that the prospect of public execution was as integral to the triumph as it would be to the spectacles that took place in the Roman arena, spectacles resonant with racial overtones in their cruel display of the life and death struggles of criminals and slaves.[118] The transient performance of the triumph also has a complex relationship to the more permanent monuments associated with such events: triumphal arches. Created not merely to memorialize a specific triumph, triumphal arches – 'which by the first century CE had become a characteristic marker of Roman presence and power across the Empire, from Britain to Syria'[119]

– nonetheless drew on similar visual strategies in conveying both the alleged accomplishments of individual generals and Rome's overall military might. Within the store of imagery on such arches was often the parade of defeated enemies, such as the Dacians depicted on the continuous frieze from the arch of Trajan at Beneventum (erected in 114 CE), part of a much larger programme on the arch that sought to communicate the economic and social gains made possible by Trajan's efforts.[120]

Although the expansion of their empire produced standard images aimed at reinforcing the claims and practices of Roman power, as Beard insists, 'the most militaristic societies can also be – and often are – those that query most energetically the nature and discontents of their own militarism'.[121] In this way, it is important to appreciate a range of responses by the Roman public itself to such sights; by one account, the sight of the defeated Arsinoe in Caesar's triumph evoked pity not scorn from her Roman viewers.[122] Images expressing both conquest of, and simultaneous admiration for, defeated 'barbarians' can likewise be witnessed in a series of earlier statues dating to the third century BCE, which commemorated the victory of King Attalos I of Pergamon, in modern-day Turkey, over the Gauls.

The precise message of the so-called 'defeated Gaul' statues is difficult to identify conclusively since the types survive primarily through later copies, although the famous Roman copy of the 'Dying Gaul' now on exhibit in the Capitoline Museum suggests some of their presumed pathos. The life-size statue has a number of features that identify the male figure as a Gaul, including his moustache, his shield, the metal collar or torque around his neck, and the trumpet broken at his side. Depicted in the nude, the Gaul is looking down, clearly a gesture of submission, and may perhaps be holding a wound on his leg. Although clearly conquered, as I. M. Ferris insists, it is impossible to see the overall message of the statue as anything 'other than a study of "dignity in defeat."'[123] In another statue type also credited to the Attalid series, a standing nude male Gaul is in the process of committing suicide with a sword to his breast while he holds the arm of his fully clothed wife with the other hand, presumably having just taken her life. Suggestive of the influence such representations of the Gauls – as primitive, but noble

– would hold on the Roman imaginary, some scholars have argued that copies of these two statues were commissioned by Julius Caesar for display in his house at Rome, helping shape the meaning and memory of his own campaigns in Gaul.[124]

Of course, even 'noble in defeat' relentlessly announces defeat, and it would be impossible here to account for all the surviving Roman sculpture and architectural monuments – erected in Rome and throughout the empire – that helped give voice to the Roman imperial mission and the conquest it inscribed on the bodies of others.[125] Still, it is worth considering briefly one innovative medium for depicting war as a taming of barbarian hordes, a medium that emphatically presented war as a prolonged and even chaotic process: the narrative column. Trajan's column, the first of such columns, was set up in his forum in Rome in 113 CE and features a continuous frieze that winds around the whole column shaft, depicting the Roman campaigns against the Dacians in 101–2 and 105–6 CE. It is unclear how much of the frieze on Trajan's column would actually have been visible to a Roman viewer in its original position (as opposed to scholars today who have the advantage of photographs), but Ferris notes that the Dacians are consciously portrayed as a distinct racial group throughout, not merely a generic type.[126]

The column of Marcus Aurelius was erected in the Campus Martius sometime after Marcus Aurelius' death in 180 CE. Modelled on Trajan's column, it, too, features a continuous frieze, albeit one portraying campaigns against the Marcomanni (in Germany) and Sarmatians in the 170s CE. The overall feel of the column departs radically from the ordered scenes on Trajan's column; indeed, on this column 'there is often almost a sense of panic and frenetic endeavour on the part of the Roman forces'.[127] Noting the scenes of extreme violence – which assail the viewer in quick succession especially since Marcus Aurelius' column omits some of the more sedate scenes of Roman camp life so important to the earlier column – Ferris concludes that on the later column:

> the barbarian has simply become a body, dehumanized pieces and fragments of bleeding and battered flesh, whose fate was dictated by

Roman imperial authority. These bodies are stabbed or hacked at, they are pushed and herded like beasts being brought in from the fields, they are pulled along by the hair, they are beheaded and their bodies piled up in heaps for the edification of the viewer.[128]

While such images clearly seek to communicate the raw exercise of Roman power, the unremitting chaos of its style nonetheless invites from its audience serious questions about Rome's empire and its claims to mastery at this point in time – do such images suggest, in fact, an empire that is progressively losing control of both self and state?

Although Trajan's earlier column presents warfare (and so Roman conquest) in more controlled terms than the later one, it nonetheless includes a scene that Sheila Dillon calls 'one of the most unusual, disturbing, and violent depictions of women in Roman art'[129]; in this scene, five women are shown torturing three men, who are naked and bound. The identification of both the women and their victims has been the subject of much debate. Dillon herself argues against any interpretation that sees the prisoners as Roman soldiers, believing it would be too shocking for a Roman audience, and posits instead that the scene shows non-Roman women (i.e. Moesian women who had suffered under the Dacians or local women attached to the Roman army) torturing captured Dacians. She similarly disputes the theory that it depicts a real event – as is often assumed given its unprecedented subject matter – and suggests instead that we understand it 'as a visual trope that was meant to portray graphically the humiliation and degradation of the Dacians in their defeat and the utter unnaturalness of their opposition to Roman imperial rule, here visualized as an inversion of the "natural order" of things, with women inflicting violence on men'.[130]

Such a scene – as also the Parthian use of womanly costume to ridicule Crassus – highlights the recurring use of gender in defining relative positions of power in ancient conquest narratives. Indeed, female forms were often used to personify Roman provinces, especially in images of defeat, a conceit that serves to 'double' the symbolic difference between the defeated forces and their Roman conquerors by casting the conquered as both racially *and* sexually 'other'.[131] Cleopatra herself, in fact, fit so perfectly into this advantageous doubling of foreign and female that, to coin a phrase, if she did not exist, the Romans would have had to invent her (which, as we have seen, in many ways they actually did). Once of the most dramatic surviving examples of the trend for depicting defeated provinces as women was found at Aphrodisias in south-west Turkey. The relief depicts the Roman emperor Claudius in heroic nude form pacifying the female form of Britannia, who struggles on the ground at his feet, one breast exposed.[132] The exposure of female flesh as a sign of vulnerability is obviously very different from the vision of the emperor's nude body, which is meant to signify his power and perfection. Such a commanding image of Claudius' masculinity, needless to say, might surprise readers and viewers of *I, Claudius,* as well as perhaps his contemporary Roman public. But the location of the find also reminds us of the complexity of Roman imperial discourse – what was the conquest of Britain meant to signify to an audience a thousand miles away?

Even as Claudius might have one British woman under foot, Martial nonetheless describes another British woman, Claudia Rufina, who apparently had the world at *her* feet. For despite the fact that Claudia was originally from the 'blue-stained' British, Martial raves that she possessed the 'Latin' heart and beauty that made everyone want to claim her: 'Italian mothers are able to believe she is Roman' and Attic women take her for 'their own'.[133] Martial's portrayal of Claudia Rufina as seamlessly crossing racial boundaries, at least in the eyes of other women, gainfully suggests the ways in which art and literary representations not only seek to establish a range of categories, but also open complementary possibilities of combating them as well. So I would like to conclude this chapter by sampling more ambivalent and at times subversive literary responses to Roman conquest, ones frequently played out in just such border crossings.

'Becoming' the 'other'?

Racial representations are not one-dimensional, and even if on one level they project absolute confidence in defining a Greek or Roman self against the barbarian, on another level, such attempts frequently threaten to unravel. While it is true that a powerful and pervasive vision of the barbarian coalesced throughout Greek fifth-century art and literature, it is also true that the very concept was simultaneously challenged and destabilized in the work of writers like Herodotus and Euripides. In addition to illustrating racial formations in all their complexity, then, racial representations supply the resources for examining the very act of producing racial categories, and, in doing so, they often expose their many weaknesses. Moreover, in certain sites in ancient art and literature, racial formation and the setting of racial boundaries are investigated not through the barbarian – including his or her capacities to become 'more civilized', especially when faced with over-whelming force – but rather the stability of individuals within the categories of 'Greek' and 'Roman' themselves. What might the porousness of such racial boundaries mean in the other direction? Could they testify to the challenges not of keeping people out, but rather keeping people in?

As we have seen, visual elements like clothing and weaponry often demar-cate racial differences in Greek art. Yet, as Beth Cohen points out, Athenian men were at times shown donning elements of foreign costume. Thus, on some Greek vases, hoplite soldiers wear what appear to be Persian caps under the helmets. Such gestures might simply reflect utilitarian measures practiced in real life (these caps might simply make their helmets more comfortable), but they might also make a subtle statement about mastery, that is, such tactics might visually provide 'a means for Athenian men of *taming* the Other – of exercising control and asserting superiority in a diverse, even threatening world'.[134] To go even further, we might read such touches as conscious appropriations of disempowered status, a way of 'playing' the 'other' and so exploring a range of power relations in more intimate ways, perhaps in order to communicate sympathy for the plight of the 'other' or to experience a kind of vicarious pleasure in disempowerment. We can see something of the latter dynamic in Roman love poetry, where the male narrator often professes delight in acting as 'slave' to his female beloved – a conceit whose carefully contained manner of debasement seems especially exposed on occasions where *real* slaves show up.[135]

We can witness other incidents of Romans 'becoming' the 'other' in Roman literature, the opposite, as it were, of the much-heralded process of Romanization. In one of his love poems, Propertius angrily chastises his 'mad' lover Cynthia for dying her hair like the British and using a 'Belgian colour' that he calls 'unnatural' to her Roman face. Provocatively using a verb meaning 'play' or 'masquerade' of such imitation, Propertius seems to worry that his lover is attempting to become the barbarian right in front of his eyes.[136] In a later poem, Ovid responds by portraying a similar attempt by his lover, but Ovid depicts Corinna's actions as much more superficial, expressing greater confidence in the ultimate failure of such 'play'. Now Corinna, having destroyed her own hair with chemical dyes, is forced to wear 'captured hair' sent by Germany (presumably a wig made from the hair of a German slave), meaning that she garners the praise rightly meant for 'some Sygambrian woman'. But by wearing the hair of someone else rather than altering her own features, Corinna only 'seems' rather than 'becomes' the foreign woman. And, to be sure, Corinna's natural state remains only temporarily marred, for Ovid promises that her 'native' hair will soon grow back.[137]

Throughout Roman literature, women were often seen as more susceptible to foreign influence, and given their explicit reference to specific foreign groups, Propertius and Ovid seem to be using the female body and its limits here as a way of testing the stability of the burgeoning Roman empire in its encounters with, and appropriations of, 'others' – with Propertius demonstrably less confident about the overall exchange. Commentators on both poems have also suggested that they reflect actual trends among women at Rome, that blonde hair in particular became popular as the Romans came increasingly into contact with slaves from the north.[138] As real practices, such fads raise crucial questions about why appropriations from less powerful groups take place within certain social and political structures. Why would Roman women choose to emulate the look of northern slaves? What is at stake in such performances? For Ovid and Propertius, moreover, such possibilities have a specifically literary dimension – they present not so much 'real' female performance, but male fantasy about women's bodies and their presumed propensity for 'going native' at the very heart of Rome itself. But while Ovid seems to enjoy exploring the notion when it comes to his lover's body, he later treats it with much greater distress when he finds himself subject to his own transformation at the world's edge.

After a diverse and lively career, for reasons not quite clear, Ovid was evidently sent into exile at Tomis along the Black Sea in 8 CE, at what is today Constanza in Romania. Ovid's poetry from Tomis (the *Tristia* and *Epistulae ex Ponto*) is the only source for this event, and he himself claims that Augustus was offended by the lascivious nature of a work he published some years earlier, the *Art of Love* (*Ars Amatoria*). Although Ovid bitterly complains about his life in exile, including the remoteness of Tomis,[139] in fact, the area had a long history of contact with the Greco-Roman world. The Greeks had reached Tomis during their efforts at colonization along the Black Sea,[140] and the Romans eventually conquered much of the area along the western Pontic shore with Tomis itself occupying a key position economically. Administratively, Tomis was placed first under the control of the proconsul of Macedonia, and later transferred to Moesia when that became a province in 15 CE.[141]

Despite such events, Ovid depicts not a territory defined by its history of contact with the Greeks and Romans, but rather an isolated world replete with longstanding ethnographic stereotypes. He refers to the location of his exile in general terms as Scythia, and the people surrounding him as the Getae and Sarmatians.[142] Although he acknowledges that the Greeks settled colonies in that area and that some Greek cities remain ('who would believe it', he asks),[143] he perceives the population as 'mixed' at best, with the 'native' element clearly winning out.[144] Ovid utilizes the ancient environmental theory throughout his poems, closely linking the region's cold climate to the character of the 'barbarians' who surround him – 'trousered' and warlike groups among whom his life is constantly precarious.[145] Emphasizing the uncivilized nature of the place, in one poem, Ovid even claims that cannibals live close by.[146] He further evokes literary figures like Odysseus, Medea, and even Iphigenia at 'nearby' Tauris to dramatize his plight. Whether Ovid's miserable depiction is accurate is, in many ways, beside the point; my interest is rather the ways Ovid presents his own Roman identity itself as constantly jeopardized by exile, irrevocably eroding in the new landscape.

Early in the *Tristia* (literally the 'sorrows'), Ovid memorably compares his initial departure from Rome to a kind of death, and later calls himself a 'shadow' of the man he once was.[147] Noting the centrality of Rome to his identity, he proclaims that he first died when deprived of his homeland, and – even more openly resonant of the 'rightful' process of Roman empire-building – begs that as a Roman citizen he not be made to fear capture by the enemy, declaring 'divine right forbids anyone born from Latin blood to endure barbarian shackles as long as Caesars rule'.[148] What Ovid's anxiety portends, it seems, is the threat of Romanization's inverse, for it is not the barbarian whose identity is transformed by Roman rule, but rather the Roman who is becoming increasingly barbaric.[149] Proclaiming in one poem that his body has been hardened by exile, Ovid proposes, in contrast, that his mind has been weakened.[150] He rues in particular the loss of his Latin (his verse he says in one poem is no more 'barbaric than the place it's from'),[151] and ultimately bemoans that 'here *I* am the barbarian, understood by no one, and the dim-witted Getae make fun of my Latin speech'.[152]

Ovid's admission that there are contexts in which he stands as the barbarian is designed to elicit a kind of panic from its Roman reader, at least in the ways it signals the failure of his intrinsic Romanness to survive in the wild; for as Ovid is finding out, his Roman identity is something that can be lost without the geographic and political stability he once derived from the Roman state: how secure was it to begin with? But Ovid's reference to the gaze of the racial 'other' for whom *he* is the 'barbarian' also reminds us of the role of perspective – how different a Roman might seem from the other side of the looking-glass. In related ways, although Persian sources do not survive to nearly the same degree as Greek ones, some historians are now asking both how the ancient Persians saw themselves and how *they* defined the Greeks throughout their cataclysmic encounters, an adversary the Persians named 'Yauna'.[153]

It would be impossible to conclude this attempt to chart the role of ancient art and literature in both advancing and subverting ancient racial formations without turning once more to Alexander the Great and his own textual legacy, which reaches even further than the limits of the ancient *oikumene* that once inspired him. For the exploits of Alexander were embellished in innumerable outlets, including a colourful novel known as the *Alexander Romance*, which survives in many different versions and perhaps has its origins as early as the third or second century BCE in Egypt.[154] Alexander's literary image was also developed in two prominent Arabic texts, *The Sayings of Philosophers* and *The Secret of Secrets*, the former based in part on a text in Syriac – and both texts, like the rest of the Alexander corpus, would be transmitted into multiple languages over time, and read and reproduced in an array of national contexts.[155] Surely such a richly diverse afterlife begs the question: to whom does Alexander ultimately belong?

CHAPTER IV

WHOSE HISTORY?

Germans are tourists and Frenchman are tourists but <u>Englishmen are Greeks</u>. Such was the sense of their discourse, and we must take their word for it that it was very good sense indeed.

Virginia Woolf

In her story 'A Dialogue upon Mount Pentelicus', Virginia Woolf details the pretensions of six Englishmen on a visit to Greece. At one point, the group of tourists – a label they themselves eschew – attempt to speak to their 'escort of dirty Greek peasant boys' in Greek, or, as Woolf phrases it, 'in their own tongue as Plato would have spoken it had Plato learned Greek at Harrow'. When faced with the incomprehension of their listeners, the reaction of the Englishmen is unanimous: 'one word came aptly to their lips; a word that Sophocles might have spoken, and that Plato would have sanctioned; they were "barbarians."' 'To denounce them,' Woolf adds, 'was not only to discharge a duty on behalf of the dead but to declare the rightful inheritors.' Using the term 'barbarian', one whose abiding power we have witnessed, as Woolf wryly notes, the Englishmen effectively align themselves with the ancient Greeks, while putting in place those modern Greek 'imposters'.[1]

The English tourists soon begin a conversation with one another, arriving 'upon the tough old riddle of the modern Greek and his position in the world today' and inspiring one of the group to 'demonstrate with great shocks of speech and of muscle what it was the Greeks had been, and what it is that they are no longer'. Another member of the group, however, calls attention to the ways in which the ancient Greeks have become a store for all manner of projection, a process by which, he proclaims, the name Greek 'can mean in short all that we do not know and as in your case all that we dream and desire'. The speaker then proposes with devastating accuracy: 'Indeed there is no reason why you should read their writings, for have you not written them?'[2]

In this final chapter, I want to examine a range of assumptions and desires that make Woolf's Englishmen identify so adamantly with the Greeks, adhering to them so closely, in fact, that they seem to have 'written' or even become the Greeks themselves. What dreams and aspirations have attended such claims to a classical inheritance? Or, perhaps more importantly, how have such identifications with – and inventions of – classical antiquity and its structures of thought shaped our modern racial ideologies? I will survey a range of appropriations of the classical world here, but most of my sites of discussion, like the controversial *Black Athena* itself, will admittedly bring us back again and again to the modern nineteenth century, a period with whose giant windmills we still endlessly seem to tilt.[3]

Although various art and architectural traces of ancient Greece and Rome had survived through the Middle Ages, the Renaissance initiated a sweeping revival of interest in the classical world.[4] (Just how certain texts were there to be 'rediscovered' is itself an intricate tale; suffice to say, that although Irish monks may have 'saved civilization',[5] Arab intellectuals were also central to the transmission of an important set of ancient texts.[6]) From that point on, the ever-widening circulation of Greek and Roman texts and translations, drawings of classical ruins, and ancient artwork would forever transform the ways in which the classical past and present were understood in relation to one another. At times, the 'old riddle' of antiquity's relation to later eras would be a difficult one to solve, especially when reverence for the ancient world was confronted by the emergent belief in progress – the conviction, reinforced by Darwinism, that younger civilizations inherently outstrip their elders.[7] Despite such intermittent challenges, dialogue with the classical world would continue to flourish over the centuries and Greek and Roman antiquity would provide an irreplaceable, if malleable resource for the articulation of a range of concepts central to modern life, not least race and nation.

The ancient environmental theory itself initially provided a key edifice for the organization of modern racial thought, surviving in both broad outline and via the Hippocratic essay *Airs, Waters, Places*.[8] A summary of *Airs, Waters, Places* was found among Montesquieu's papers, and he presumably relied heavily on it for his seminal work *On The Spirit of the Laws* (1748),[9] a treatise that 'took it as axiomatic that the character of a people depended on the climate to which they were exposed.'[10] As Mark Harrison explains, 'Classical doctrines of environmental determinism came into vogue during the eighteenth century because they offered an explanation of the material and intellectual progress experienced by European countries over the previous two centuries'.[11] The differences allegedly produced by climate also served in more direct terms to help justify a range of contemporary processes, not least empire-building: 'India, it was thought, had been subjugated because her climate had made its inhabitants supine and fatalistic, while the bracing weather of northern Europe had produced a dynamic race, fit for conquest and exploration.'[12]

By the nineteenth century, the theory of environmental determinism was starting to yield to biological theories of race based on skin colour. Indeed, Harrison argues that the British recognition that they were *not* adapting to the tropical climate of India helped precipitate a greater reliance on newer scientific theories of race throughout the British Empire.[13] Given that climate was often retained as an explanation for varying skin colours, however, these two theories at times intersected, even as their treatment of the source of racial difference – biology versus geography – emphatically diverged.[14] In the antebellum American South, as Mart Stewart notes, environmentalism lasted into the nineteenth century in part because such ideology was critical to the southern justification of slavery: '(t)hat Africans could apparently ... endure such labour better than whites was proof positive to some that different climates had moulded the races differently and to others at least that Africans were historically better "acclimated" to hot climates'.[15] Still, when environmentalism was eventually dislodged, many adherents to the newer biological theory used it not to discredit slavery, but simply to offer a different rationale. Drawing on concepts like polygenesis, Africans were no longer thought to be conditioned by climate for the gruelling labours of slavery, but rather able to undergo it because they were fundamentally different from white Southerners.[16]

Given the nineteenth century's advancement of a range of theories designed to buttress Eurocentrism and – in more material terms – European imperialism and colonialism, it is no coincidence that this century provides a key foundation for Martin Bernals's controversial study of Greek cultural origin: *Black Athena: The Afroasiatic Roots of Classical Civilization*. With one eye on the ancient world, Bernal's multi-volume project aims in part to reveal the many attempts beginning in the modern nineteenth century to portray the origins of ancient Greek civilization as an entirely autonomous phenomenon, an assertion that corresponded both with the emergence of classics itself as a modern academic discipline and new scientific theories of race.[17] Explicitly founded on attempts to connect modern Europe and ancient Greece, the actual 'doing' of classics was thus deeply implicated from its very start, in Bernal's view, in the promotion of an historical and transnational genealogy of 'whiteness'.[18]

In foregrounding the influence of specific intellectual and historical movements on the study of western antiquity, *Black Athena* has often been compared to Edward Said's *Orientalism*,[19] but Bernal strongly insists on the differences between the two, writing that 'his (i.e. Said's) work is literary and allusive, mine historical and pedestrian. More importantly, I do not accept his view that Orientalism – or for that matter ancient history – are almost entirely self-referential'.[20] As this statement suggests, Bernal's positivism and absolute belief in an historical truth are apparent throughout *Black Athena*. Bernal's attempt to dispel the racist influences on various models of Greek origin is therefore not a preface to claiming that all perceptions of history are comprised by ideology, but rather a way of clearing the fog in order to see 'what actually happened.' At the same time, the terms of Bernal's analysis, and especially the spectre of race itself, remain a sticking point for his wildly ambitious project.

Coming to terms with *Black Athena*

The subject of *Black Athena* seems deceptively straightforward; as Bernal writes: '*Black Athena* is essentially concerned with the Egyptian and Semitic roles in the formation of Greece in the Middle and Late Bronze Age.'[21] As Bernal well knew, however, by opening examination of Greece and its origins, including its putative dependency on civilizations to the east, he was lighting a powder keg – openly defying the assumption of Greek self-sufficiency or 'miraculism' that had bolstered many intellectual and nationalist projects in the west. In *Volume 1: The Fabrication of Ancient Greece 1785–1985*, Bernal conspicuously began his work not with demonstration of the actual historical origins of Greek culture, but with an extensive historiography of how that origin has been presented, beginning with the Greeks themselves. In Bernal's view, the ancient Greeks subscribed to an 'Ancient Model' of their own cultural development, one that recognized a period of Egyptian and Phoenician colonization around 1500 BCE, as well as the continuing and profound influence of these cultures on their own.

Once established, this 'Ancient Model' stood until the modern nineteenth century, at which point what Bernal calls an 'Aryan Model' was developed precisely to promote the alleged purity of Greece and its superiority over Egypt. Notably, the rise of the Aryan Model did not pivot on the discovery of any new 'internal' evidence from the ancient world, but rather, as Bernal argues, was driven by external ideas concerning race, progress, and Romanticism, including growing identification of Greece as the birthplace of modern Europe. In general terms, the Aryan Model posited that 'Greek culture developed as a result of the mixing between an aboriginal "Pre-Hellenic" population and one or more invasions from the North by Indo-European speakers'.[22] While there was little evidence for the earliest occupants of Greece – as we have seen, the Greeks themselves vaguely construed them as 'Pelasgians' or the like – classicists insisted that these 'Pre-Hellenic' groups had 'been "white" or "Caucasian", and certainly not Semitic or African'.[23] The Aryan Model itself, Bernal proposes, actually took two forms: a 'Broad' version that developed first which, while it adamantly denied the role of Egypt, continued to allow for the Phoenician (i.e. Semitic) impact on Greek culture, and an 'Extreme' one that eventually repudiated even the prospect of substantial Phoenician influence in light of contemporary anti-Semitism.[24] Ultimately, Bernal aimed to restore a 'Revised Ancient Model', which accepted both the stories of Egyptian and Phoenician colonization, albeit dating them to the first half of the 2nd millennium BCE, and an invasion of Indo-European speakers in the 4th or 3rd millennium BCE.

The discipline of classics was founded on the study of ancient languages, a practice called 'philology', and Bernal's attempts to demonstrate early foreign influence on Greek culture by examining ancient Greek remains central to his approach. Ancient Greek itself has long been classified as an Indo-European language, a classification with which Bernal generally agrees. But Bernal argues that the earlier population of Greece, the 'Pre-Hellenic' population, spoke a language that left little trace in Greek, and so contends that the significant number of non-Indo-European forms in Greek (i.e. those not attributable for linguistic reasons to the presumed Indo-European invaders) must derive from a different source.[25] In looking to foreign influences instead, Bernal thus seeks pointedly to discredit a linchpin of the Aryan Model: 'the non-Indo-European speaking "Pre-Hellenic" peoples upon whom every inexplicable aspect of Greek culture has been thrust.'[26] More specifically, Bernal claims that the non-Indo-European elements in Greek 'can be plausibly derived from Egyptian and West Semitic' in accordance with 'a long period of domination by Egypto-Semitic conquerors'.[27]

Despite more neutral-sounding claims that *Black Athena* focuses on 'Greek cultural *borrowings* from Egypt and the Levant (my emphasis)'[28] as Bernal's reference to the role of 'Egypto-Semitic conquerors' suggests, he stresses the impact of domination throughout his work. In fact, Bernal himself points out that all three models outlined in *Black Athena* – including his own Revised one – 'share one paradigm, that of the possibility of diffusion of language or culture through conquest', a prospect that 'goes against the dominant trend in archaeology today, which is to stress indigenous development.'[29] Recognizing that such assumptions are central to Bernal's approach, some critics have suggested (not without irony) that Bernal himself thus relies heavily on nineteenth-century models of top-down cultural transmission in seeking to unseat the Aryan model.[30] Arguments about colonization, in particular, remain one of the most controversial parts of *Black Athena*, raising questions we have considered in Chapter I, that is, how myth and material evidence can be used to unlock early Greek history.

Classicists have long been receptive to the idea of links between Greece and the Near East, although they have traditionally limited substantial Near Eastern influence on Greek culture to a relatively late era known as the 'Orientalizing Period', c. 750–650 BCE, a standard convention whose motives Bernal rightly questions. In recent years, though, many classical historians have been willing to push the date of contact further back, albeit generally interpreting the influence in economic rather than political terms. Sarah P. Morris writes of *Black Athena* that '(m)y treatment of the same period (the Late Bronze Age) and some of the same evidence . . . imagines not conquest or colonization, those military encounters exaggerated by ancient rulers and overestimated by modern historians, but regular and mutually profitable transactions.'[31] In a similar vein, David O'Connor acknowledges that although there is evidence of people from the Aegean – most likely traders – travelling to Egypt by the time of the Egyptian Eighteenth Dynasty (c. 1574–1293 BCE), it is unclear whether Egyptians, in turn, were in the Aegean.[32] More broadly, O'Connor argues that 'Egyptian objects (or objects reflecting Egyptian styles) found in the Aegean, and Aegean objects found in Egypt' are not sufficient to confirm the particular phenomenon of colonization, especially when ancient Egyptian colonization in Lower and Upper Nubia left clear evidence of its arrival in the material record.[33]

Invasions and migrations have long featured prominently in discussions of Greek racial origins because they provide a useful device for explaining dramatic changes in the archaeological record, not to mention positing a single source of group identity. Among his sequence of historical invasions, Bernal includes the 'Dorian Invasion' from northwest Greece – an event associated with the so-called myth of the 'Return of the Heraklids' (children of Hercules), which he dates to the twelfth century BCE.[34] While this invasion is not central to his own work, Bernal's perfunctory mention of it belies the fact that the 'Dorian invasion' has been hotly contested by modern scholars, and such debates shed light on the hazards of reconstructing early Greek history from later mythic narratives.

The Dorians, one of the major Greek ethnic sub-groups, were commonly associated with the Peloponnese in antiquity. Sparta would eventually serve as the quintessential Dorian city, and in the shadow of the Peloponnesian War, this identification gave a powerful structure for elucidating Sparta's antagonism with Athens, the paradigmatic Ionian city, suggesting that their conflict derived from fundamental differences of character and not merely their respective political aspirations. The work of Karl Otfried Müller, a nineteenth-century German philologist, helped shape modern perceptions of the so-called 'moderation, simplicity, frugality, and steadfastness' of the Dorians, qualities that not only allegedly distinguished them from the Ionians, but also made them, like Müller, 'uncannily Protestant.'[35] Significantly, German identification with the Dorians would continue into the Nazi period.[36]

But where did the Dorians come from? Relying on myths that claimed the Dorians had invaded the Peloponnese following the Trojan War, archaeologists at the end of the nineteenth century conflated the alleged invasion of the Dorians with the fall of the Mycenaean palace civilization, a wide-scale destruction that was readily visible in the archaeological record, as was a subsequent transformation of material culture that quickly became attributed to the Dorians.[37] Much of this archaeological evidence has been re-evaluated, however, and Jonathan Hall responds to the barbed question of whether the Dorian invasion 'ever actually happened' by clarifying the different possible meanings behind such phrasing:

> If . . . by the 'Dorian migration' we mean a single, massive influx of immigrants from central Greece, then the answer must be no. If we mean that every member of the population of Dorian cities in the Classical period was genetically descended from an original inhabitant

of central Greece, then again – no. And if we mean that 'real blood ties' existed between the populations of cities as distant as Argos, Melos and Halikarnassos, then – almost certainly not . . . This is not to say, however, that there was no reality to 'being Dorian' in the sixth or fifth centuries.[38]

Hall's sense that the 'Dorian migration' was 'real' in that it provided the grounds for 'being Dorian' in the sixth or fifth centuries marks the importance he places on interpreting Greek myth within the context of its mobilization rather than the murky past it purports to explain. Looking more closely, Hall notes the inconsistencies between stories of the Dorian invasion and those of the 'Return of the Heraklids' and argues that there were initially two distinct myths – 'that of the Dorians of Erineos, perhaps first developed at Sparta, and that of the Herakleidai, engineered in the Argolid' – which were eventually fused.[39] The version of the myth that we find in our evidence thus 'dates back no further than the mid-sixth century – that is, some five or six centuries after the supposed date of the migration'.[40] Given such gaps in time, any core truth behind the myth seems forever out of reach, but, as Hall proposes, we can still try to illuminate the ways in which the transmissions of these myths of origin served those telling them. To take a more modern (if hackneyed) example: we may never know the historical basis, if any, of a story like George Washington's chopping down of the cherry tree, but surely we can trace the role of the re-telling of such a tale in the bolstering of our perceptions of America's first President, and so perhaps American identity itself.

Bernal, on the other hand, places a fundamental 'truth' at the heart of Greek myth, even if its trappings have been obscured over time, and he employs foundational figures from Greek myth in arguing more concretely for episodes of foreign colonization. Bernal thus treats Danaus as an historical personage, dating his arrival in Argos to around 1720 BCE as part of a general 'Hyksos Egypto-Canaanite conquest' (the Hyksos being a Semitic-speaking group who conquered Egypt at around that time after which, according to Bernal, they infiltrated the Aegean).[41] Using Aeschylus'

Suppliant Women to support his theory, Bernal argues that while the play's surface may mask Danaus' actual role as colonizer (portraying him as dependent on Greek help instead), Aeschylus nonetheless employs persistent wordplay alluding to the Egyptian and Hyksos subtext in the myth.[42] In short, despite certain adjustments to suit the Greek audience's sensibilities, Bernal believes that Aeschylus' play holds traces of a real historical event: Greek colonization at the hands of Hyksos invaders arriving from Egypt.

Many classicists have argued strenuously against such literal treatment of Greek myth. Edith Hall, as we have seen, asserts that the meaning of foreign origin changes over time in myth; more specifically, she argues that such foundation myths emerge not from a context of Egyptian (or Hyksos) colonization, but '*Greek* colonization, as the poet-genealogists sought to provide their Hellenophone public, now spread over all corners of the Mediterranean, with mythical progenitors and founders who had prefigured their own activities in foreign parts (*sic*).'[43] Such arguments underscore the fact that perceptions of colonization themselves must be strictly historicized (how would Greek audiences make sense of episodes of foreign colonization in their distant past given their own colonization efforts beginning in the eighth century?), as well as the function of mythic narrative at any one point in time. Given his tendency to focus on what is told via myth rather than why or when and to what audience – surely, first and foremost, Aeschylus' play addresses not a generic Greek audience, but a specifically Athenian one – Bernal's handling of Greek myth remains a major point of contention in evaluations of his work, and some scholars have similarly challenged his complementary use of Egyptian legends about the pharaoh Sesotris.[44]

On the other hand, the most unconditional praise for *Black Athena* tends to emphasize the broader service Bernal has performed in bringing modes of knowledge construction, and more specifically the pervasiveness of Eurocentrism, to public awareness.[45] Robert Young has insisted that 'Bernal's most significant intervention, *though to some extent unacknowledged even by himself,* is the fact that he places race, racism and the racialization of knowledge at the core of his argument' (my emphasis).[46] Significantly, despite his attempt to indict centuries of scholarly racism,

Bernal himself primarily employs the terminology of cultural contact and cultural formation when talking about antiquity itself; yet, as Michaels has pointed out, the affect of 'culture' is frequently supplied by race, and controversies over the racial connotations of Bernal's project continue to proliferate – encouraged in no small part by Bernal's provocative title and the spotlight it placed on the goddess Athena's presumptive 'blackness.'

Coming to terms with 'black' Athena

Observing the power of Bernal's title, Molly Myerowitz Levine has argued that *Black Athena* extends far beyond Athena – a potent figure in her own right – to 'impl(y) an unequivocal stand on the skin colour and/or race of the ancient Egyptians'[47] (a phrase whose hedging reliance on 'and/or' should not go unremarked). Bernal has nonetheless sought to counter such presumptions and at one point asserted that the title 'African Athena' would have more accurately reflected his aims.[48] Yet, Bernal did little to help his cause when he 'explained' that his 'publisher insisted on retaining it, arguing: "Blacks no longer sell. Women no longer sell. But black women still sell!"'[49] Still, in Volume 1, Bernal did attempt to provide a brief explanation of the rationale behind his titular goddess' skin colour:

> ... the earliest Greek representation of Athena is that from Mycenae, in which her limbs are painted, in line with Minoan convention – taken from Egypt – of representing men as red/brown and women as yellow/white. Nevertheless, it is the conjunction of Neit/Athena's Egypto-Libyan origins, Herodotus' awareness of the connection, and his portrayal of the Egyptians as black, that has inspired the title of this series.[50]

Bernal later elaborated his specific claim about Herodotus stating, in essence, that, although classical writers applied various skin colour terminology to the ancient Egyptians, Herodotus had described Egyptians specifically with 'black skins and woolly hair' (a passage briefly discussed in Chapter I).[51]

Even more, Bernal outlined his own views concerning the ancient Egyptians, professing that he was both 'dubious of the utility of the concept "race" in general' and 'even more sceptical about the possibility of finding an answer in this particular case'. Stating that he believed 'Egyptian civilization was fundamentally African and that the African element was stronger in the Old and Middle Kingdoms, before the Hyksos invasion, than it later became', Bernal added: 'The actual African nature of Egyptian civilization, however, is not relevant to our present discussion, which is concerned with the ambiguities in the *perceived* "racial" position of the Egyptians' (sic).[52] Bernal's designation of race as a socially constructed phenomenon – one whose complexities are only magnified when applying it to historical populations – has been almost universally overlooked by his critics. Indeed, many scholars have harshly criticized his assertion in the same passage that there were some pharaohs 'whom one can usefully call black',[53] meaning that, if alive today, certain Egyptian pharaohs would invariably fall into that modern category, regardless of the racial structures that mattered in their own lifetimes. Bernal's attempt to place the debates about ancient Egypt within modern racial formations is admirable in some ways (albeit potentially misleading as we have seen), but, as he rightly declares, the topics of Egyptian civilization and 'actual' race of the Egyptians are actually quite peripheral to his approach. In point of fact, Bernal shows little interest in whether – or how – the ancient Greeks defined the Egyptians and Phoenicians racially nor does he pause to consider the skin colour of the Greeks either as he outlines the relentless methods by which whiteness has been assigned to them. It is perhaps with no little irony, then, that *Black Athena* has been plunged headlong where her appearance seems to lead, that is, into longstanding debates about the skin colour of the ancient Egyptians.

Following its publication, *Black Athena* rapidly entered the American consciousness, and it was often connected specifically to the field of Afrocentrism. The September 23, 1991 issue of *Newsweek* that placed Cleopatra on its cover (see Introduction) sought to answer its own question about her racial identity by probing both the controversies surrounding

Black Athena and what it considered Afrocentrism's related attempts to transform the American school curriculum. Molefi Kete Asante has been a central figure in Afrocentrism since the 1980s,[54] but its doctrines with regard to ancient Egypt have a much longer genealogy. Stephen Howe has identified a substantial body of writing about ancient Egypt among African–American clergymen beginning in the mid-nineteenth century; and, by that time, such interpretations of Egypt

> already contained the themes which were to re-echo through all the subsequent decades: identification with ancient Egypt as a great black civilization, at least partly the creation of 'Ethiopians', 'Negroes', 'Cushites' or 'sons of Ham'; belief that civilization originated in Africa and was carried thence to Greece and the world; (and) assertion that this past greatness was a source both of racial pride and of hope for future achievement.'[55]

By the twentieth century, the conviction that Egyptian culture was itself indebted to its southern neighbour Ethiopia would gain even further popularity, circumventing the prickly debates about the race of the ancient Egyptians, while also transferring priority to a Christian country, one that had been able to rebuff Italian attempts at colonization.[56] In the decades following, a number of prominent black leaders such as W.E.B. Du Bois and Marcus Garvey would continue to evoke ancient Egypt and ancient Africa in addressing contemporary racial concerns, references that often sought explicitly to assert, by illustration, the potential capacity of black populations.[57]

Edward Wilmot Blyden (1832–1912), a native of St. Thomas who, when denied an advanced education in the United States, moved to Liberia, has been credited with the formulation of Pan-Africanism, and Blyden at times alluded to the classical world's positive treatment of Blacks in calling attention to the extreme racism of the modern west.[58] The origins of Afrocentrism as a distinct intellectual and educational movement, on the other hand, are most closely associated with Cheikh Anta Diop (1923–1986), a Senegalese scholar and advocate of Pan-African unity whose insistence on the links between Greece and Egypt, including belief in early Egyptian colonization of Greece, in many ways anticipated *Black Athena*.[59] One prominent trademark of Afrocentrism – its explicit critique of Eurocentrism and western culture – has infuriated many critics. Such open antagonism is captured well by the title of a work that has been central to Afrocentrism: George G. M. James' *Stolen Legacy* (1954) – a work whose title Michaels seemingly evokes in his assertion of the racial pathos behind claims about 'stealing culture'.

Decisively linking Egypt and Africa, James' work bluntly declared that its objective was 'to show that the true authors of Greek philosophy were not the Greeks; but the people of North Africa, commonly called the Egyptians; and the praise and honour falsely given to the Greeks for centuries belong to the people of North Africa, and therefore to the African Continent'.[60] *Stolen Legacy* remains a passionate if problematic treatise, not only indicting Aristotle and Alexander the Great for robbing a library that was built only after their deaths, the famed library at Alexandria, but also seeming to rely on a vision of a mystical Egypt that comes straight out of Masonic literature.[61] On the other hand, critics of Afrocentrism are not immune from their own distortions and emotionally-charged rhetoric. The classicist Mary Lefkowitz has written somewhat puzzlingly that '(t)he Greeks, *least of all peoples*, deserve the fate to which the Afrocentrists have subjected them (my emphasis),'[62] and the title of Glen Bowersock's review of Lefkowitz's *Not Out of Africa* and her jointly-edited volume *Black Athena Revisited* likewise demonstrates – or perhaps parodies – her general anguish: '*Rescuing* the Greeks (my emphasis).'[63]

Despite launching a much-needed challenge to the deep-rooted historical and intellectual biases that have sustained Eurocentrism, Afrocentrism at times nevertheless reveals its own set of precarious foundations. Its insistence on the universal meanings of 'blackness', for example, advocates a dangerous racial essentialism, one that is not avoided by reference to a collective and homogenous 'black culture' instead. So, too, some of its more extreme adherents have practiced an ominous return to earlier racial science, offering a range of 'theories' about the role of melanin and climate in dictating human destiny.[64] Not without some merit, then, does Kwame Anthony Appiah observe about Afrocentrism that 'the most striking thing . . . is how thoroughly at home it is in the frameworks of nineteenth-century European thought', making Afrocentrism, in short, 'simply Eurocentrism turned upside down'.[65] Like Bernal himself, Afrocentrism thus seems to run up against the inescapability of nineteenth-century thought, even when pursuing an aggressive critique of its continuing legacy in modern thought. And finding new frameworks for approaching the ancient Egyptians has proven to be an equally onerous task.

Coming to terms with the ancient Egyptians

As *Black Athena* well demonstrates, debates about race and the 'capacity' for producing advanced civilizations have long placed ancient Egypt at their centre. By the mid-nineteenth century – alongside attempts to promote Greece over Egypt – there were also increasing efforts to make Egypt 'white' as an alternate way of 'explaining' its accomplishments. Turning to the American context, Young has argued that such a project found 'its rationale not in a general conspiracy of European racism in nineteenth-century academia, but in the particular context of nineteenth-century American racial theory in its attempt to justify and rationalize slavery in the years leading up to the American Civil War.'[66] In their seminal work *Types of Mankind* (1854) the American anthropologists J. C. Nott and George R. Gliddon thus adapted the research of S.G. Morton, who had sought through skull analysis to prove that the ancient Egyptians were Caucasian.[67] This method of analysis was patently circular, for it defined 'Egyptian as Asiatic Caucasian' and so made it seem that only those 'crania approaching the "Caucasian" ideal were truly Egyptian.'[68] Conversely, skulls that correlated with a 'Negro' type were interpreted as evidence of an ancient slave population in Egypt: 'Here, then, was an ancient historical precedent for a white society with black slaves.'[69] Meanwhile, other scholars sought to deny Egyptian achievement by suggesting that its culture was reliant on foreign invasions – that racial cure-all for many historians – either by a 'dynastic race' (whose origins varied)[70] or a foreign group known as the Hamites, a term whose referent evolved as it moved away from the original idea of a group suffering from the biblical curse of Noah.[71] Such a 'Hamitic hypothesis', not coincidentally, often identified the Hamites explicitly as 'Caucasian'.[72]

Anthropologists still study the physical remains of ancient Egyptians today, although they generally deny that their methods aim to demonstrate a causal relationship between who the Egyptians were biologically and how they achieved their impressive civilization.[73] In comparing the physical features of ancient Egyptians with other groups, most scholars conclude that ancient Egypt was a 'mixed population', even though there is debate over precisely what types composed that 'mix' (especially to what degree the Egyptian population shows affinity with populations further south) and how that 'mix' may have changed over time. Howe summarizes one prevailing view: 'as the evidence of self-depiction would lead us to expect – this was a people predominantly of indigenous African origin, whose skin hues may have exhibited just, or almost, as wide a range as do those of peoples across the contemporary "Saharo-tropical" region, from Algerian Berbers to southern Sudanese.'[74]

As the comparison to people inhabiting the region today implies, when describing the ancient Egyptians, scholars often draw on both implicit and explicit comparisons to modern populations. Frank Yurco accordingly argues for a range of skin colours among ancient Egyptians by using language that strongly intimates an unbroken continuity with the present:

> The ancient Egyptians, *like their modern descendants*, were of varying complexions of colour, from the light Mediterranean type (like Nefertiti) to the light brown of Middle Egypt, to the darker brown of Upper Egypt, to the darkest shade around Aswan and the First Cataract region, *where even today*, the population shifts to Nubian (my emphasis).[75]

Perceptions about modern Egyptians clearly hold a significant, if often tacit, position in debates about the Egyptian past. Although there is some attempt to restore Egyptian agency through such analogy, modern Egyptians have nonetheless also been subjected – like Woolf's modern Greeks – to accusations of presumed 'decline'. Thus, for many outside observers, '(t)he fact that by the nineteenth century Egypt's population was clearly made up of a mixture of Arabs and Africans (was) held not to disprove the Caucasian thesis, but rather to explain Egypt's long decline'.[76] Furthermore, as Soheir A. Morsy has shown, the stakes continue to be high for residents of Egypt since debates over ancient Egyptian skin colour still stalk the political status of contemporary Egypt, including the treatment of Egyptian identity by US immigration.[77]

But what would it mean to restore agency to ancient Egyptians in these debates as well? Levine, a classical scholar, applauds the intervention of physical anthropologists in the *Black Athena* debate, advocating that physical anthropology is 'especially critical for prehistory – a time long before any written records existed – where the mute remains of bodies and bones wait silently until given their voice as historical witnesses by the physical anthropologist'.[78] But is the restoration of past voices really that simple? What if ancient bodies prefer to remain silent on this matter or, indeed, do not speak our language? Yurco has insisted that '(t)he whole matter of black or white Egyptians is a chimera, cultural baggage from our own society that can only be imposed artificially on ancient Egyptian society'.[79] Rather than superimposing our values onto deceased Egyptian bodies, can we turn instead to the 'evidence of self-depiction' that Howe cites? The ancient Egyptians themselves called Egypt *Kmt*, 'Black Land', a term that has often been used to suggest their identification as 'Black', although it seems more likely an attempt to draw a distinction between the fertile soil of the Nile Valley and the 'red land' of the arid desert.[80]

Egyptian art itself presents a complicated medium for determining what ancient Egyptians 'really' looked like – or thought of themselves – given that certain traditional conventions governed figural representation, including the practice of using different skin colours to represent men versus women, with women (as in ancient Greek art) generally depicted with lighter skin tones. In the same way, it is not always possible to discern the motive behind the choice of materials: are two figures of Tutankhamen covered in black resin in order to approximate his skin colour or was black resin used because it was a valuable commodity and helped display the pharaoh's grandeur? The question is made more complicated when comparing these figures to other representations that show Tutankhamen with lighter skin.[81] In general, pharaonic art does not seem to attempt realism (at least the way we define it today), especially when it comes to individual appearance. In contrast, albeit centuries later, scores of mummy portraits from Roman Egypt have been discovered, portraits which, given their variety, seem to convey the appearance of actual individuals. Significantly, these individuals are shown with a range of skin colours, and there is no suggestion that the difference in skin colour correlates to any difference in social status.[82]

Although it remains difficult to pinpoint the precise racial meaning of individual portraits, pharaonic art did depict foreign groups in ways that marked them as visually different, both from the Egyptians and from one another. 'Nubians' and 'Asiatics' are frequently shown in New Kingdom art with recurring physical features that seem to distinguish them, and the message of Egyptian superiority in these contexts is often explicitly announced by showing these other groups in postures of submission or defeat. In one eighteenth-century tomb, an image portrays a series of foreign groups (e.g., 'Asiatics, Cretans, and Nubians') bringing tribute to Tuthmoses III, and the 'Nubians, from the Nile Valley south of the First Cataract at Aswan, are painted in darker skin tones than the Asiatics, and are depicted with more prognathous jaws than the Egyptians.'[83] A more unusual scene on Queen Hatshepsut's mortuary at Deir-el-Bahri depicts an expedition to 'Punt' (presumably 'located along and to the west of the Sudanese/Eritrean coast'), whose figures include 'a grossly obese "queen"' and her bearded husband.[84]

Persistent debates about the ancient Egyptians signal the prominent place they have been accorded in thinking about race and past civilizations. When seeking better understanding of the ancient Egyptian view of themselves and others, however, it is important not to suspend Egypt in some kind of romanticized and unchanging world, but rather to acknowledge the changing socio-historical contexts in which the ancient Egyptians encountered other groups, including the extent and manner of their engagement with civilizations to the south and east, and not merely their north, i.e. Greece. In contrast to the current enthusiasm for treating Egypt as strictly 'Mediterranean' – a turn S.O.Y. Keita rightly suggests needs more investigation, especially if it serves merely to re-encode Egyptian 'whiteness' under different guise[85] – van Binsbergen notes that we have yet 'to situate Ancient Egypt within the full range of great African civilisations, from that of Kush . . . to the great civilisations of West, East, and Southern Africa throughout history right up to the present times'.[86]

Although surviving evidence suggests that civilizations to the south of Egypt developed later, there are a number of cultures – located in what is today southern Egypt, the Sudanese Republic, and Ethiopia – that need to be added to our map of ancient history. Kush, as we saw in Chapter I, was the Egyptian name for a series of states that developed in the upper Nile Valley beginning in the second millennium BCE. Generally speaking, developments in Kush followed the ebbs and flows of Egyptian history, flourishing when the Egyptian state faltered and vice versa;[87] the pharaohs of the Twenty-fifth Dynasty were, in fact, all Kushite.[88] A strong Kushite capital had developed at Kerma in the second millennium BCE, but that territory was later colonized by Egyptian pharaohs of the Eighteenth and Nineteenth dynasties. Later Kushite centres would develop in Napata then, beginning around 250 BCE, in Meroë.[89] Meroë itself finally collapsed in the fourth century CE when faced with various pressures, not least the rise of Axum in the north of present day Ethiopia and Eritrea. The city of Axum subsequently controlled a vast empire, and even after its political importance waned, it remained a major hub of Christianity.[90]

From ancient to modern empire

In 1937, ancient Axum was catapulted into the modern world when Benito Mussolini brought an obelisk from the ancient Ethiopian city to

Rome to memorialize the recent Italian invasion, erecting the obelisk prominently in Rome's Circus Maximus. As part of a peace settlement, the Italians agreed to return the obelisk to Ethiopia in 1947, but it would take nearly sixty years to finalize the process.[91] The obelisk has had a long history of appropriations by the west; one century before Mussolini, Napoleon had 'revive(d) the obelisk's glamour, and by the late 1880s the US government had just erected its own, in the form of the Washington Monument.'[92] Later, the Ethiopians would dedicate their own obelisk to mark the end of Italian rule.[93] The inspiration for Mussolini's theft can be traced even further back, however, for Mussolini often portrayed his political efforts as an attempt to restore the glory of ancient Rome, an empire once ruled by that original obelisk-stealer: Augustus. Central to Mussolini's claims were massive construction projects designed to 'remake' the city of Rome in all its former grandeur, ironically destroying many historical remains in the process.[94]

Adolf Hitler made a six-day state visit to Rome in May 1938, during which he spent time visiting the city's monuments and attending a special exhibit celebrating 'the bimillenniary of Rome's "second founder"', the Roman emperor Augustus, an event clearly designed for 'the political advantage of Rome's "third founder," the Duce.'[95] In Volume 1 of *Black Athena*, Bernal traces the evolution of German ideas about Greece between the years 1790 and 1830, and Greece certainly retained its impressive hold on German intellectual and political life in the years following.[96] Hitler himself professed great admiration for the Spartans and at the end of the war apparently 'drew courage from the recollection of Leonidas's last stand at Thermopylae.'[97] But Nazi emulation of ancient Rome was also pervasive. Keenly aware of the problems presented by Rome's so-called 'decline and fall' (which Nazi ideology attributed to both 'race-mixing' in the later empire and the rise of Christianity), Hitler nonetheless drew repeatedly on the Roman empire as a model of ultimate state power.[98] Roman echoes appear throughout Nazi architecture, not least in the emulation of its sheer monumentality, which Hitler believed communicated the insignificance of the individual in relation to the group.[99] In 1936, Hitler charged Albert

Speer with designing a new plan for the capital, which he intended to rechristen 'Germania' at its planned completion in 1950.[100]

The idea of 'Germania' is without question the most powerful Roman legacy in German thought; as with many Roman geographic labels, 'Germania' acquired female form in antiquity, and she later personified both the abstract idea of a German people and, after German unification in 1871, that nation in practice. While the form and meaning of 'Germania' would continue to evolve throughout German art and literature,[101] its origins can be traced to a single Latin text: Tacitus' *Germania*. The reception of Tacitus' historical writings took many turns over the centuries, depending in large part on whether his perceived views conformed to contemporary intellectual movements. Tacitus' cynicism about political power, for example, caused him at times to be associated with Machiavelli. In other periods, Tacitus was seen as a revolutionary, and his popularity took a noticeable leap in France during the late eighteenth century. Across the Atlantic, he was both John Adams and Thomas Jefferson's favorite classical writer.[102]

In contrast to Tacitus' other historical writings, the *Germania* occupied a fairly stable position across the centuries. The *Germania* had been 'redis-covered' in Italy in the fifteenth century and soon reached Germany, where it was widely circulated and accepted not only as a literal record of Germany's past but also as an *Ur*-account of what made Germans essentially German. From Tacitus came the idea that the Germans were a kind of 'noble savage', innately characterized by a love of liberty, a fierceness in battle, a kingship that ruled by election and consent, the equal treatment of women in marriage, and – more than anything else – a purity of blood. Tacitus' interest in contrasting the 'simple' Germans and 'over-civilized' Romans further helped German intellectuals draw a distinction between 'Romanists' and 'Germanists' in their own time – a divide that was essential to Reformation thought.[103] The notion of racial purity, of course, eventually found its way into Nazi Germany with devastating consequences, and acknowledging such dire results, Arnaldo Momigliano once proposed that the *Germania* 'should be given high priority among the hundred most dangerous books ever written.'[104]

Separating out conflicting strands of historical thought among Nazi leaders, Volker Losemann has observed that '(t)here was undoubtedly a contradiction between Hitler's own positive assessment of Roman antiquity and the extreme admiration for German pre-history by other leading Nazi ideologists'.[105] Still, both views were presumably accommodated, perhaps because the Romans had never been able to vanquish the Germans, enabling a plausible, if uneasy, truce between the two historical archetypes. It would require a much trickier negotiation for nineteenth-century British writers and politicians, who were progressively forced to confront their own conquest at the hands of Rome, even as they were aggressively pursuing an empire to call their own.

Coming to terms with Roman conquest

In identifying with classical antiquity, would-be claimants face a series of choices, not least whether Greece or Rome better serve their purpose. Greek and Roman antiquity have each held sway at different times and in different places, acquiring radically different connotations and conveying not only divergent political messages, but also different features presumed to epitomize each society, such as Greek aestheticism or Roman engineering. Roman antiquity, moreover, presents not only the possibility of pagan versus Christian identifications, but also two opposing forms of state structure, one that violently emerged from the other: the Republic and empire. The fall of the Roman Republic was itself subjected to a shifting set of interpretations in Britain beginning in the eighteenth century, closely following changes in contemporary political thought, with Julius Caesar often pitted directly against his eventual successor Augustus in assessing Rome's greatness.[106] The Victorian admiration for ancient Greek culture has attracted considerable scholarly attention,[107] but British intellectuals and politicians also turned to ancient Rome for a very specific purpose: to weigh the merits of their own imperial vision.

While the idea of empire had been discredited in much of Europe by the exploits of Napoleon and his successors, by around 1870, the British nonetheless started to investigate more openly the terms of their own growing empire, a process that was increasingly public following the debate in Parliament over whether Queen Victoria should assume the title of Empress of India in 1876.[108] As part of these deliberations, comparisons to ancient Rome became increasingly prominent, and the analogy lasted in various forms into the twentieth century.[109] In its most overt form, this strategy involved direct identification with the Romans, a connection facilitated by the emphasis placed on classics in the contemporary British education system.[110] Even more, the putative bond between the two empires drew on British perceptions of the so-called civilizing mission of Roman expansion, an idea central to the British justification of its advances in the British Isles and later its presence in India.[111]

Still, the modern British appropriation of ancient Rome required considerable dexterity. British writers, for example, were acutely aware of Rome's eventual decline and sought to account for that possibility in the conduct of their own empire, discussions that became more fraught as anxieties about their own success grew.[112] In earlier eras, allusions to Rome's fall had been cloaked in romantic fantasy; thus, Joseph Michael Gandy's 1830 painting could lovingly portray the Bank of England as it would look in ruins in thousands of years' time.[113] But later the prospect wrought greater unease and a more explicit opening for critique of British imperial policies. Norman Vance has identified a number of parodies of Edward Gibbon's hugely influential *History of the Decline and Fall of the Roman Empire* (1776–88) that purported to be looking back on the fall of the British empire, including one that presented itself as a twenty-first century Japanese text book.[114]

Of particular concern was the way in which the Romans had allegedly been corrupted internally over the course of their foreign expansion, and some British writers expressed awareness that British rule in India was far more despotic than the political system practiced at home, seeking to frame their own harsh methods as necessity rather than a harbinger of internal decay.[115] Following the Indian Mutiny of 1857, the remains of a male skeleton still holding his lance – discovered decades earlier in Pompeii – became 'a celebrity' in British art and fiction, epitomizing the virtues of extreme duty and self-sacrifice.[116] By the end of the century, however, the British would be much more concerned with the defenders of the British empire in flesh. Believing Roman decline had been precipitated by its increasing embrace of luxury and decadence, the current British constitution was scrutinized closely: 'Was Britain, were the British, still fit to rule, physically and mentally as well as morally?'[117] To assuage such concerns, public discourse increasingly turned to ways of developing the ideal (male) British imperial body and moral practice;[118] it was to meet these demands that General Baden-Powell conceived the Boy Scouts.[119]

The spectre of decadence and accompanying anxiety over the masculine body, however, also allowed Irish figures like George Moore and Oscar Wilde to use 'strategic alignment with Rome as a way of getting back at the mad dogs and Englishmen who sometimes saw themselves as neo-Roman world-rulers as well as the colonists of Ireland'.[120] Wilde, in particular, publicly imitated the Roman emperor Nero, pointedly going to Paris in 1882 to have his hair styled in the fashion depicted on surviving busts of the emperor.[121] Appropriations of Rome were thus both dynamic and potentially subversive, demonstrating that while 'on one level allusions to imperial Rome did serve as a "heuristic reinforcement" in British imperial ideology, on another level, they also served to unravel and confront much that was rigid about categories in imperial ideology'.[122] In addition to querying masculinity, the comparative vision of Rome also raised troubling questions about race, a term central to British rule in India.

India played a complex role in the nineteenth-century European engagement with antiquity, for it was in India in 1786 that the idea of an Indo-European language group was first developed when a British supreme court justice serving there 'realized that definite resemblances could be detected in the grammatical structure of Sanskrit (the classical language of ancient India), Latin, ancient Greek, Gothic, Celtic, and Persian'.[123] Following the initial classification of Indo-European, 'enthusiasm for all aspects of Indian culture . . . raged from the 1790s to the 1820s.'[124] The reception and motives, however, varied; in England, interest in India correlated closely with its own imperial project – in fact, study of India was first initiated by the East India Company, and, as Javed Majeed has shown, at least one committee would advocate the inclusion of Sanskrit as one of the possible examination subjects for the Indian Civil Service[125] – while in Germany, where there were no such political aspirations, the project took a distinctly romanticized tone.[126] Despite the historical affiliations that might be deduced from Indo-European as a concept, British rule nonetheless maintained stringent boundaries between the British and native Indians, at least in theory; ideologies of race were critical to British strategies,[127] and the fear of miscegenation featured prominently in narratives throughout the colonial period.[128]

When looking at the Roman empire, British writers were tested in particular by the ways the Romans had presumably been able to assimilate their conquered subjects. Recognizing that they were not doing the same in India, British writers believed that the Romans had not been forced to deal with populations racially different from themselves (a theory the Romans would not themselves endorse, as we have seen, but which seemed self-evident from the perspective of modern Europeans), and that the Romans had achieved such an end through their extension of citizenship, that is, by opening the gates in political rather than racial terms.[129] Even as they faced concerns about their own racial practice of empire, the British were also forced to come to terms with the complexity of their own Roman past. For identification with the Romans was undermined by one simple fact: Britain itself had once been conquered by Rome, making Roman Britain and British India uncomfortably close.[130] Richard Hingley has carefully documented the role of the Roman past in British imperial thought, and he argues that two specific solutions were developed specifically to counter this dilemma, both of which were pursued simultaneously: the attempt to reclaim a heroic British (i.e. Celtic) past and the attempt to move even closer to Rome.[131] Both strategies would require reconstituting racial ideas about 'Englishness' itself.

The Romans had left Britain in 410 CE, and, although Britain subsequently experienced invasions by the Normans and Danish, the Victorian era placed greatest emphasis on the invasion of the Anglo-Saxons when reconstructing racial origins, positing that the Anglo-Saxons, arriving after the Romans had left, had either killed the native Britons or driven them to the north and west. Such a narrative served not only to link the English to 'superior' Teutonic (i.e. German) roots,[132] but also allowed them to distinguish themselves from other populations in the British Isles, i.e. the perceived descendants of the lowly 'Celts' in Ireland, Scotland and Wales. When contemplating Roman Britain initially, then, English writers did not see themselves as descended from the conquered population of Britain, whom they conceptualized in derogatory fashion as a kind of 'Celtic subaltern'.[133]

As Germany became an increasing threat to Britain, however, there was a concomitant need to downplay German roots, and English writers soon promoted a theory of 'mixed-race' origins instead. In this version, while it was acknowledged that a number of groups had come together to form the modern British population, emphasis shifted to the role of two key components: the native population and their Roman conquerors. In order to make the native blood more 'attractive', the idea of a weak 'Celtic subaltern' was thereafter replaced by strong native figures who, it was thought, had actively resisted Rome, such as Boadicea, Caratacus, and Calgacus, as well as the newly-invented Beric.[134] So, too, while British authors had previously fashioned Britain as the heir to the Roman empire in an abstract sense,[135] it was now further claimed that the Romans had contributed to the genetic pool, so the British could conceive of their Roman inheritance 'in racial as well as moral terms.'[136]

The impetus to refine views of racial identity in regard to the Roman past was precipitated by another significant trend: the increasing availability of material culture from Roman Britain. Visible remains of the Roman past in Britain had long been recorded,[137] but Francis Haverfield initiated the growth of Roman archaeology as a professional practice in the 1900s and 1910s'.[138] Strongly influenced by the writings of Theodor Mommsen, Haverfield's work focused on questions of 'Romanization',[139] i.e. the impact of Roman conquest on the Britons as witnessed in material terms. Haverfield firmly believed that the study of material culture was critical given that 'Roman culture carried with itself Roman identity'[140] – an assumption that, as we have seen in Chapter II, still structures many treatments of ancient material culture. Culture, then, became an important way of defining the Roman legacy and bolstering ideas about race. More specifically, the native British population, or at least its upper class, could be conceptualized as fully 'Romanized', meaning that 'the stigma of conquest' was alleviated.[141] That the Romans had not reached every part of the British Isles likewise meant that the English could use ancient material culture to define themselves against those 'proximate others' who had not received the uplifting benefits of Romanization.[142]

Even as English writers were denying sites like Ireland equal rights to the Roman heritage, by the eighteenth and nineteenth centuries Irish 'hedge schools' were themselves teaching Greek and Latin. The classical past, moreover, had its own place in Irish identifications; Laurie O'Higgins contends that '(a)ll sectors of eighteenth-century Irish society held that a bond with the classics was constitutive of Irish identity'[143] – that classics could be a source of enrichment and not merely, as the English would have, a mode of Irish deprivation. Bernal has asserted that 'from the beginning, the chief purpose of those advocating a humanistic education . . . was to forestall or avoid revolution'; he added: 'Indeed, the cult of the Classics served quite effectively to maintain the status quo'.[144] While depressingly true at many historical moments, exclusive concentration on the powerful when evaluating classical influences on the modern world has recently been challenged by scholars looking more closely at other sites of reception, such as Ireland, where structures of class, race, and power made very different demands on antiquity. Arguing that Irish peasants interpolated their own lives into classical texts, Siobhán McElduff proposes that '(w)hile Irish peasants might have been somewhat unusual in their relationship to the classics, they were by no means unique',[145] meaning that it is time to radically rethink the possibilities of 'our' classical heritage, maybe it is even time – as Woolf might phrase it – to write new Greeks and Romans.

Yet, as Bernal has demonstrated, classical antiquity has often been asked to draw insistent lines between 'black' and 'white', and I would like to re-examine this particular charge from another angle – through the eyes of Phillis Wheatley, a young American slave whose knowledge of Latin helped challenged the boundaries between slave and free, challenging contemporary assumptions about who could qualify as human.

Setting new terms: *Classica Africana*

On March 10, 1742, a lecture entitled 'Is slavery compatible with Christian freedom or not' was delivered in Latin at the University of Leiden in the Netherlands.[146] Drawing on classical writings on slavery, as well as biblical passages, the author concluded that the two were, in fact, compatible – not an unusual thesis for its time. But the speech could be considered remarkable because its writer, Jacobus Elisa Johannes Capitein, had himself formerly been a slave. Grant Parker, meticulously locating the lecture in its broader historical context, notes that Capitein has occupied an ambivalent place in modern study of slave narratives. Parker, however, places special emphasis on the dominant role of Christianity in Capitein's views, asserting '(i)t would be a wilful and inaccurate reading of the treatise to imagine that it sought in the first instance to justify slavery when the goal of Christian conversion is so clearly at its core'.[147]

Christianity provided a major source of identification for another classically educated slave, Phillis Wheatley, whose sometime defence of slavery has also provoked mixed response. Wheatley, likely 'a native Wolof speaker from the Senegambian coast' was taken into slavery in 1761, at around the age of seven or eight.[148] She was purchased upon her arrival in Boston by the merchant John Wheatley, after which she received the name 'Phillis' and converted to Christianity. Taught by her owner's daughter, Wheatley evidently learned English quickly, and, as John Wheatley later wrote, she had 'a great Inclination to learn the Latin tongue'.[149] Having published her own poetry as early as 1767, Wheatley first received international attention for an elegy she wrote on the occasion of the Reverend George Whitefield's death in 1770. Around 1773, Wheatley travelled to London with her mistress, where she published *Poems On Various Subjects, Religious and Moral*, the first 'by a person of African descent in the English language, marking the beginning of an African–American literary tradition.'[150] She was manumitted upon her return,[151] but with the advent of the Revolutionary war in 1775, she had difficulty getting more of her work in print. Wheatley eventually died in poverty in 1784 at the age of thirty or thirty-one.

In her writing, Wheatley was greatly influenced by Latin authors like Vergil, Ovid, and Terence, as well as the neoclassical writer Alexander Pope, and Tracey Walters suggests that, to Wheatley, 'classical revision was about artistic license as well as poetic validation'.[152] In the poem, 'To Maecenas', Wheatley pointedly evokes Terence – presumably well aware of accounts that Terence had once himself been a slave – whose paired glory from the Muses and origins in 'Afric's sable race' were critical to her affiliations.[153] On a few occasions, Wheatley openly refers to herself when defining her poetic voice, even calling attention to her slave status. In a poem addressed to Harvard students, Wheatley markedly portrays her passage into slavery in positive terms because it had provided the route to Christianity. Thus, in contrast to the 'Father of mercy' with a 'gracious hand' who receives her, Wheatley portrays her 'native shore' as 'the land of errors and *Egyptian* gloom (*sic*)' and 'dark abodes'.[154] Later in the same poem, she declares that it is '(a)n *Ethiop* tells you (*sic*)'. In another poem addressed to the Earl of Dartmouth, however, Wheatley evokes a more painful image of slavery, using her own separation from her family to illuminate the threat of British tyranny:

> I, young in life, by seeming cruel fate
> Was snatch'd from *Afric*'s fancy'd happy seat:
> What pangs excruciating must molest,
> What sorrows labour in my parent's breast?
> Steel'd was the soul that by no misery mov'd
> That from a father seiz'd his babe belov'd:
> Such, such my case. And can I then but pray
> Others may never feel tyrannic sway?[155]

Wheatley's poetry was published on both sides of the Atlantic, and she became known to many major figures of her era; Voltaire, for one, praised her talent. So dangerous to the ideology of slavery, which relied on seeing slaves as sub-human, was her ability to compose original poetry, however, that she was forced to undergo a public examination in 1772 by eighteen prominent Boston men, who were charged with determining whether she was actually the author of her work; they eventually issued a statement confirming her authorship.[156] Perhaps her most notorious critic was Thomas Jefferson, whom she never met in person but who remained sceptical about the capacities her poetry evinced, dismissively writing that '(r)eligion, indeed, has produced a Phyllis Whately (sic); but it could not produce a poet'.[157] And the gap between the two is worth underscoring, for while Wheatley used her knowledge of classics to define her literary voice, a deeply personal commitment, it was also necessary for claiming the status of human being itself. Her white male contemporaries like Jefferson, on the other hand, felt nothing like the same pressure. Jefferson's abilities in classics could be harnessed with great public acclaim to the charting of a new nation.[158]

Throughout the nineteenth and early twentieth centuries, American slavery continued to inform the relationship between classics and many African–American intellectuals. Michele Valerie Ronnick has devoted particular attention to the writings of William Sanders Scarborough (1852–1926), who was born into slavery in Georgia, but eventually became Chair of Greek and Latin at Wilberforce University.[159] In the early part of the twentieth century, W. E. B. Du Bois, a one-time professor of Greek and Latin at Wilberforce, would engage in very public debates about the relevance of classical education with Booker T. Washington, a former slave who had founded the Tuskegee Institute, with Washington placing greater value on vocational training for rising black students.[160] At the same time, a number of black women like Anna Julia Cooper were also pursuing a classical education, often continuing their engagement with the classics by becoming teachers – one of the few professions open to women at that time – of Latin or other ancient subjects.[161]

Alongside such debates about whether classics should (or did) mean different things to black and white Americans, black artists were also developing their own creative responses to the classical tradition. As Tracey Walters has shown, it is possible to trace a distinct set of conversations black women writers, following in the footsteps of Phillis Wheatley, forged with the classical tradition, including Henrietta Cordelia Ray, Pauline Hopkins, Gwendolyn Brooks, Toni Morrison, and Rita Dove.[162] In particular, Walters has pointed out the recurring use of 'mythic mothers' like Demeter and Niobe in their writings.[163] Patrice Rankine, on the other hand, makes a very different character from Greek myth central to his rich study of Ralph Ellison: Ulysses. While Ulysses provides inspiration in many parts of Ellison's work, Ulysses (Odysseus to the Greeks) also serves well, Rankine notes, as 'a metaphor for black classicism' more broadly[164] – a proposition whose possibilities find infinite echo in the series of vibrant paintings created by the African–American artist Romare Bearden based on the *Odyssey*.[165]

Beyond the United States, classicists are now exposing other sites of black classicism.[166] Barbara Goff and Michael Simpson have explored the particular draw of the mythic house of Laius – and its two most prominent figures, Oedipus and Antigone – on black writers in both Africa and the African diaspora.[167] Beginning with the eighteenth-century Jamaican poet Francis Williams, whose work predates Wheatley's, scholars from a range of disciplines are also exploring both Caribbean classical education and its literary traditions,[168] traditions the Greek Odysseus has also frequented through Derek Walcott's epic poem *Omeros*. In reflecting on his own literary dialogue with the *Odyssey*, Walcott lyrically reflects that 'it is perfectly valid for me to think of an archipelago in which there are boats and pigs and men, scared people and a succession of islands – home to me – to think of the *Odyssey* in terms of the Caribbean'.[169] Unusual, but by no means unique: such black writers illustrate beautifully that although the Greek and Roman world has often been a place of alienation to those without power, it can also offer a place to come home to and rest.

Conclusion: coming to terms with the classical past

One attempt to ascertain the cause of Rome's demise phrases the question with great aplomb: did Rome fall or was it pushed? Reports of the end of the classical world have been greatly exaggerated. But by way of closing, I would like to return to Woolf's short story, and consider how the 'dirty Greek peasant boys' might take ownership of their own history. For even as Bernal purports to find in classics a wholly anti-revolutionary impulse from its very inceptions, he is forced to acknowledge one powerful nineteenth century exception: the Greek War of Independence.[170] The story of the War of Independence, which broke out in 1821, is often told through the 'philhellenes', that band of romantic idealists – estimated at between 1100–1200 total volunteers[171] – who travelled from all parts of Europe to help liberate Greece from its Turkish oppressors. The narrative's impact derives in no small part from the disillusion and death many of the young men faced when actually arriving in Greece, and continuing veneration of their romantic sacrifice is surely fostered by the death of Byron at Missalonghi. Such poignant images, of course, conceal a series of more complicated facts – for one, that religious difference was the source of much of the western anxiety about the conflict and that many of the philhellenes were, in fact, professional soldiers who found Greece their only possible destination given the anti-revolutionary wave sweeping other parts of Europe.[172]

I do not intend to debunk conventional narratives of the Greek War of Independence here, but I do want to reconsider our reliance on classics itself as the primary intellectual framework for making sense of the war and its aftermath, especially since such devotion to the ancient Greeks was a much more ambivalent prospect within Greece itself. The Greek poet George Seferis captures beautifully both the pride and the burden wrought by the classical past when he writes of waking 'with a marble head in his hands', one he 'did not know where to put down'.[173] And, as Michael Herzfeld has shown, the Greeks developed their own academic modes of investigating Greek identity after the wars, in part as a response to the burdensome demands of 'performing' Hellenism for outsiders. Herzfeld explains:

The development of an indigenous folklore discipline was . . . a sustained, often painful attempt to discern order in chaos, on the part of a people whose national identity was often threatened by the very nations which had appointed themselves as its guardians. It gave the Greeks a chance of applying one of their most celebrated ancient proverbs – 'know thyself' – by providing a framework for discovery. In this sense, Greek folklore studies were an organic part of the making of modern Greece.[174]

Through folklore studies, the Greeks (or certain Greeks), then, were able to come to terms with their own past in a way that complemented – and at times eluded – the burdens of a 'Greekness' that had been imposed externally, a form of study that sought not to reinstate a restrictive continuity with the past, but to understand more fully who they had become in their own right in the present.

AFTERWORD

I, too, sing America.

According to family history, my grandfather only just missed making the 1936 US Olympic team. What would he have felt watching Jesse Owens' stunning performance in the face of such hostility and racism? My grand-father has left an even more enduring mark on me, however, for as a young man he decided to change his last name from the decidedly Polish 'Markowski' to 'McCoskey' in order to make it easier for the local Pittsburgh sportswriters to spell, or so the story goes. But I think the act was really about whiteness – and how could my grandfather have known that in the complex racial terrain of early twentieth-century America, one of the only European immigrant groups less 'white' than the Polish was the Irish? Later, when they met, perhaps my Irish grandfather would have told him.

The material in this book has been with me for a long time. I have advo-cated a return to race in classical studies on a number of occasions. The response of many of my colleagues is often the same – race, they say, is such an American preoccupation. To which, I suppose, the answer is: yes, of course, but not only American. In his poem 'I, too, sing America', Langston Hughes writes of being the 'darker brother', one who grows strong despite his exclusion and who will soon be strong enough to demand his own place. His beauty, he says, will put America to shame. As he announces in the final line: 'I, too, am America'. To confront race, to understand the roots and consequences of our own blackness and whiteness, requires first that we know our own histories and then that we find our own voice.

As I hope this book has shown, it is essential to document scrupulously the operation of race, including both the strenuous ways it sets about its work and the ways we might help it come undone. By gaining a more firm foothold on race historically, including its roots in classical antiquity (both real and invented), I think we can begin to combat its clandestine power and also see that our modern version of race is far from inevitable or neutral, it is simply a structure of belief that has been so powerful as to convince us that it is the only possible one.

SOME SUGGESTIONS FOR FURTHER READING

For a general introduction to race theory, especially in historical perspective:

Back, Les and John Solomos (eds), *Theories of Race and Racism: A Reader*, (New York and London, 2000).

Bernasconi, Robert and Tommy L. Lott (eds), *The Idea of Race*, (Indianapolis, 2000).

Dain, Bruce, *A Hideous Monster of the Mind: American Race Theory in the Early Republic*, (Cambridge, Mass, 2002).

Mills, Charles W., *Blackness Visible: Essays on Philosophy and Race*, (Ithaca, 1998).

Smedley, Audrey, *Race in North America: Origin and Evolution of a Worldview*, third edition (Boulder, 2007).

Stepan, Nancy, *The Idea of Race in Science: Great Britain 1800–1960*, (Hamden, Conn, 1982).

For approaches to identity and difference in classical antiquity:

Balsdon, J. P. V. D., *Romans and Aliens*, (London, 1979).

Bilde, Per *et al.* (eds), *Ethnicity in Hellenistic Egypt*, (Aarhus, 1992).

Burstein, Stanley M., *Graeco-Africana: Studies in the History of Greek Relations with Egypt and Nubia*, (New Rochelle, 1995).

Hall, Edith, *Inventing the Barbarian: Greek Self-Definition through Tragedy*, (Oxford, 1989).

Hall, Jonathan M., *Ethnic Identity in Greek Antiquity*, (Cambridge and New York, 1997).

———, *Hellenicity: Between Ethnicity and Culture*, (Chicago, 2002).

Harrison, Thomas (ed), *Greeks and Barbarians*, (New York, 2002).

Isaac, Benjamin, *The Invention of Racism in Classical Antiquity*, (Princeton, 2004).

Johnson, Janet H. (ed), *Life in a Multi-Cultural Society: Egypt from Cambyses to Constantine and Beyond*, Studies in Ancient Oriental Civilization, no. 51 (Chicago, 1992).

Malkin, Irad (ed), *Ancient Perceptions of Greek Ethnicity*, (Cambridge, Mass, 2001).

Mudimbe, V. Y, *The Idea of Africa*, (Bloomington, 1994).

Sherwin-White, A. N., *Racial Prejudice in Imperial Rome*, (Cambridge, 1967).

Snowden, Frank M., Jr., *Before Color Prejudice: the Ancient View of Blacks*, (Cambridge, Mass, 1983).

———, *Blacks in Antiquity: Ethiopians in the Greco-Roman Experience*, (Cambridge, Mass, 1970).

Thompson, Lloyd A., *Romans and Blacks*, (Norman, 1989).

Yamauchi, Edwin M. (ed), *Africa and Africans in Antiquity*, (East Lansing, 2001).

For race and classical receptions:

Bridges, Emma *et al.* (eds), *Cultural Responses to the Persian Wars: Antiquity to the Third Millennium*, (Oxford and New York, 2007).

Cook, William W. and James Tatum, *African American Writers and Classical Tradition*, (Chicago, 2010).

Greenwood, Emily, *Afro-Greeks: Dialogues Between Anglophone Caribbean Literature and Classics in the Twentieth Century*, (Oxford and New York, 2010).

Goff, Barbara and Michael Simpson, *Crossroads in the Black Aegean: Oedipus, Antigone, and Dramas of the African Diaspora*, (Oxford and New York, 2007).

Howe, Stephen, *Afrocentrism: Mythical Pasts and Imagined Homes*, (London and New York, 1998).

Rankine, Patrice, *Ulysses in Black: Ralph Ellison, Classicism and African American Literature*, (Madison, 2006).

Trafton, Scott, *Egypt Land: Race and Nineteenth-Century American Egyptomania*, (Durham, 2004).

On *Black Athena:*

Berlinerblau, Jacques, *Heresy in the University: The Black Athena Controversy and the Responsibilities of American Intellectuals*, (New Brunswick, 1999).

Bernal, Martin, *Black Athena: The Afroasiatic Roots of Classical Civilization, Volume 1: The Fabrication of Ancient Greece 1785-1985*, (New Brunswick, 1987).

———, *Black Athena: The Afroasiatic Roots of Classical Civilization, Volume 2: The Archaeological and Documentary Evidence*, (New Brunswick, 1991).

———, *Black Athena: The Afroasiatic Roots of Classical Civilization, Volume 3: The Linguistic Evidence*, (New Brunswick, 2006).

———, *Black Athena Writes Back: Martin Bernal Responds to his Critics*, edited by David Chioni Moore, (Durham and London, 2001).

Lefkowitz, Mary R. and Guy MacLean Rogers (eds), *Black Athena Revisited*, (Chapel Hill, 1996).

Orrells, Daniel *et al.* (eds), *African Athena: New Agendas*, (Oxford, forthcoming).

NOTES

Introduction

1 Goldberg, David Theo, *Racial Subjects: Writing on Race in America*, (New York and London, 1997), p. 27.

2 Omi, Michael and Howard Winant, *Racial Formation in the Unites States: From the 1960s to the 1990s*, second edition (New York and London, 1994), p. 55.

3 Omi and Winant: *Racial Formation*, p. 55.

4 See Ignatiev, Noel, *How the Irish Became White*, (New York and London, 1995). Also Roediger, David R., 'Irish–American Workers and White Racial Formation in the Antebellum United States', in E. N. Gates (ed), *Racial Classification and History*, (New York and London, 1997), pp. 247–277.

5 Donald, James and Ali Rattansi, 'Introduction', in J. Donald and A. Rattansi (eds), *'Race', Culture and Difference*, (London, Thousand Oaks, and New Delhi, 1992), p. 1.

6 Omi and Winant: *Racial Formation*, p. 55.

7 See especially Gilroy, Paul, *'There Ain't No Black in the Union Jack: The Cultural Politics of Race and Nation*, (Chicago, 1991).

8 Smedley, Audrey, *Race in North America: Origin and Evolution of a Worldview*, third edition, (Boulder, 2007), p. 25. Too many scholars have contributed to ongoing work in the field of race and race theory to give a complete list of references here; for an excellent anthology of key writings, begin with Bernasconi, Robert and Tommy L. Lott (eds), *The Idea of Race*, (Indianapolis, 2000). Also Back, Les and John Solomos (eds), *Theories of Race and Racism: A Reader*, (London and New York, 2000). For philosophical approaches specifically, Mills, Charles W., *Blackness Visible: Essays on Philosophy and Race*, (Ithaca and London, 1998) and Outlaw, Lucius T., Jr., *On Race and Philosophy*, (New York and London, 1996).

9 Omi and Winant: *Racial Formation*, pp. 61–64. See also Bernal, Martin, 'Race in History', in W. A. Van Horne (ed), *Global Convulsions: Race, Ethnicity, and Nationalism at the End of the Twentieth Century* (Albany, 1997), pp. 75–92.

10 Stepan, Nancy, *The Idea of Race in Science: Great Britain 1800–1960*, (London and Hamden, 1982), pp. 1–6. Also Gould, Stephen Jay, 'American Polygeny and Craniometry before Darwin: Blacks and Indians as Separate, Inferior Species', in S. Harding (ed), *The 'Racial' Economy of Science: Toward a Democratic Future*, (Bloomington and Indianapolis, 1993), pp. 90–93.

11 Smedley: *Race in North America*, pp. 27–28.

12 Mudimbe, V. Y., 'African Athena?', *Transition* 58 (1992), p. 121.

13 Bernal, Martin, *Black Athena: The Afroasiatic Roots of Classical Civilization, Volume 1: The Fabrication of Ancient Greece 1785–1985*, (New Brunswick, 1987).

14 See Williams, Vernon J. Jr., *The Social Sciences and Theories of Race*, (Urbana and Chicago, 2006), a reassessment of Franz Boas and Booker T. Washington among others.

15 Diller, Aubrey, *Race Mixture Among the Greeks Before Alexander*. Illinois Studies in Language and Literatures, vol. 20, pt. 1, (Urbana, 1937), p. 10.

16 Diller: *Race Mixture*, p. 11.

17 Diller: *Race Mixture*, p. 157.

18 Diller: *Race Mixture*, p. 160.

19 Frank, Tenney, 'Race Mixture in the Roman Empire', *American Historical Review* 21.4 (1916), pp. 702–703 and 705.

20 Duff, A. M., *Freedmen in the Early Roman Empire* (Oxford, 1928), p. 209.

21 Rostovzeff, Michael Ivanovitch, *The Social and Economic History of the Roman Empire* (Oxford, 1926), p. 485. See also G. M. Bongard-Levin, 'M. I. Rostovtzeff in England: a Personal Experience of West and East,' in G. R. Tsetskhladze, (ed), *Ancient Greeks West and East* (Leiden, Boston, and Köln, 1999), pp. 1–45.

22 Toynbee, Arnold J., *A Study of History, volume 1*, (Oxford and London, repr. 1939), p. 238.

23 Toynbee: *Study of History*, p. 239.

24 Diller: *Race Mixture*, p. 13.

25 For example, Davis, S., *Race-Relations in Ancient Egypt: Greek, Egyptian, Hebrew, Roman*, (New York, 1952) and Saddington, D. B., 'Race Relations in the Early Roman Empire', in *Aufstieg und Niedergang der Römischen Welt* II.3 (1975), pp. 112–137.

26 Snowden, Frank M., Jr, *Blacks in Antiquity: Ethiopians in the Greco-Roman Experience*, (Cambridge, Massachusetts and London, 1970), p. 218. Some important work by William Leo Hansberry from roughly the same period is collected at Harris, Joseph E. (ed), *Pillars in Ethiopian History: The William Leo Hansberry African History Notebook, volume 1*, (Washington D.C., 1974) and Harris, Joseph E., (ed), *Africa and Africans as Seen by Classical Writers: The William Leo Hansberry African History Notebook, volume 2*, (Washington D.C. 1977).

27 Thompson, Lloyd A., *Romans and Blacks*, (Norman and London, 1989), p. 157. See also Thompson, Lloyd, 'Roman Perceptions of Blacks', *Scholia* n.s. 2 (1993), pp. 17–30 and Kelly, David H., 'Egyptians and Ethiopians: Color, Race, and Racism', *Classical Outlook* (Spring 1991), pp. 77–82.

28 Indicative of some of the confusion in terminology, Mary Lefkowitz asserts that 'the Greeks classified people by nationality rather than skin colour, as Frank Snowden pointed out a quarter-century ago', in 'Ancient History, Modern Myths', in M. R. Lefkowitz and G. M. Rogers (eds), *Black Athena Revisited* (Chapel Hill and London, 1996), p. 21.

29 For example, Balsdon, J. P. V. D., *Romans and Aliens*, (London, 1979) and Ruggini, Lellia Cracco, 'Intolerance: Equal, and Less Equal in the Roman World,' *Classical Philology* 82.3 (1987), pp. 187–205.

30 Begley, Sharon, *et al.*, 'Out of Egypt, Greece', *Newsweek* (September 23, 1991), p. 50.

31 But see Gruen, Erich, 'Cleopatra in Rome: Facts and Fantasies', in D. Braund and C. Gill (eds), *Myth, History and Culture in Republican Rome* (Exeter, 2003), pp. 264–65.

32 Quoted in Llewellyn-Jones, Lloyd, 'Celluloid Cleopatras or Did the Greeks Ever Get to Egypt?', in D. Ogden (ed), *The Hellenistic World: New Perspectives* (London, 2002), p. 283.

33 A general introduction to Egypt under Ptolemaic rule can be found at Chauveau, Michel, *Egypt in the Age of Cleopatra*, trans. D. Lorton, (Ithaca and London, 2000).

34 Llewellyn-Jones: 'Celluloid Cleopatras', pp. 282–96.

35 Llewellyn-Jones: 'Celluloid Cleopatras', p. 294.

36 Hamer, Mary, *Signs of Cleopatra: Reading an Icon Historically*, second edition (Exeter, 2008), pp. 120–121.

37 Wyke, Maria, *Projecting the Past: Ancient Rome, Cinema, and History* (New York and London, 1997), p. 99. See also Hamer: *Signs of Cleopatra*, pp. 120–124.

38 Haley, Shelley P., 'Black Feminist Thought and Classics: Re-membering, Re-claiming, Re-empowering', in N. S. Rabinowitz and A. Richlin (eds), *Feminist Theory and the Classics*, (New York and London, 1993), pp. 27 and 29.

39 Cameron, Alan, 'Two Mistresses of Ptolemy Philadelphus', *Greek, Roman, and Byzantine Studies* 31 (1990), pp 287–311.

40 Recently an effort has emerged to find Cleopatra's actual burial site, see Brown, Chip, 'The Search for Cleopatra', *National Geographic* 220. 1 (July 2011), pp. 40–63.

41 Montserrat, Dominic, 'Unidentified Human Remains: Mummies and the erotics of biography', in D. Montserrat (ed), *Changing Bodies, Changing Meanings: Studies on the human body in antiquity* (London and New York, 1998), p. 163.

42 McKenzie Judith, *The Architecture of Alexandria and Egypt c. 300 BC to 700 AD*, (New Haven and London, 2007), pp. 119–136.

43 Goddio, Franck and Manfred Clauss (eds), *Egypt's Sunken Treasures*, second edition (Munich, Berlin, London, and New York, 2008), pp. 370–383.

44 Stiebing, William H, Jr., *Uncovering the Past: A History of Archaeology*, (New York and Oxford, 1993), pp. 69–74.

45 Plutarch, *Life of Antony*, 27. 4.

46 See, for example, Hamer: *Signs of Cleopatra*, plate 1.1 and plate 1.2.

47 Illustrated at Hamer: *Signs of Cleopatra*, plate 1.6.

48 Llewellyn-Jones: 'Celluloid Cleopatras', p. 277.

49 Daugherty, Gregory N., 'Her First Roman: A Cleopatra for *Rome*', in M. S. Cyrino (ed), *Rome, Season One: History Makes Television*, (Malden and Oxford, 2008), pp. 141 and 144.

50 Wyke: *Projecting the Past*, pp. 95–96.

51 Gruen: 'Cleopatra in Rome', pp. 268–273.

52 Cicero, *Letters to Atticus*, 15.15.2.

53 Propertius, *Elegies*, 3.11. 29–46; cf. Cassius Dio, *Roman History*, 50.5.4.

54 Reinhold, Meyer, 'The Declaration of War Against Cleopatra', *Classical Journal* 77.2 (1981–1982), pp. 97–103.

55 Cassius Dio, *Roman History*, 50. 33.

56 Plutarch, *Life of Antony*, 27. 2–3.

57 For more on Cleopatra's reception in later eras, see Hamer: *Signs of Cleopatra* and Hughes-Hallett, Lucy, *Cleopatra: Histories, Dreams and Distortions*, (New York, 1990). Walker, Susan and Peter Higgs (eds), *Cleopatra of Egypt: from History to Myth*, (London, 2001) features an impressive collection of essays and images published in conjunction with a major exhibition on Cleopatra.

58 Flory, Marleen B., 'Pearls for Venus', *Historia: Zeitschrift für Alte Geschichte* 37.4 (1988), p. 502.

59 Zanker, Paul, *The Power of Images in the Age of Augustus*, trans. A. Shapiro (Ann Arbor, 1990), p. 144. See also Iversen, Erik, *Obelisks in Exile, volume 1: The Obelisks of Rome*, (Copenhagen, 1968), pp. 142–160.

60 Curl, James Stevens, *Egyptomania: The Egyptian Revival: a Recurring Theme in the History of Taste*, (Manchester and New York, 1994), p. 29.

61 Curl: *Egyptomania*. Also Bowman, Alan, 'Recolonising Egypt', in T. P. Wiseman (ed), *Classics in Progress: Essays on Ancient Greece and Rome*, (Oxford and New York, 2002), pp. 193–223.

62 Said, Edward W., *Orientalism* (New York, 1979), pp. 1–2.

63 Pliny, *Panegyricus*, 31–32.

64 Mitchell, Timothy, *Colonising Egypt*, (Berkeley, Los Angeles, and London, 1988), p. 2.

65 Colla, Elliott, *Conflicted Antiquities: Egyptology, Egyptomania, Egyptian Modernity*, (Durham and London, 2007), pp. 172–177. For Carter's account of the discovery, see: Carter, Howard, 'The Tomb of Tutankhamun', in B. M. Fagan (ed), *Eyewitness to Discovery: First-Person Accounts of More than Fifty of the World's Greatest Archaeological Discoveries*, (Oxford and New York, 1996), pp. 105–115. See also Reid, Donald Malcolm, *Whose Pharaohs? Archaeology, Museums, and Egyptian National Identity from Napoleon to World War I*, (Berkeley, Los Angeles, and London, 2002).

66 See Gregory, Derek, 'Colonial Nostalgia and Cultures of Travel: Spaces of Constructed Visibility in Egypt', in N. AlSayyad (ed), *Consuming Tradition, Manufacturing Heritage: Global Norms and Urban Forms in the Age of Tourism*, (London and New York, 2001), pp. 111–151.

67 For example, Holt, Frank L., *Into the Land of Bones: Alexander the Great in Afghanistan*, (Berkeley, Los Angeles, and London, 2005), which draws explicit attention to the modern events that drive the book, pp. xi–xii.

68 Kristof, Nicholas, 'Cassandra Speaks', *New York Times*, March 18, 2003), section A, col. 1, p. 33. For a different perspective, see the account of Fick, Nathaniel, *One Bullet Away: the Making of a Marine Officer*, (Boston and New York, 2005), a former classics major at Dartmouth College who served in both Afghanistan and Iraq.

69 Cieply, Michael, 'That Film's Real Message? It Could Be: "Buy a Ticket"', *New York Times*, (March 5, 2007), section E, col. 5, p. 1; and Moaveni, Azadeh, '*300* Sparks an Outcry in Iran', *Time.com*, (March 13, 2007). For more about the lengthy reception of the Persian Wars, see Bridges, Emma, Edith Hall, and P. J. Rhodes (eds), *Cultural Responses to the Persian Wars: Antiquity to the Third Millennium*, (Oxford and New York, 2007).

70 Snowden: *Blacks in Antiquity*, p. 179.

71 Petronius, *Satyricon*, 102.

72 See Hill, Mike (ed), *Whiteness: A Critical Reader*, (New York and London, 1997) and Delgado, Richard and Jean Stefanic (eds), *Critical Whiteness Studies: Looking Behind the Mirror*, (Philadelphia, 1997). Also Painter, Nell Irvin, *The History of White People*, (New York and London, 2010).

73 Sweet, Frank W., *Legal History of the Color Line: The Rise and Triumph of the One-Drop Rule*, (Palm Coast, 2005).

74 See McCoskey, Denise, 'By Any Other Name? Ethnicity and the Study of Ancient Identity,' *The Classical Bulletin* 79.1 (2003), pp. 93–109.

75 Quoted at Sollors, Werner, 'Foreword: Theories of American Ethnicity', in W. Sollors (ed), *Theories of Ethnicity: A Classical Reader*, (New York, 1996?), p. xxxviii, n. 4.

76 For an excellent overview, see Cornell, Stephen and Douglas Hartman, *Ethnicity*

and Race: Making Identities in a Changing World, (Thousand Oaks, London, and New Delhi, 1998), pp. 16–38.

77 Discover, vol. 15, no. 11, (November 1994).

78 Cited at Sollors: 'Foreword', p. xxxv.

79 See McInerney, Jeremy, 'Ethnos and Ethnicity in Early Greece', in I. Malkin (ed), Ancient Perceptions of Greek Ethnicity (Cambridge and London, 2001), pp. 53–57 and Morgan, Catherine, 'Ethne, Ethnicity, and Early Greek States, c. 1200–480 BCE: an Archaeological Perspective', in Malkin: Ancient Perceptions, pp. 75–112. Also, Morgan, Catherine, Early Greek States Beyond the Polis, (London and New York, 2003).

80 Sollors: 'Foreword', p. xxix. See also Smedley: Race in North America, pp. 37–41.

81 McInerney: 'Ethnos and Ethnicity', p. 56.

82 Hall, Jonathan M., Ethnic Identity in Greek Antiquity (Cambridge and New York, 1997), p. 34.

83 Xenophon's Socrates uses 'ethnos' of rhapsodes at Symposium 3.6.

84 Jones, C. P., 'Ethnos and genos in Herodotus', Classical Quarterly 46 (1996), pp. 315–320.

85 See Graf, Fritz, Greek Mythology: An Introduction, trans. T. Marier (Baltimore and London, 1993), pp. 125–131. Also Dowden, Ken, The Uses of Greek Mythology, (London and New York, 1992).

86 Morgan: 'Ethne, Ethnicity, and Early Greek States', p. 83.

87 Jones: 'Ethnos', p. 317.

88 Jones: 'Ethnos', p. 318.

89 Barker, Chris, Television, Globalization and Cultural Identities, (Buckingham and Philadelphia, 1999), p. 63.

90 For helpful discussions of how race and ethnicity relate to one another, see also Cornell and Hartman: Ethnicity and Race, pp. 25–37 and Sollors: 'Foreword', p. xxix–xxxv.

91 For interdisciplinary approaches to racism, see Harris, Leonard, Key Concepts in Critical Theory: Racism, (New York, 1999).

92 Also, but using 'ethnic' terminology: Coleman, John E., 'Ancient Greek Ethnocentrism', in J. E. Coleman and C. A. Walz (ed), Greeks and Barbarians: Essays on the Interactions between Greeks and Non-Greeks in Antiquity and the Consequences of Eurocentrism, (Bethesda, 1997), pp. 175–220; and Tuplin, Christopher, 'Greek Racism? Observations on the Character and Limits of Greek Ethnic Prejudice', in Tsetskhladze: Ancient Greeks West and East, pp. 47–75.

93 Sherwin-White, A.N., Racial Prejudice in Imperial Rome, (Cambridge, 1967), p. 1.

94 Isaac, Benjamin, The Invention of Racism in Classical Antiquity, (Princeton and Oxford, 2004), p. 16.

95 Isaac: Invention, p. 2.

96 Isaac: Invention, pp. 17–39. See a review of Isaac at McCoskey, Denise, 'Naming the Fault in Question: Theorizing Racism among the Greeks and Romans', The International Journal of the Classical Tradition, 13.2 (Fall 2006), pp. 243–267.

Chapter I

1 For an excellent introduction to Greek and Roman geographic thought, see Harley, J. B. and David Woodward (eds), The History of Cartography, volume 1: Cartography

in Prehistoric, Ancient, and Medieval Europe and the Mediterranean, (Chicago and London, 1987), pp. 130–257. Also Dilke, O. A. W., *Greek and Roman Maps* (Ithaca, 1985) and Casson, Lionel, *Travel in the Ancient World*, (Baltimore, 1994). For a more thematic approach to ancient travel and geography, Hartog, François, *Memories of Odysseus: Frontier Tales from Ancient Greece*, trans. J. Lloyd (Chicago, 2001).

2　See, for example, Strabo, *Geography*, 1.1.3 and 1.1.8.

3　On ancient continental division, Thomas, Rosalind, *Herodotus in Context: Ethnography, Science and the Art of Persuasion* (Cambridge, 2000), pp. 75–101; also on ancient geography generally, Clarke, Katherine, *Between Geography and History: Hellenistic Constructions of the Roman World* (Oxford, 1999). For a critical reading of geographic conventions, see Lewis, Martin W. and Kären E. Wigen, *The Myth of Continents: A Critique of Metageography*, (Berkeley, Los Angeles, and London, 1997); on Europe specifically, Pagden, Anthony, 'Europe: Conceptualizing a Continent', in A. Pagden (ed), *The Idea of Europe: From Antiquity to the European Union*, (Cambridge and New York, 2002), pp. 33–54.

4　Modern historians often use the concept of the 'frontier' in discussing the boundaries of the Roman world. See, for example, Whittaker, C.R., *Rome and Its Frontiers: The Dynamics of Empire*, (London and New York, 2004) and Dyson, Stephen L, *The Creation of the Roman Frontier*, (Princeton, 1985).

5　Philostratus' *Life of Apollonius of Tyana* presents a later geographic survey of the Mediterranean world in its account of the extensive travels of the Neopythagorean sage Apollonius, active in the first century CE.

6　See Malkin, Irad, 'Greek Ambiguities: Between "Ancient Hellas" and "Barbarian Epirus"', in Malkin: *Ancient Perceptions*, pp. 187–212.

7　See Braund, D., 'Greeks, Scythians and *Hippake*, or "Readings Mare's-Cheese"', in Tsetskhladze: *Ancient Greeks West and East*, pp. 521–530.

8　For example, Whitehouse, Ruth D. and John B. Wilkins, 'Greeks and natives in south-east Italy: approaches to the archaeological evidence', in T. C. Champion (ed), *Centre and Periphery: Comparative studies in archaeology*, (London and Boston, 1989). On the role of marriage, Shepherd, Gillian, 'Fibulae and Females: Intermarriage in the Western Greek Colonies and the Evidence from the Cemeteries', in Tsetskhladze: *Ancient Greeks West and East*, pp. 267–300. For consideration of Greek contact with others outside formal colonial structures, see de Hoz, Javier, 'The Greek Man in the Iberian Street: Non-colonial Greek Identity in Spain and Southern France', in K. Lomas (ed), *Greek Identity in the Western Mediterranean: Papers in Honour of Brian Shefton*, (Leiden and Boston, 2004), pp. 411–427.

9　For an excellent introduction, see Antonaccio, Carla M., 'Colonization: Greece on the Move, 900–480', in H. A. Shapiro (ed), *The Cambridge Companion to Archaic Greece*, (Cambridge and New York, 2007), pp. 201–224.

10　For example, Strabo, *Geography*, 1.2.1; see also Polybius, *Histories*, 3.59.

11　See Syme, Ronald, 'Military Geography at Rome', *Classical Antiquity* 7.2 (1988), pp. 227–251 and Sherk, Robert K., 'Roman Geographical Exploration and Military Maps', *Aufstieg und Niedergang der Römischen Welt* II.1 (1974), pp. 534–562. For a more expansive discussion of the evolution of Roman spatial ideology, Nicolet, Claude, *Space, Geography, and Politics in the Early Roman Empire*, (Ann Arbor, 1991).

12　Beard, Mary and Michael Crawford, *Rome in the Late Republic: Problems and Interpretations*, (London, 1985), p. 80.

13　Hall, Edith, *Inventing the Barbarian: Greek Self-Definition through Tragedy* (Oxford, 1989), p. 56.

14 Alcock, Susan E., 'Breaking up the Hellenistic world: survey and society,' in I. Morris (ed), *Classical Greece: ancient histories and modern archaeologies* (Cambridge, 1994), p. 171.

15 Millar, Fergus, *The Roman Near East 31 BC-AD 337* (Cambridge, Massachusetts and London, 1993), p. 5. See also Isaac, Benjamin, *The Limits of Empire: The Roman Army in the East*, revised edition, (Oxford and New York, 1990).

16 Parker, Grant, *The Making of Roman India* (Cambridge, 2008), pp. 14–18 and 28–33.

17 Romm, James S., *The Edges of the Earth in Ancient Thought: Geography, Exploration, and Fiction*, (Princeton, 1992), p. 88.

18 Walbank, F. W., *The Hellenistic World*, revised edition (Cambridge, Massachusetts, 1993), pp. 199–200.

19 Parker: *Roman India*, pp. 147–198.

20 *Res Gestae Divi Augusti*, 31.

21 Leslie, D. D. and K. H. J. Gardiner, *The Roman Empire in Chinese Sources*, (Rome, 1996). For a different look at ancient China relative to the world of classical antiquity, see Kim, Hyun Jin, *Ethnicity and Foreigners in Ancient Greece and China*, (London, 2009).

22 Mudimbe, V. Y., *The Idea of Africa*, (Bloomington and Indianapolis, 1994), p. 71.

23 Evans, Rhiannon, 'Ethnography's Freak Show: The Grotesques at the Edges of the Roman Earth', *Ramus* 21 (1999), pp. 56–57.

24 See Brantlinger, Patrick, 'Victorians and Africans: The Genealogy of the Myth of the Dark Continent', *Critical Inquiry* 12.1, '"Race," Writing, and Difference' (1985), pp. 166–203.

25 Romm: *Edges*, p. 88.

26 Herodotus, *Histories*, 4. 42–43.

27 Romm: *Edges*, p. 83.

28 Dilke: *Greek and Roman Maps*, p. 131.

29 Romm: *Edges*, pp. 19–20.

30 Vasunia, Phiroze, *The Gift of the Nile: Hellenizing Egypt from Aeschylus to Alexander* (Berkeley, Los Angeles and London, 2001), pp. 275–282.

31 Walbank: *Hellenistic World*, pp. 200–202.

32 See Mitchell, Barbara, 'Cyrene: Typical or Atypical?' in R. Brock and S. Hodkinson (eds), *Alternatives to Athens: Varieties of Political Organization and Community in Ancient Greece* (Oxford and New York, 2000), pp. 82–102.

33 Sallust (c. 86–35 BCE) describes the event in his *Jugurthine War*.

34 Raven, Susan, *Rome in Africa*, third edition (London and New York, 1993). Another helpful introduction can be found at MacKendrick, Paul, *The North African Stones Speak*, (Chapel Hill, 1980).

35 See Rosenmeyer, P. A. 'A Greek Inscription on the Memnon Colossus: The Mysterious "Mister T"', *Classical Quarterly*, n.s. 54.2 (2004), pp. 620–24 and Rosenmeyer, Patricia, 'Greek Verse Inscriptions in Roman Egypt: Julia Balbilla's Sapphic Voice', *Classical Antiquity* 27.2 (2008), pp. 334–58

36 For a general introduction, see O'Connor, David, *Ancient Nubia: Egypt's Rival in Africa*, (Philadelphia, 1993) and Burstein, Stanley M., *Graeco-Africana: Studies in the History of Greek Relations with Egypt and Nubia*, (New Rochelle, Athens and Moscow, 1995).

37 Plutarch, *Life of Antony*, 27. 3.

38 Strabo, *Geography*, 17.1.54 provides an infamous description of the queen as

'masculine and blind in one eye'. For modern perspectives on Candace, see Williams, Larry and Charles S. Finch, 'The Great Queens of Ethiopia,' in I.Van Sertima (ed), *Black Women in Antiquity*, Journal of African Civilizations 6.1, (New Brunswick and London, 1988), pp. 30–31.

39 Thompson, L. A., 'Eastern Africa and the Graeco-Roman world (to A.D. 641)', in L. A. Thompson and J. Ferguson (eds), *Africa in Classical Antiquity: Nine Studies* (Ibadan, 1969), p. 34. For the sources themselves, see Burstein, Stanley (ed), *Ancient African Civilizations: Kush and Axum*, (Princeton, 2009).

40 Swanson, Maynard W., 'Colonizing the Past: Origin Myths of the Great Zimbabwe Ruins,' in E. M. Yamauchi (ed), *Africa and Africans in Antiquity*, (East Lansing, 2001), p. 292. See also Howe, Stephen, *Afrocentrism: Mythical Pasts and Imagined Homes*, (London and New York, 1998), pp. 117–119.

41 Garlake, Peter, 'Prehistory and ideology in Zimbabwe', *Africa* 52.3 (1982), pp. 1–19. Also Garlake, Peter, *Great Zimbabwe*, (London, 1973).

42 Homer, *Iliad*, 23. 205–206 and Homer, *Odyssey*, 1.22–25.

43 Snowden, Frank M. Jr., 'Greeks and Ethiopians' in Coleman and Walz (eds), *Greeks and Barbarians*, p. 107.

44 Snowden: *Blacks*, p. 103.

45 Mudimbe: *Idea of Africa*, pp. 79–80. See Didodorus Siculus, *Library of History*, Book 3.

46 Dilke: *Maps*, p. 27.

47 For example, Aristotle, *Politics*, 1327b; cf. Plato, *Timaeus* 24c.

48 Text and translation at Kirk, G.S., J. E. Raven and M. Schofield (eds), *The Presocratic Philosophers*, second edition (Cambridge and New York, 1983), pp. 168–169.

49 Thomas: *Herodotus in Context*, pp. 47–48.

50 Balsdon: *Romans and Aliens*, p. 60.

51 See: Evans 'Ethnography's Freak Show'.

52 Tyrrell, Wm. Blake, *Amazons: A Study in Athenian Mythmaking* (Baltimore and London, 1984), p. 56. Given their alleged location at the edges of the *oikumene* the Amazons appear in intriguing ways in other accounts of geographic exploration, including Alexander the Great's campaigns. See Baynham, Elizabeth, 'Alexander and the Amazons', *Classical Quarterly* 51.1 (2001), pp. 115–126.

53 Harari, Maurizio, 'A Short History of Pygmies in Greece and Italy', in Lomas: *Greek Identity in the Western Mediterranean*, p. 164.

54 Dilke: *Maps*, p. 27.

55 Isaac: *Invention*, p. 94. In ancient sources, for example: Vitruvius, *On Architecture*, 6.1.3.

56 Pliny, *Natural History*, 2.80.189–190.

57 Wheeler, Roxann, *The Complexion of Race: Categories of Difference in Eighteenth-Century British Culture*, (Philadelphia, 2000), pp. 24–28.

58 Strabo, *Geography*, 2.5.8.

59 For background on the corpus and its authorship, Lloyd, G. E. R., 'The Hippocratic Question', *Classical Quarterly* n.s. 25 (1975), pp. 171–192.

60 For example, Jouanna, Jacques, *Hippocrates*, trans. M. B. DeBevoise (Baltimore and London, 1999), p. 375; cf. Chiasson, Charles, 'Scythian Androgyny and Environmental Determinism in Herodotus and the Hippocratic *peri aeron hudaton topon*', *Syllecta Classica* 12 (2001), p. 45 and n. 30. For a general introduction, see also McCoskey, Denise Eileen, 'On *Black Athena*, Hippocratic Medicine, and Roman Imperial Edicts: Egyptians and the Problem of Race in Classical Antiquity',

in R. D. Coates (ed), *Race and Ethnicity: Across Time, Space and Discipline*, (Leiden and Boston, 2004), pp. 313–324.

61   *Airs, Waters, Places*, 24. Trans. J. Chadwick and W. N. Mann.

62   *Airs Waters, Places*, 16.

63   On the Sauromatae and Amazons, Herodotus, *Histories*, 4. 110–117. Also Hartog, François, *The Mirror of Herodotus: The Representation of the Other in the Writing of History*, trans. J. Lloyd (Berkeley, Los Angeles, London, 1988), pp. 216–224. On historical evidence for the Amazons, begin with Davis-Kimball, Jeannine, *Warrior Women: An Archaeologist's Search for History's Hidden Heroines*, with M. Behan, (New York, 2002).

64   *Airs Waters, Places*, 16.

65   *Airs Waters, Places*, 23.

66   So, also, the text's odd use of 'serving wenches' to epitomize the physical qualities needed for hyper-fertility at chapter 21.

67   Thomas: *Herodotus in Context*, p. 97.

68   *Airs Waters, Places*, 16.

69   For example, Toynbee: *Study of History*, p. 253 and Appiah, Kwame Anthony, *In My Father's House: Africa in the Philosophy of Culture*, (New York and Oxford, 1992), p. 11.

70   On Rome's ideal position and so imperial mission, see Vitruvius, *On Architecture*, 6.1.10–11. and Strabo, *Geography*, 2.5.26; on Italy's favorable position and natural resources, 6.4.1–2; and for the advantageous topography of Greece, 8.1.3.

71   Gere, Cathy, *The Tomb of Agamemnon* (Cambridge, Massachusetts, 2006), p. 137.

72   Gere: *Tomb of Agamemnon*, pp. 60–80.

73   See especially Veyne, Paul, *Did the Greeks Believe in Their Myths?: An Essay on the Constitutive Imagination*. trans. P. Wissing (Chicago, 1988).

74   Hall: *Ethnic Identity*, p. 87.

75   Hall: *Inventing the Barbarian*, pp. 36–37.

76   Hall, Jonathan M., *Hellenicity: Between Ethnicity and Culture* (Chicago and London, 2002), p. 56.

77   For more in-depth discussion, see Hall: *Hellenicity*, pp. 56–89.

78   Hall, Jonathan M., 'Contested Ethnicities: Perceptions of Macedonia within Evolving Definitions of Greek Identity', in Malkin: *Ancient Perceptions*, p. 166.

79   Herodotus, *Histories*, 7. 150.

80   Some biblical interpretations of Noah's three sons have similarly treated each one as the founder of a different racial group. Most notably, Noah's son Ham was considered the ancestor of all African groups, providing a religious justification for slavery through Noah's so-called 'curse'; see Whitford, David M., *The Curse of Ham in the Early Modern Era: the Bible and the Justifications for Slavery*, (Farnham and Burlington, 2009). Also Yamauchi, Edwin M., 'The Curse of Ham', *Criswell Theological Review* n.s. 6.2 (2009), pp. 45–60.

81   Smith, Jonathan Z., 'What a Difference A Difference Makes', in J. Neusner and E. S. Frerichs (eds), *"To See Ourselves as Others See Us": Christians, Jews, "Others" in Latin Antiquity* (Chico, California, 1985), p. 5.

82   Hall: *Hellenicity*, pp. 126–128.

83   Thucydides, *History of the Peloponnesian War*, 1. 3. 3. Trans. R. Warner. See discussion of the passage at Hall: *Hellenicity*, pp. 125–26.

84   Hall: *Hellenicity*, pp. 132–33.

85   E. Hall: *Inventing*, p. 11 and *passim*.

86   Hall: 'Contested Ethnicities', p. 166.

87   E. Hall: *Inventing*, p. 11.

88   E. Hall: *Inventing*, pp. 4–5 and 10–11. See also Dauge, Yves Albert, *Le Barbare: Recherches sur la conception romaine de la barbarie et de la civilisation*, Collection Latomus, volume 176 (Brussels, 1981).

89   Aristotle, *Politics* 1252b and *passim*. For evaluation of Aristotle's views and continuing influence, begin with Garnsey, Peter, *Ideas of Slavery from Aristotle to Augustine*, The W.B. Stanford Memorial Lectures (Cambridge and New York, 1996).

90   See Rosivach, Vincent J., 'Enslaving "Barbaroi" and the Athenian Ideology of Slavery', *Historia: Zeitschrift für Alte Geschichte* 48.2 (1999), pp. 129–157.

91   On Greek slavery, begin with Garlan, Yvon, *Slavery in Ancient Greece*, revised and expanded edition, trans. J. Lloyd, (Ithaca and London, 1988). Also duBois, Page, *Slavery: Antiquity and its Legacy*, (London, 2010).

92   Thompson, F. Hugh, *The Archaeology of Greek and Roman Slavery*, (London, 2003), pp. 3–4; see also Harris, W. V., 'Demography, Geography and the Sources of Roman Slaves', *Journal of Roman Studies* 89 (1999), pp. 62–75

93   Hopkins, Keith, *Conquerors and Slaves*, (Cambridge and New York, 1978).

94   Balsdon: *Romans and Aliens*, p. 81.

95   Begin with Bradley, K. R., 'On the Roman Slave Supply and Slavebreeding', in M. I. Finley (ed), *Classical Slavery*, (London and Portland, 1987), pp. 53–81.

96   Thompson: *Archaeology*, p. 9.

97   Montserrat, Dominic, 'Experiencing the male body in Roman Egypt', in L. Foxhall and J. Salmon (eds), *When Men Were Men: Masculinity, power and identity in classical antiquity*, (London and New York, 1998), p. 159.

98   Balsdon: *Romans and Aliens*, p. 215.

99   Balsdon: *Romans and Aliens*, p. 79.

100 See Bradley, K. R., *Slaves and Masters in the Roman Empire: A Study in Social Control*, (New York and Oxford, 1984), pp. 81–112.

101 Watson, Alan, *Roman Slave Law*, (Baltimore and London, 1987), pp. 35–45. The most notorious representation of a freedman in Roman literature is Trimalchio in Petronius' *Satyricon*. F. Scott Fitzgerald reportedly used 'Trimalchio in West Egg' as the working title for his novel that eventually became *The Great Gatsby*. For discussion of Augustus' views of manumission, see Thompson, L. A., 'The concept of purity of blood in Suetonius' life of Augustus', *Museum Africum* 7 (1981), pp. 35–46.

102 For example, Aristotle, *Politics* 1285a.

103 Hall: 'Contested Ethnicities', p. 166.

104 See Nicole Loraux, *Born of the Earth: Myth and Politics in Athens,* trans. S. Stewart (Ithaca and London, 2000).

105 Osborne, Robin, 'Law, the Democratic Citizen and the Representation of Women in Classical Athens', *Past and Present* 155 (1997), pp. 3–9.

106 Konstan, David, '*To Hellenikon ethnos*: Ethnicity and the Construction of Ancient Greek Identity,' in Malkin: *Ancient Perceptions*, p. 35. Pericles' speech is recounted at Thucydides, *History of the Peloponnesian War*, 2. 35–46. In the *Menexenus*, seemingly a response to – or parody of – Pericles' speech, Plato distinguishes Athenians as 'pure-blooded' and professes them unwilling to 'mix' with barbarians like other Greeks, 245c–d. See Kahn, Charles H., 'Plato's Funeral Oration: The Motive of the *Menexenus*', *Classical Philology* 58.4 (1963), pp. 220–234. A papyrus connected to Philodemus records a conversation from Plato's deathbed in which he is asked what

it means to be a 'barbarian:' see Gaiser, Konrad, *Philodems Academica: Die Berichte über Platon und die Alte Akademie in zwei herkulanensischen Papyri*, (Stuttgart, 1988), pp. 176–180. For Greek thought more broadly, Saxonhouse, Arlene W., *Fear of Diversity: The Birth of Political Science in Ancient Greek Thought*, (Chicago and London, 1992).

107 Thomas, Rosalind, 'Ethnicity, Genealogy, and Hellenism in Herodotus,' in Malkin: *Ancient Perceptions*, pp. 226.

108 Herodotus, *Histories*, 8.144.2. Trans. A. de Sélincourt.

109 Thomas: *Herodotus in Context*, pp. 71–72.

110 Chiasson: 'Scythian Androgyny', p. 57.

111 Herodotus, *Histories*, 2.35.2. See also West, Stephanie, 'Cultural antitheses: reflections of Herodotus 2.35–36', *International Journal of the Classical Tradition* 5.1 (1998), pp. 3–19.

112 Thomas: 'Ethnicity, Genealogy', pp. 227–28.

113 Hartog: *Mirror of Herodotus*, pp. xxi and 371.

114 Karttunen, Klaus, 'The Ethnography of the Fringes,' in E. J. Bakker, I. J. F. De Jong, and H. Van Wees (eds), *Brill's Companion to Herodotus* (Leiden, Boston, and Köln, 2002), p. 460.

115 For the place of such structures in Greek thought more broadly, Lloyd, G. E. R., *Polarity and Analogy: Two Types of Argumentation in Early Greek Thought*, (Cambridge, 1966).

116 Herodotus, *Histories*, 1.131–140.

117 Redfield, James, 'Herodotus the Tourist,' *Classical Philology* 80 (1985), p. 109. On the Scythians in Herodotus, see also Hartog: *Mirror of Herodotus*, pp. 3–206.

118 Redfield: 'Herodotus the Tourist', p. 117.

119 Thomas: 'Ethnicity, Genealogy', pp. 215–17.

120 Thomas: 'Ethnicity, Genealogy', p. 215.

121 Thomas: *Herodotus in Context*, pp. 131–33; cf. Plato, *Statesman* 262d-e.

122 Thomas: *Herodotus in Context*, p. 122.

123 Plutarch, *On the Malice of Herodotus*, 12.

124 Herodotus, *Histories*, 2.35.1.

125 Vasunia: *Gift of the Nile*, p. 2.

126 Vasunia: *Gift of the Nile*, p. 31 and *passim*.

127 Vasunia: *Gift of the Nile*, p. 116.

128 Herodotus, *Histories*, 2.85–90.

129 Herodotus, *Histories*, 3.12.

130 Herodotus, *Histories*, 2.57 and 2.104.

131 Snowden, Frank M. Jr., 'Bernal's "Blacks" and the Afrocentrists', in Lefkowitz and Rogers: *Black Athena Revisited*, pp. 113–114.

132 Herodotus, *Histories*, 3. 101.

133 See Martin, Catherine Gimelli, 'Orientalism and the Ethnographer: Said, Herodotus, and the Discourse of Alterity', in J. Herron, *et al.*, (eds), *The Ends of Theory*, (Detroit, 1996), pp. 86–103. For ancient receptions of Herodotus, see Hornblower, Simon, 'Herodotus' influence in antiquity', in C. Dewald and J. Marincola (eds), *The Cambridge Companion to Herodotus* (Cambridge and New York, 2006), pp. 306–318 .

134 Hulme, Peter, *Colonial Encounters: Europe and the Native Caribbean 1492–1797* (London and New York, 1986), pp. 20ff. See also Smith, 'What a Difference', pp. 3–48.

135   Wiesen, David S., 'Herodotus and the Modern Debate Over Race and Slavery,' *The Ancient World* 3 (1980), p. 3.

136   Vasunia: *Gift of the Nile*, pp. 248–88.

137   Bowersock, G. W., *Hellenism in Late Antiquity* (Ann Arbor, 1990), p. xi. Also Momigliano, Arnaldo, *Alien Wisdom: The Limits of Hellenization*, (Cambridge, 1975).

138   Isocrates, *Panegyricus*, 50. Trans. S. Usher.

139   Whitmarsh, Tim, 'The Birth of a Prodigy: Heliodorus and the Genealogy of Hellenism', in R. Hunter (ed), *Studies in Heliodorus*, Proceedings of the Cambridge Philological Society, supplementary volume, n. 21 (Cambridge, 1998), p. 100.

140   Moore, Alan and Dave Gibbons, *Watchmen* (New York 1987), ch. 11, pp. 7–9.

141   Green, Peter, 'The Metamorphosis of the Barbarian: Athenian Panhellenism in a Changing World', in R. W. Wallace and E. M. Harris (eds), *Transitions to Empire: Essays in Greco-Roman History, 360–146 BCE, in honor of E.Badian* (Norman and London, 1996), p. 21.

142   Green: 'Metamorphosis', p. 24.

143   Borza, Eugene N., 'Greeks and Macedonians in the Age of Alexander: The Source Traditions,' in Wallace and Harris: *Transitions to Empire*, p. 135.

144   Arrian, *Anabasis*, 2.10.7. But, in contrast, he uses the phrasing 'Macedonia and the rest of Greece' at 2.14.4.

145   Herodotus, *Histories*, 5.22. 1–2.

146   Hall: 'Contested Ethnicities', pp. 168–69.

147   Plutarch, *Life of Alexander*, 51.4.

148   Danforth, Loring. M., 'Alexander the Great and the Macedonian Conflict', in J. Roisman (ed), *Brill's Companion to Alexander the Great* (Leiden and Boston, 2003), pp. 347–364. See also Mackridge, P. and E. Yannakakis (eds), *Ourselves and Others: The Development of a Greek Macedonian Cultural Identity Since 1912* (Oxford and New York, 1997). For perceptions of Alexander's legacy in Pakistan, see Sidky, H., 'Alexander the Great, the Graeco-Bactrians, and Hunza: Greek Descents in Central Asia', *Central Asiatic Journal* 43.2, (1999), pp. 232–249.

149   See Flower, Michael, 'Alexander the Great and Panhellenism', in A.B. Bosworth and E. J. Baynham (eds), *Alexander the Great in Fact and Fiction* (Oxford and New York, 2000), pp. 96–135.

150   For a different perspective on his campaigns, see Heckel, Waldemar, 'Resistance to Alexander the Great', in L. A. Tritle (ed), *The Greek World in the Fourth Century: From the Fall of the Athenian Empire to the Successors of Alexander*, (London and New York, 1997), pp. 189–227.

151   Tarn, W. W., 'Alexander the Great and the Unity of Mankind', *Proceedings of the British Academy*, (London, 1933), pp. 123–166. See also Tarn's response to initial criticism at Tarn, W.W., 'Alexander, Cynics and Stoics,' *The American Journal of Philology* 60.1 (1939), pp. 41–70. Merlan, Philip, 'Alexander the Great or Antiphon the Sophist?', *Classical Philology* 45.3 (1950), pp. 161–166 credits Antiphon the Sophist with proposing these ideas before Alexander.

152   Badian, Ernst, 'Alexander and the Unity of Mankind', *Historia: Zeitschrift für Alte Geschichte* 7.4 (1958), p. 425.

153   For a summary of scholarly views, see Stoneman, Richard, *Alexander the Great*, second edition (London and New York, 2004), pp. 7–11.

154   Strabo, *Geography*, 1.4.9; cf. Roller, Duane W., *Eratosthenes' Geography*, (Princeton and Oxford, 2010), pp. 220–221.

155 Plutarch, *On the Fortune or Virtue of Alexander the Great*, 1.6.

156 For an introduction to the ancient sources on Alexander, see Baynham, Elizabeth, 'The Ancient Evidence for Alexander the Great', in Roisman: *Brill's Companion to Alexander the Great*, pp. 3–29; also Carney, Elizabeth, 'Artifice and Alexander History', in Bosworth and Baynham: *Alexander the Great*, pp. 263–285.

157 Borza, Eugene N., 'Ethnicity and Cultural Policy at Alexander's Court', *The Ancient World* 23 (1992), p. 24.

158 Fredricksmeyer, Ernst, 'Alexander the Great and the Kingship of Asia', in Bosworth and Baynham: *Alexander the Great*, p. 160.

159 Stewart, Andrew, *Faces of Power: Alexander's Image and Hellenistic Politics*, (Berkeley, Los Angeles, and Oxford, 1993), p. 176.

160 Green, Peter, 'Alexander's Alexandria', in *Alexandria and Alexandrianism*, (Malibu, 1996) p. 8.

161 Polybius, *Histories*, 5.104.10.

162 Woolf, Greg, 'Beyond Romans and Natives', *World Archaeology* 28.3 (1997), p. 347.

163 Cornell, T. J., *The Beginnings of Rome: Italy and Rome from the Bronze Age to the Punic Wars (c. 1000–264 BC)* (London and New York, 1995), p. 96.

164 See Hemker, Julie, 'Rape and the Founding of Rome', *Helios* 12.1 (1985), pp. 41–47.

165 Cornell: *Beginnings of Rome*, p. 41.

166 Florus, *Epitome*, 2.6. 1–2.

167 Farney, Gary D., *Ethnic Identity and Aristocratic Competition in Republican Rome* (Cambridge and New York, 2007), p. 77.

168 Cornell: *Beginnings of Rome*, p. 351.

169 Laurence, Ray, 'Introduction', in R. Laurence and J. Berry (eds), *Cultural Identity in the Roman Empire* (London and New York, 1998), p. 2. For a general introduction to Roman citizenship, see Gardner, Jane F., *Being a Roman Citizen*, (London and New York, 1993) or Sherwin-White, A. N., *The Roman Citizenship*, second edition (Oxford, 1973).

170 Velleius Paterculus, *Roman History*, 1.14.1.

171 Cicero, *On Duties*, 3.47.

172 Balsdon: *Romans and Aliens*, p. 101.

173 Cicero, *On Duties*, 1.53. For discussion of the passage, see Walbank, F. W., 'Nationality as a Factor in Roman History', *Harvard Studies in Classical Philology* 76 (1972), p. 145.

174 Cicero, *On Duties*, 1.53.

175 Quintilian, *Institutio Oratoria*, 8.1.3.

176 Balsdon: *Romans and Aliens*, p. 130.

177 For perceptions of difference even later in the Roman period, see Heather, Peter, 'The Barbarian in Late Antiquity: Image, reality, and transformation', in R. Miles, *Constructing Identities in Late Antiquity*, (London and New York, 1999), pp. 234–258.

178 Farney: *Ethnic Identity*, p. 4.

179 Farney: *Ethnic Identity*, p. 101.

180 Cornell: *Beginnings of Rome*, p. 151. See also Hall, J. F. (ed), *Etruscan Italy: Etruscan Influences on the Civilizations of Italy from Antiquity to the Modern Era*, (Provo, 1996).

181 I first encountered the romance of the Etruscans through Emmy Richardson; see Richardson, Emeline Hill, *The Etruscans, their art and civilization*, (Chicago, 1964).

182 Farney: *Ethnic Identity*, p. 127.
183 Cornell: *Beginnings of Rome*, pp. 158–59.
184 Cornell: *Beginnings of Rome*, pp. 169–170.
185 Williams, J.H.C., *Beyond the Rubicon: Romans and Gauls in Republican Italy*, (Oxford and New York, 2001), pp. 128–129. For specific aspects of the consolidation of Italy, see Torelli, Mario, *Studies in the Romanization of Italy*, ed and trans. by H. Fracchia and M. Gualtieri, (Edmonton, 1995).
186 Velleius Paterculus, *Roman History*, 2.15. 2.
187 Cornell: *Beginnings of Rome*, pp. 242–244.
188 Gruen, Erich S., *Culture and National Identity in Republican Rome* (Ithaca, 1992), pp. 6–21.
189 Gruen: *Culture and National Identity*, pp. 6–8.
190 On Roman Greece itself, see Alcock, Susan E., *Graecia Capta: The Landscapes of Roman Greece*, (Cambridge and New York, 1993).
191 Horace, *Epistles*. 2.1.156–157; cf. Velleius Paterculus, *Roman History* 2. 34. 3, where Cicero is praised in terms that reinterpret Horace's conceit.
192 Woolf, Greg, 'Becoming Roman, Staying Greek: Culture, Identity and the Civilizing Process in the Roman East', *Proceedings of the Cambridge Philological Society* 40 (1994), p. 120. See, for example, Pliny, *Letters*, 8.24.
193 Whitmarsh, Tim, *Greek Literature and the Roman Empire: The Politics of Imitation*, (Oxford, 2001), p. 2. See also Konstan, David and Suzanne Saïd (eds), *Greeks on Greekness: Viewing the Greek Past Under the Roman Empire*, *Proceedings of the Cambridge Philological Society*, supplementary vol. 29 (Cambridge, 2006) and Goldhill, Simon (ed), *Being Greek Under Rome: Cultural Identity, the Second Sophistic, and the Development of Empire*, (Cambridge, 2001).
194 Woolf: 'Becoming Roman, Staying Greek', p. 130.
195 Cicero, *On the Responses of the Haruspices*, 19.
196 Cicero, *De Finibus*. 2. 49.
197 Saavedra, Tina, 'Women as Focalizers of Barbarism in Conquest Texts', *Echos du Monde Classique* n.s. 18 (1999), p. 60. There is an interesting comparison of four different categories of individual (poet, lawyer, soldier, artist) and their experience of the Roman/barbarian divide at Williams, Derek, *Romans and Barbarians: Four Views from the Empire's Edge 1st Century AD*, (New York, 1998).
198 Thompson: *Romans and Blacks*, p. 87.
199 Isaac: *Invention*, p. 405.
200 Polybius, *Histories*, 3. 2. 6. On Polybius' place in defining for modern readers the dynamics of the Hellenistic period and the rise of Rome, see Walbank, Frank W., *Polybius, Rome and the Hellenistic World: Essays and Reflections*, Cambridge and New York, 2002) and Champion, Craige B., *Cultural Politics in Polybius's Histories*, (Berkeley, Los Angeles, and London, 2004).
201 See O'Connell, Robert L., *The Ghosts of Cannae: Hannibal and the Darkest Hour of the Roman Republic*, (New York, 2010).
202 See also Saddington, D. B., 'Roman Attitudes to the "Externae Gentes" of the North' *Acta Classica* 4 (1961), pp. 90–102.
203 Williams: *Beyond the Rubicon*, p. 140.
204 Williams: *Beyond the Rubicon*, p. 9. See also Shore, Cris, 'Imagining the New Europe: Identity and Heritage in European Community Discourse', in P. Graves-Brown, S. Jones, and C. Gamble (eds), *Cultural Identity and Archaeology: The Construction of European Communities*, (London and New York, 1996), pp. 96–115 and Wood,

Stephen, 'A Classical Heritage?: Perspectives on "Europe" as Cultural Entity', in U. E. Beitter (ed), *The New Europe at the Crossroads: Europe's Classical Heritage in the Twenty-First Century* (New York, 2001), pp. 323–339. Also Webster, Jane, 'Ethnographic barbarity: colonial discourse and "Celtic warrior societies"', in J. Webster and N. J. Cooper (eds), *Roman Imperialism: Post-Colonial Perspectives*, Leicester Archaeology Monographs No 3, (Leicester, 1996), pp. 111–123.

205 Williams: *Beyond the Rubicon*, pp. 13–14.
206 Murdoch, Adrian, 'Germania Romana', in B. Murdoch and M. Read, (eds) *Early Germanic Literature and Culture* (Rochester, 2004), p. 60. Also Wells, Peter S., 'Manufactured Objects and the Construction of Identities in Late La Tene Europe', *Eirene* 31 (1995), pp. 129–150.
207 Woolf, Greg, *Becoming Roman: The Origins of Provincial Civilization in Gaul* (Cambridge and New York, 1998), p. 32.
208 Williams: *Beyond the Rubicon*, p. 127.
209 Tacitus, *Annals*, 11.23–25.1.
210 Ruggini: 'Intolerance', p. 192. Caesar briefly describes the Britons at 5.12–14. Later, Tacitus provides his own ethnography of Britain at *Agricola*, 10–12.
211 Caesar, *Gallic Wars*, 6. 11.
212 Caesar, *Gallic Wars*, 6. 13–15.
213 Caesar, *Gallic Wars*, 6. 16–20.
214 Caesar, *Gallic Wars*, 6. 21–23.
215 Caesar, *Gallic Wars*, 24.
216 See the three volume exhibition catalogue, *2000 Jahre Varusschlacht*, (Stuttgart, 2009).
217 Suetonius, *Augustus*, 23.
218 Murdoch: 'Germania Romana', p. 57.
219 Murdoch: 'Germania Romana', pp. 58–60.
220 Tacitus, *Annals*, 1.62.
221 Tacitus, *Germania*, 1–27.
222 Tacitus, *Germania*, 28–46.
223 Tacitus, *Germania*, 2–4.
224 Isaac: *Invention*, pp. 436, 498–499, and 515.
225 Saddington: 'Race Relations', pp. 114–15. See also Baldry, H.C., *The Unity of Mankind in Greek Thought* (Cambridge, 1965).
226 Although Kevin Osterloh (work in progress) discusses the mobilization of the notion of a 'human race' by Nicolaus of Damascus in response to Roman rule.
227 King, Martin Luther, Jr., 'I Have a Dream', repr. in J. M. Washington (ed), *I Have a Dream: Writings and Speeches that Changed the World*, (San Francisco, 1992), p. 102.

Chapter II

1 Achebe, Chinua, 'Named for Victoria, Queen of England', *New Letters*, 40.1 (1973), pp. 17–18.
2 Achebe: 'Named for Victoria', p 17.
3 Cassius Dio, *Roman History*, 52.15. Trans. I. Scott-Kilvert.
4 de Certeau, Michel, *The Practice of Everyday Life*, trans. S. Rendall (Berkeley, Los Angeles, and London, 1984), p. 36.

5   de Certeau: *Practice*, pp. 37 and 38–39.

6   McClintock, Anne, *Imperial Leather: Race, Gender and Sexuality in the Colonial Context*, (New York and London, 1995), p. 15.

7   Woolf: 'Becoming Roman, Staying Greek', p. 130.

8   See Hides, Shaun, 'The Genealogy of Material Culture and Cultural Identity', in P. Graves-Brown, S. Jones, and C. Gamble (eds): *Cultural Identity and Archaeology*, pp. 25–47.

9   For a useful overview of the term's use, see Hingley, Richard, *Globalizing Roman Culture: Unity, diversity and empire* (London and New York, 2005), pp. 14–18. Applied to ancient evidence, see, for example: MacMullen, Ramsay, *Romanization in the Time of Augustus*, (New Haven and London, 2000) and Keay, Simon and Nicola Terrenato (eds), *Italy and the West: Comparative Issues in Romanization*, (Oxford, 2001).

10 Mattingly, David, 'Cultural Crossovers: Global and Local Identities in the Classical World,' in S. Hales and T. Hodos (eds), *Material Culture and Social Identities in the Ancient World* (Cambridge and New York, 2010), pp. 285–86.

11 For a response to such assumptions, Cooper, Nicholas J., 'Searching for the blank generation: consumer choice in Roman and post-Roman Britain', in Webster and Cooper: *Roman Imperialism*, pp. 85–98.

12 Hingley: *Globalizing Roman Culture*, p. 15. For a related look at Roman archaeology in the Maghreb, see Mattingly, David J., 'From one colonialism to another: imperialism and the Magreb,' in Webster and Cooper: *Roman Imperialism*, pp. 49–69.

13 Hingley: *Globalizing Roman Culture*, p. 30.

14 Laurence: 'Introduction', p. 2. See also Revell, Louise, *Roman Imperialism and Local Identities*, (Cambridge and New York, 2009) and Millar, Fergus, 'Local Cultures in the Roman Empire: Libyan, Punic and Latin in Roman Africa', *Journal of Roman Studies* 58 (1968), pp. 126–134.

15 Antonaccio, Carla M., '(Re)defining Ethnicity: Culture, Material Culture, and Identity,' in Hales and Hodos: *Material Culture and Social Identities*, p. 38.

16 See, for example, Shennan, Stephen, 'Introduction: Archaeological Approaches to Cultural Identity', in S. Shennan (ed), *Archaeological Approaches to Cultural Identity*, (London, 1989), pp. 5–14. 'Ethnic style' performs a similar function; see Pasztory, Esther, 'Identity and Difference: The Uses and Meanings of Ethnic Styles', in S. J. Barnes and W. S. Melion (eds), *Cultural Differentiation and Cultural Identity in the Visual Arts*, (Hanover and London, 1989), pp. 15–38. For another potential source of bias in archaeological interpretation, see Nixon, Lucia, 'Gender Bias in Archaeology', in L. J. Archer, S. Fischler, and M. Wyke (eds), *Women in Ancient Societies: An Illusion of the Night*, (New York, 1994), pp. 1–23.

17 See Shennan: "Introduction: Archaeological Approaches', pp. 1–32 and Jones, Siân, *The Archaelogy of Ethnicity: Constructing Identities in the Past and Present*, (London and New York, 1997).

18 See Lomas, Kathryn, 'Urban elites and cultural definition: Romanization in southern Italy', in T. Cornell and K. Lomas (eds), *Urban Society in Roman Italy* (New York, 1995), pp. 107–120 and Brunt, P.A., 'The Romanization of the Local Ruling Classes in the Roman Empire' in *Roman Imperial Themes*, (Oxford, 1990), pp. 267–281.

19 Hall: *Ethnic Identity*, p. 3.

20 Hall: *Ethnic Identity*, p. 182.

21 See initial reactions to Hall's work, including his response, at 'Review Feature', *Cambridge Archaeological Journal* 8.2 (1998), pp. 265–283.

22 Antonaccio, Carla M., 'Ethnicity and Colonization', in Malkin: *Ancient Perceptions*, p. 125.

23 Green: 'Alexander's Alexandria', pp. 3–25.

24 For one account, Turner, Eric, 'The Graeco-Roman Branch', in T.G.H. James (ed), *Excavating in Egypt: The Egypt Exploration Society 1882–1982*, (London, 1982), pp. 161–178. Also Bianchi, Robert S., 'From Dusk to Dawn: The American Discovery of Ptolemaic and Roman Egypt', in N. Thomas (ed), *The American Discovery of Ancient Egypt*, (Los Angeles, 1996), pp. 131–139.

25 Reynolds, Margaret, *The Sappho Companion*, (New York, 2000), pp. 19–20.

26 For discussion of how papyri can be integrated into historical studies, see Hobson, Deborah, 'Towards a Broader Context of the Study of Greco-Roman Egypt', *Echos du Monde Classique* 33, n.s. 7 (1988), pp. 353–363.

27 For an excellent and engaging introduction to the discipline of papyrology, see Hanson, Ann Ellis, 'Papyrology: Minding Other People's Business', *Transactions of the American Philological Association* 131 (2001), pp. 297–313.

28 Morris, R. L. B., 'Reflections of Citizen Attitudes in Petitions from Roman Oxyrhynchus', in R.S. Bagnall, G. M. Browne, A. E. Hanson, and L. Koenen (eds), *Proceedings of the Sixteenth International Congress of Papyrology, New York, 24–31 July 1980*, American Studies in Papyrology, vol. 23, (Chico, 1981), pp. 363–370.

29 Ritner, Robert K., 'Implicit Models of Cross-Cultural Interaction: A Question of Noses, Soap, and Prejudice,' in J. H. Johnson, (ed), *Life in a Multi-Cultural Society: Egypt from Cambyses to Constantine and Beyond*, Studies in Ancient Oriental Civilization, no. 51 (Chicago, 1992), p. 286. For Rostovtzeff's views: Rostovtzeff, M., 'Roman Exploitation of Egypt in the First Century A.D.,' *Journal of Economic and Business History* 1 (1929), pp. 337–364.

30 Summarized at Bagnall, Roger S., 'Decolonizing Ptolemaic Egypt', in P. Cartledge, P. Garnsey, and E. Gruen (eds), *Hellenistic Constructs: Essays in Culture, History, and Historiography* (Berkeley, Los Angeles, and London, 1997), pp. 225–28.

31 A succinct outline of the modern meanings can be found at Horvath, Ronald J., 'A Definition of Colonialism', *Current Anthropology* 13.1 (1972), pp. 45–57. For more discussion of the differences between ancient and modern colonialism, Hurst, Henry and Sara Owen (eds), *Ancient Colonizations: Analogy, Similarity and Difference*, (London, 2005).

32 Bagnall: 'Decolonizing Ptolemaic Egypt', p. 228.

33 Bagnall: 'Decolonizing Ptolemaic Egypt', pp. 229–231.

34 Green: 'Alexander's Alexandria', pp. 3–25; also Thompson, Dorothy J., 'Alexandria: The City By The Sea,' *Alexandrian Studies II in Honour of Mostafa El Abbadi*, Sociéte D'Archéologie D'Alexandrie Bulletin 46, (Alexandria, 2001), pp. 73–79.

35 For a close reading of the term, see Bell, H. I., 'Alexandria ad Aegyptum', *Journal of Roman Studies* 36 (1946), pp. 130–32.

36 Bagnall: 'Decolonizing Ptolemaic Egypt', pp. 231 and 238–239.

37 Thompson, Dorothy J., *Memphis Under the Ptolemies*, (Princeton, 1988), pp. 82–105.

38 On Ptolemaic Egypt as an 'expatriate society', see Selden, Daniel L., 'Alibis', *Classical Antiquity* 17.2 (1998), pp. 290–300.

39 Samuel, A. E., 'The Ptolemies and the Ideology of Kingship', in P. Green (ed), *Hellenistic History and Culture*, (Berkeley, Los Angeles and Oxford, 1993), p. 175.

40 Bagnall, Roger S., 'Greeks and Egyptians: Ethnicity, Status, and Culture,' in *Cleopatra's Egypt: Age of the Ptolemies*, (Brooklyn?, 1988), p. 21.

41 Ritner: 'Implicit Models', pp. 286–287.

42 Azoulay, Katya Gibel, 'Outside Our Parents' House: Race, Culture, and Identity', *Research in African Literatures* 27.1 (1996), p. 134.

43 Michaels, Walter Benn, 'Race into Culture: A Critical Genealogy of Cultural Identity', repr. in K. A. Appiah and H. L. Gates, Jr., (eds), *Identities* (Chicago and London, 1995), pp. 61–62.

44 For an introduction to what is at stake in the term, see Hall, Stuart and Paul du Gay (eds), *Questions of Cultural Identity*, (London, Thousand Oaks, and New Delhi, 1996).

45 Bagnall: 'Greeks and Egyptians', p. 24.

46 Willy Clarysse considers important dedications from Greek individuals to Egyptian gods at Clarysse, Willy, 'Some Greeks in Egypt', in Johnson: *Life in a Multi-Cultural Society*, p. 53.

47 Bowman, Alan K., *Egypt after the Pharaohs, 332 BC-AD 642*, (Berkeley and Los Angeles, 1986), pp. 175–176.

48 Bowman: *Egypt after the Pharaohs*, p. 188.

49 For this image in wider context (including a gendered analysis), see Venit, Marjorie Susan, 'The Stagni Painted Tomb: Cultural Interchange and Gender Differentiation in Roman Alexandria', *American Journal of Archaeology* 103.4 (1999), pp. 641–669.

50 Lewis, Naphtali, *Greeks in Ptolemaic Egypt: Case Studies in the Social History of the Hellenistic World*, (Oakville, 2001), p. 32; also Manning, J. G., *Land and Power in Ptolemaic Egypt: The Structure of Land Tenure*, (Cambridge and New York, 2003).

51 Cribiore, Raffaella, *Gymnastics of the Mind: Greek Education in Hellenistic and Roman Egypt*, (Princeton and Oxford, 2001), p. 3.

52 Cribiore: *Gymnastics of the Mind*, pp. 22–23. See also Tassier, Emmanuel, 'Greek and Demotic School-Exercises,' in Johnson: *Life in a Multi-Cultural Society*, pp. 311–315 and Clarysse, Willy, 'Egyptian Scribes Writing Greek' *Chronique D'' Egypte* 68 (1993), pp. 187–188.

53 Quoted at Cribiore: *Gymnastics of the Mind*, p. 23.

54 Dean, Mitchell, *Governmentality: Power and Rule in Modern Society* (London, Thousand Oaks, and New Delhi, 1999), p. 32.

55 Goldberg: *Racial Subjects*, p. 30.

56 Goldberg: *Racial Subjects*, p. 34.

57 Goldberg: *Racial Subjects*, p. 39.

58 Goldberg: *Racial Subjects*, p. 32.

59 Roberts, Sam and Peter Baker, 'Asked to Declare His Race for Census, Obama Checks "Black", *New York Times* April 3, 2010, section A, col. 0, p. 9.

60 Thompson, Dorothy, J., 'The Infrastructure of Splendour: Census and Taxes in Ptolemaic Egypt', in Cartledge, Garnsey and Gruen: *Hellenistic Constructs*, pp. 243–44.

61 Beard and Crawford: *Rome in the Late Republic*, pp. 42–47.

62 Thompson: 'Infrastructure of Splendour', p. 244. The Ptolemaic documents have been published in two volumes: Clarysse, Willy, Dorothy Thompson, *et al.*, *Counting the People in Hellenistic Egypt*, (Cambridge and New York, 2004). For the Roman period, see Bagnall, Roger S. and Bruce W. Frier, *The Demography of Roman Egypt*, (Cambridge and New York, 1994).

63 Clarysse, Willy, 'Greeks and Persians in a bilingual census list', *Egitto e Vicino Oriente* 17 (1994), pp. 75–76.

64 Clarysse: 'Some Greeks in Egypt', p. 52.
65 Thompson: 'Infrastructure of Splendour', p. 247.
66 Thompson: 'Infrastructure of Splendour', pp. 246–247.
67 Thompson: 'Infrastructure of Splendour', p. 248.
68 Quoted at Ritner: 'Implicit Models', p. 290.
69 Dean: *Governmentality*, p. 32.
70 Thompson, Dorothy J., 'Literacy and Power in Ptolemaic Egypt', in A. K. Bowman and G. Woolf (eds), *Literacy and Power in the Ancient World*, (Cambridge, 1994), pp. 72–73.
71 Thompson: 'Literacy and power', p. 82.
72 Shipley, Graham, *The Greek World After Alexander 323–30 BC*, (London and New York, 2000), p. 211.
73 Bagnall: 'Greeks and Egyptians', p. 22.
74 Discussed briefly at Koenen, Ludwig, 'The Ptolemaic King as a Religious Figure', in A. Bulloch, E. S. Gruen, A. A. Long, and A. Stewart (eds), *Images and Ideologies: Self-definition in the Hellenistic World*, (Berkeley, Los Angeles, and London, 1993), pp. 37–38.
75 Lewis: *Greeks in Ptolemaic Egypt*, p. 60.
76 Lewis: *Greeks in Ptolemaic Egypt*, p. 61.
77 Lewis: *Greeks in Ptolemaic Egypt*, p. 85.
78 Lewis: *Greeks in Ptolemaic Egypt*, p. 86.
79 Thompson, Dorothy J., 'Literacy and the Administration in Early Ptolemaic Egypt', in Johnson: *Life in a Multi-Cultural Society*, p. 326.
80 Clarysse, Willy, 'Greeks and Egyptians in the Ptolemaic Army and Administration', *Aegyptus* 65 (1985), pp. 58–60.
81 Lewis: *Greeks in Ptolemaic Egypt*, p. 121.
82 See the discussion following Samuel: 'Ptolemies and Ideology', pp. 207–209.
83 Clarysse: 'Ptolemaic Army and Administration', p. 60.
84 Miles, Gary B., 'The First Roman Marriage and the Theft of the Sabine Women', in R. Hexter and D. Selden (eds), *Innovations of Antiquity*, (New York and London, 1992), pp. 161–196.
85 Montserrat, Dominic, *Sex and Society in Graeco-Roman Egypt*, (London and New York, 1996), pp. 89–91. Also Shaw, Brent D., 'Explaining Incest: Brother-Sister Marriage in Graeco-Roman Egypt', *Man* 27.2 (1992), pp. 267–299.
86 Thompson, Dorothy J, 'Families in Early Ptolemaic Egypt' in Ogden: *The Hellenistic World*, pp. 140–43.
87 Thompson: 'Families in Early Ptolemaic Egypt', pp. 142 and 149–53.
88 See Massey, Douglas S. and R. J. Sampson (eds), *The Moynihan Report revisited: lessons and reflections after four decades* (Thousand Oaks, California, 2009).
89 Montserrat: *Sex and Society*, p. 87.
90 Lewis: *Greeks in Ptolemaic Egypt*, pp. 27–28.
91 Thompson: 'Families in Early Ptolemaic Egypt', p. 153.
92 Lewis: *Greeks in Ptolemaic Egypt*, p. 28.
93 Ritner: 'Implicit Models', p. 289.
94 Bagnall: 'Greeks and Egyptians', p. 21.
95 Lewis: *Greeks in Ptolemaic Egypt*, pp. 88–101.
96 Lewis: *Greeks in Ptolemaic Egypt*, p. 103.
97 Pomeroy, Sarah, 'Women in Roman Egypt: A Preliminary Study Based on Papyri', in H.P. Foley (ed), *Reflections of Women in Antiquity*, (New York, London, and

Paris, 1981), pp. 317–318 and Hobson, Deborah, 'The Role of Women in the Economic Life of Roman Egypt: A Case Study from First Century Tebtunis', *Echos du Monde Classique* 28.3 (1984), pp. 389–390. A more general overview can be found at Rowlandson, Jane, 'Gender and Cultural Identity in Roman Egypt', in F. McHardy and E. Marshall (eds), *Women's Influence on Classical Civilization*, (London and New York, 2004), pp. 151–166. Original sources pertaining to women in both periods have been collected in Rowlandson, Jane (ed), *Women and Society in Greek and Roman Egypt*, (Cambridge and New York, 1998).

98   Smyth, Gerry, 'The Politics of Hybridity: Some Problems with Crossing the Border', in A. Bery and P. Murray (eds), *Comparing Postcolonial Literatures: Dislocations* (New York, 2000), p. 52.

99   See McCoskey, Denise, 'Race Before "Whiteness": Studying Identity in Ptolemaic Egypt', *Critical Sociology* 28 (2002), pp. 13–39.

100   Bowman, Alan K. and D. Rathbone, 'Cities and Administration in Roman Egypt', *Journal of Roman Studies* 82 (1992), p. 111. Rostovtzeff: 'Roman Exploitation' pp. 337–364.

101   Cassius Dio, *Roman History*, 57.10.5.

102   Lewis, Naphtali, '*Merismos Anakechorekoton*: An Aspect of Roman Oppression in Egypt', repr. in *On Government and Law in Roman Egypt: Collected Papers of Naphtali Lewis*, (Atlanta 1995), pp. 1–13 and Lewis, Naphtali, 'A Reversal of Tax Policy in Roman Egypt' repr. in *On Government and Law*, pp. 357–374.

103   Rostovtzeff: 'Roman Exploitation', pp. 363–364.

104   Quoted at Lewis, Naphtali, *Life in Egypt under Roman Rule*, (Atlanta, 1999), p. 202.

105   Quoted at Lewis: *Life in Egypt*, p. 202.

106   Lewis: *Life in Egypt*, p. 31.

107   Wallace-Hadrill, Andrew, 'Family and Inheritance in the Augustan Marriage Laws,' *Proceedings of the Cambridge Philological Society* n.s. 27 (1981), pp. 58–80. For a general introduction to Roman marriage, see Treggiari, Susan, *Roman Marriage: Iusti Coniuges from the Time of Cicero to the Time of Ulpian* (Oxford, 1991).

108   Lewis: *Life in Egypt*, p. 32.

109   On 'passing', see, for example, Appiah, Kwame Anthony, 'Reconstructing Racial Identities,' *Research in African Literatures* 27.3 (1996), p. 69.

110   Selections from the document appear in English translation at Lewis, Naphtali and Meyer Reinhold (eds), *Roman Civilization: Selected Readings, Volume II: the Empire*, third edition (New York, 1990), pp. 298–302.

111   Isaac: *Invention*, pp. 305, 315–316, and 322.

112   Lewis: *Life in Egypt*, pp. 19–25.

113   Richard Alston, *Soldier and Society in Roman Egypt: A social history* (London and New York, 1995), pp. 121–123 and 139.

114   Alston: *Soldier and Society*, p. 141.

115   Alston: *Soldier and Society*, pp. 139 and 141–142.

116   Alston: *Soldier and Society*, p. 130.

117   Alston: *Soldier and Society*, p. 128.

118   Alston: *Soldier and Society*, p. 136.

119   Alston: *Soldier and Society*, p. 127.

120   Balsdon: *Romans and Aliens*, p. 72; also Campbell, Brian, 'The Marriage of Soldiers Under the Empire', *Journal of Roman Studies* 68 (1978), pp. 153–166 and Cherry, David, 'Marriage and Acculturation in Roman Algeria', *Classical*

Philology 92.1 (1997), pp. 71–83. For brief discussion of soldiers marrying within group, see Noy, David, *Foreigners at Rome: Citizens and Strangers*, (London, 2000), p. 83, n. 90. For attitudes towards other 'boundary-crossing' marriages, see Evans-Grubbs, Judith, '"Marriage More Shameful Than Adultery": Slave-Mistress Relationships, "Mixed Marriages," and Late Roman Law', *Phoenix* 47.2 (1993), pp. 125–154.

121 Horace, *Odes*, 3.5.5–12.

122 Young, Robert, 'Egypt in America: *Black Athena*, Racism and Colonial Discourse,' in A. Rattansi and S. Westwood (eds), *Racism, Modernity and Identity: On the Western Front*, (Cambridge, 1994), p. 167.

123 Vasunia, Phiroze, 'Greater Rome and Greater Britain,' in B. Goff (ed), *Classics and Colonialism*, (London, 2005), p. 51.

124 Kleiner, Diana E. E., *Cleopatra and Rome*, (Cambridge, Massachusetts and London, 2005), p. 159; cf. Plutarch, *Life of Antony*, 87.1 and Cassius Dio, *Roman History*, 51.15.

125 Juvenal, *Satires*, 6. 597–601 and Martial, *Epigrams*, 6. 39.

126 Balsdon: *Romans and Aliens*, p. 218. Cf. Pliny, *Natural History*, 7.12.51, which comments on the Ethiopian appearance of the boxer Nicaeus, whose mother (although not herself showing it in her appearance) had allegedly been born from an adulterous union with an Ethiopian.

127 Pliny, *Letters*, 10. 5–7.

128 Bowman and Rathbone, 'Cities and Administration', pp. 120ff.

129 Dio Chrysostom, *Discourses*, 32. 36–40.

130 Aelius Aristides, *To Rome*, xi–xiii.

131 Martial, *Epigrams*, 7. 30.

132 de Certeau: *Practice*, p. 94.

133 See also Dyson, Stephen L., *Rome: A Living Portrait of an Ancient City* (Baltimore, 2010), Coulston, J. and H. Dodge (eds), *Ancient Rome: The Archaeology of the Eternal City*, Oxford University School of Archaeology Monograph 54, (Oxford, 2000), Parkins, Helen (ed), *Roman Urbanism: Beyond the Consumer City*, (London and New York, 1997), and Stambaugh, John E., *The Ancient Roman City*, (Baltimore and London, 1988).

134 Noy: *Foreigners at Rome*, p. 16. For more extensive treatment of ancient population estimates, see Scheidel, Walter, 'Demography', in W. Scheidel, I. Morris, and R. Saller (eds), *The Cambridge Economic History of the Greco-Roman World*, (Cambridge and New York, 2007), pp. 38–86.

135 On the racial origin of slaves in Rome, see MacMullen, Ramsay, 'The Unromanized in Rome', in S. J. D. Cohen and E. S. Frerichs (eds), *Diasporas in Antiquity*, (Atlanta, 1993), pp. 49–51.

136 See Noy: *Foreigners at Rome*, pp. 53–84, for detailed discussion of immigration to Rome and pp. 205–284 for the different groups residing in Rome.

137 Balsdon: *Romans and Aliens*, p. 16; although cf. Lott, J. Bert, *The Neighborhoods of Augustan Rome*, (Cambridge, 2004), pp. 22–23. See also Noy, David, 'Being an Egyptian in Rome: Strategies of Identity Formation', in J. Zangenberg and M. Labahn (eds), *Christians as a Religious Minority in a Multicultural City*, Journal for the Study of the New Testament Supplement Series 243, (London and New York, 2004), pp. 47–54. For a comprehensive account of Rome's topography, see Richardson, L., jr, *A New Topographical Dictionary of Ancient Rome*, (Baltimore, 1992).

138 Seneca, *On Consolation to Helvia*, 6.2–4. But cf. Martial's short epigram in which

a 'barbarian basket' has come from Britain, but now Rome prefers to call it 'its own' (*suam*), *Epigrams*, 14.99.

139 Wyke, Maria, 'Augustan Cleopatras: Female Power and Poetic Authority', in A. Powell (ed), *Roman Poetry and Propaganda in the Age of Augustus*, (London, 1992), p. 107. Also Solmsen, Friedrich, *Isis Among the Greeks and Romans*, (Cambridge, 1979).

140 Balsdon: *Romans and Aliens*, pp. 106–108.

141 Gruen, Erich S., *Diaspora: Jews amidst Greeks and Romans*, (Cambridge, Massachusetts and London, 2002), pp. 29–41. Also Rutgers, Leonard Victor, 'Roman Policy towards the Jews: Expulsions from the City of Rome during the First Century CE', *Classical Antiquity* 13.1 (1994), pp. 56–74.

142 Noy: *Foreigners at Rome*, p. 159.

143 MacMullen: 'Unromanized in Rome', pp. 47–48.

144 Juvenal, *Satires*, 3. 60–61.

145 Shumate, Nancy, *Nation, Empire, Decline: Studies in Rhetorical Continuity from the Romans to the Modern Era*, (London, 2006), p. 136.

146 Juvenal, *Satires*, 3.13–16.

147 Juvenal, *Satires*, 6. 542–47.

148 Juvenal. *Satires*, 14. 96–106.

149 MacMullen: 'Unromanized in Rome', p. 54. See also Williams, Margaret H., 'The Shaping of the Identity of the Jewish Community in Rome in Antiquity', in Zangenberg and Labahn: *Christians as a Religious Minority*, pp. 33–46.

150 Cicero, *On Behalf of Flaccus*, 66–69. Cf. Gruen: *Diaspora*, pp. 19–22.

151 Cohen, Shaye J. D., *The Beginnings of Jewishness: Boundaries, Varieties, Uncertainties*, (Berkeley, Los Angeles, and London, 1999), pp. 70–82.

152 Sherwin-White: *Racial Prejudice*, p. 99.

153 Cohen: *Beginnings*, p. 52. To put the protection of the male citizen body in greater relief, see Edwards, Catharine, 'Unspeakable Professions: Public Performance and Prostitution in Ancient Rome', in J. P. Hallett and M. B. Skinner (eds), *Roman Sexualities*, (Princeton, 1997), pp. 66–95.

154 Gilman, Sander L., 'The Visibility of the Jew in the Diaspora: Body Imagery and Its Cultural Context', in A. L. Berger (ed), *Judaism in the Modern World*, (New York and London, 1994), p. 91.

155 Cohen: *Beginnings*, p. 28.

156 Schäfer, Peter, *Judeophobia: Attitudes toward the Jews in the Ancient World*, (Cambridge and London, 1997), pp. 9 and 34–118.

157 Cohen: *Beginnings*, pp. 67–68.

158 Cohen, Shaye J. D., '"Those Who Say They Are Jews and Are Not": How Do You Know a Jew in Antiquity When You See One?', in Cohen and Frerichs: *Diasporas in Antiquity*, p. 41.

159 For a discussion of the importance of Jewish synagogues in the diaspora, see, for example, Rajak, Tessa, 'Synagogue and Community in the Graeco-Roman Diaspora,' in J. R. Bartlett (ed), *Jews in the Hellenistic and Roman Cities*, (London and New York, 2002), pp. 22–38. Also Fine, Steven (ed), *Sacred Realm: The Emergence of the Synagogue in the Ancient World*, (New York and Oxford, 1996).

160 Suetonius, *Domitian*, 12.

161 Cohen: *Beginnings*, pp. 39–49.

162 Barclay, John M. G., *Jews in the Mediterranean Diaspora: From Alexander to Trajan (323 BCE–117 CE)* (Berkeley, Los Angeles, and London, 1996), p. 77.

163   Cohen: *Beginnings*, p. 68.

164   Cohen: *Beginnings*, pp. 156–174. Also Goodman, Martin, *Mission and Conversion: Proselytizing in the Religious History of the Roman Empire*, (Oxford, 1994).

165   Cohen: *Beginnings*, p. 27.

166   Gruen: *Diaspora*, p. 2. See also McCoskey, Denise Eileen, 'Diaspora in the Reading of Jewish History, Identity, and Difference', *Diaspora* 12.3 (2003), pp. 387–418; for a more extensive treatment, Barclay: *Jews in the Mediterranean Diaspora* and Collins, John J., *Between Athens and Jerusalem: Jewish Identity in the Hellenistic Diaspora*, (New York, 1986); and for original sources, Williams, Margaret H. (ed), *The Jews among the Greeks & Romans: A Diasporan Sourcebook* (Baltimore, 1998) and Feldman, Louis H. and Meyer Reinhold (eds), *Jewish Life and Thought among Greeks and Romans: Primary Readings*, (Minneapolis, 1996).

167   Gruen, Erich S., 'Jewish Perspectives on Greek Culture and Ethnicity', in Malkin: *Ancient Perceptions*, p. 348. Also Gruen, Erich. S., *Heritage and Hellenism: The Reinvention of Jewish Tradition* (Berkeley, Los Angeles, and London, 1998).

168   Gruen: *Diaspora*, pp. 106–108. See also Smallwood, E. Mary, 'The Jews in Egypt and Cyrenaica during the Ptolemaic and Roman Periods', in Thompson and Ferguson: *Africa in Classical Antiquity*, pp. 110–131.

169   Lewis: *Greeks in Ptolemaic Egypt*, p. 117. See also Hanson, Ann Ellis, 'Egyptians, Greeks, Romans, *Arabes*, and *Ioudaioi* in the First Century A.D. Tax Archive from Philadelphia: P. Mich. inv. 880 Recto and *P. Princ.* III 152 Revised,' in Johnson: *Life in a Multi-Cultural Society*, pp. 133–145.

170   Bartlett, John R., *Jews in the Hellenistic World: Josephus, Aristeas, The Sibylline Oracles, Eupolemus*, Cambridge Commentaries on Writings of the Jewish and Christian World 200 BC to AD 200, vol. I.i, (Cambridge and New York, 1985), pp. 11–34.

171   See, for example, Buell, Denise Kimber *Why this new race: ethnic reasoning in early Christianity* (New York, 2005). For more discussion of the complexity of Egypt in later antiquity, especially following the advent of Christianity, see Bagnall, Roger S., *Egypt in Late Antiquity*, (Princeton, 1993) and Gagos, Traianos and Peter van Minnen, *Settling a Dispute: Toward a Legal Anthropology of Late Antique Egypt*, (Ann Arbor, 1994).

172   Strabo, *Geography*, 17.1.12.

173   Ritner: 'Implicit Models', pp. 287–288.

174   Philo, *Against Flaccus*, 55.

175   Barclay: *Jews in the Mediterranean Diaspora*, pp. 64–66.

176   Kasher, Aryeh, 'The Civic Status of the Jews in Ptolemaic Egypt', in P. Bilde, T. Engberg-Pedersen, L. Hannestad, and J. Zahle (eds), *Ethnicity in Hellenistic Egypt* (Aarhus, 1992), p. 112.

177   Macrobius, *Saturnalia*, 2.4.11. Gruen notes that the pun was presumably originally made in Greek, where the words 'pig' and 'son' are much closer in sound, Gruen: *Diaspora*, p. 276, n. 240.

178   Narrated at length in Philo, *Against Flaccus*. See also Pearce, Sarah J. K., *The Land of the Body: Studies in Philo's Representation of Egypt*, (Tübingen, 2007) and Borgen, Peder, 'Philo and the Jews in Alexandria', in Bilde, Engberg-Pedersen, Hannestad, Zahle: *Ethnicity in Hellenistic Egypt*, pp. 122–138.

179   Philo, *Against Flaccus*, 54 and 78–81.

180   Philo, *Against Flaccus*, 108–191.

181   See Rives, James, B., 'Diplomacy and Identity among Jews and Christians', in

C. Eilers (ed), *Diplomats and Diplomacy in the Roman World*, (Leiden and Boston, 2009), pp. 99–126.

182   Translations from Lewis, Napthali and Meyer Reinhold (eds), *Roman Civilization: Selected Readings, volume II, the Empire*, third edition, (New York, 1990), pp. 285–288.

183   On anti-Semitism in antiquity generally, begin with Schäfer: *Judeophobia* and Feldman, Louis H., *Jew and Gentile in the Ancient World: Attitudes and Interactions from Alexander to Justinian*, (Princeton, 1993). Also Stern, Sacha, 'Dissonance and Misunderstanding in Jewish-Roman Relations', in M. Goodman (ed), *Jews in a Graeco-Roman World*, (Oxford, 1998), pp. 241–250.

184   Berlin, Andrea M. and J. Andrew Overman, 'Introduction', in A. M. Berlin and J. A. Overman (eds), *The First Jewish Revolt: Archaeology, history, and ideology* (London and New York, 2002), pp. 5–6.

185   Gruen: *Diaspora*, p. 6.

186   Barclay: *Jews in the Mediterranean Diaspora*, pp. 78–81.

187   Bowman: *Egypt after the Pharaohs*, p. 43.

188   See: Rutgers, Leonard Victor, *The Jews in Late Ancient Rome: Evidence of Cultural Interaction in the Roman Diaspora*, (Leiden, 2000).

189   Musurillo, Herbert A., *The Acts of the Pagan Martyrs Acta Alexandrinorum* (Oxford, 1954). Also Lewis: *Life in Egypt*, pp. 198–201.

190   For Alexandria in later eras, Haas, Christopher, *Alexandria in Late Antiquity: Topography and Social Conflict*, (Baltimore and London, 1997).

191   Gruen: *Diaspora*, pp. 63–65.

192   On Exodus narratives, see Gruen: *Heritage and Hellenism*, pp. 41–72.

193   Griffiths, J. Gwyn, 'Apocalyptic in the Hellenistic Era,' in D. Hellholm (ed), *Apocalypticism in the Mediterranean World and the Near East*, second edition (Tübingen, 1989), p. 273.

194   Kerkeslager, Allen, 'The Apology of the Potter: A Translation of the Potter's Oracle' in I. Shirun-Grumach (ed), *Jerusalem Studies in Egyptology* (Wiesbaden, 1998), pp. 67–79.

195   Johnson, Janet, 'Is the Demotic Chronicle an Anti-Greek Tract?" in H.-J. Thissen and K.-Th. Zauzich (eds), *Grammata Demotika: Festschrift für Erich Lüddeckens zum. 15. Juni 1983*, (Würzburg, 1984), pp. 107–124.

196   Griffiths: 'Apocalyptic', pp. 279–290. See also Sorensen, Jorgen Podemann, 'Native Reactions to Foreign Rule and Culture in Religious Literature,' in Bilde, Engberg-Pedersen, Hannestad, and Zahle: *Ethnicity in Hellenistic Egypt*, pp. 164–181.

197   Gruen, Erich S., 'Jews, Greeks and Romans in the Third Sibylline Oracle', in Goodman: *Jews in a Graeco-Roman World*, pp. 24–36. See also Bartlett: *Jews in the Hellenistic World*, pp. 35–55.

198   Scott, James C., *Domination and the Arts of Resistance: Hidden Transcripts*, (New Haven and London, 1990), p. 86.

199   See also discussion at Toney, Jerry, *Popular Culture in Ancient Rome* (Cambridge and Malden, Massachusetts, 2009), pp. 162–84.

200   Strabo, *Geography*, 8.6.18.

201   Strabo, *Geography*, 8.6.23.

202   Lewis: *Greeks in Ptolemaic Egypt*, p. 165, n. 6.

203   Bagnall: 'Decolonizing Ptolemaic Egypt', pp. 237–38.

204   Lewis: *Greeks in Ptolemaic Egypt*, p. 116.

205   Shipley: *Greek World*, pp. 203–205.

206 Polybius, *Histories*, 5.107. 1–3; Translation from Shipley: *Greek World*, p. 204.

207 Smyth: 'The Politics of Hybridity', p. 53.

208 For example, MacMullen, Ramsay, 'Nationalism in Roman Egypt', *Aegyptus* 44 (1964), pp. 179–199.

209 S. L. Dyson, 'Native Revolts in the Roman Empire', *Historia* 20 (1971), p. 239.

210 Dyson: 'Native Revolts', pp. 239–240.

211 Hingley, Richard, *Roman Officers and English Gentlemen: The Imperial Origins of Roman Archaeology*, (London and New York, 2000), pp. 73–81.

212 Goodman, Martin, 'Opponents of Rome: Jews and Others', in L. Alexander (ed), *Images of Empire*, Journal for the Study of the Old Testament Supplement Series 122 (Sheffield, 1991), pp. 224–225. Josephus' *Jewish War* is a crucial ancient account of the wars, although Josephus' point of view was strongly informed by his own activities during that time. See Mader, Gottfried, *Josephus and the Politics of Historiography: Apologetic and Impression Management in the Bellum Judaicum*, (Leiden, Boston, and Köln, 2000).

213 See Ben-Yehuda, Nachman, *The Masada Myth: Collective Memory and Mythmaking in Israel* (Madison, 1995) and Zerubavel, Yael, 'The Death of Memory and the Memory of Death: Masada and the Holocaust as Historical Metaphors', *Representations* 45 (1994), pp. 72–100.

214 See Urbainczyk, Theresa, *Slave Revolts in Antiquity* (Berkeley and Los Angeles, 2008) and Bradley, Keith R., *Slavery and Rebellion in the Roman World 140 B.C.– 70 B.C.*, (Bloomington and Indianapolis, 1998).

215 Goodman: 'Opponents of Rome', p. 228.

216 Goodman: 'Opponents of Rome', p. 225.

217 Barclay: *Jews in the Mediterranean Diaspora*, p. 79.

218 Alston: *Soldier and Society*, p. 136.

219 For a general introduction, see Freund, Richard A., *Secrets of the Cave of Letters: Rediscovering a Dead Sea Mystery* (Amherst, 2004). For the texts themselves, Lewis, Naphtali, Yigael Yadin and Jonas C. Greenfield (eds), *The Documents from the Bar Kokhba Period in the Cave of Letters*, (Jerusalem, 1989).

220 On representations in Jewish sources, see Marks, Richard G., *The Image of Bar Kokhba in Traditional Jewish Literature: False Messiah and National Hero*, (University Park, 1994).

221 Thompson, Dorothy J, 'Ptolemaios and the "Lighthouse": Greek Culture in the Memphite Serapeum' *Proceedings of the Cambridge Philological Society* 213 (n.s. 33) (1987), pp. 107–113. To place the collection in context, Tait, John, 'Egyptian Fiction in Demotic and Greek', in J. R. Morgan and R. Stoneman (eds), *Greek Fiction: The Greek Novel in Context*, (London and New York, 1994), pp. 203–222.

222 Thompson: 'Ptolemaios and the "Lighthouse"', pp. 116–117.

223 Thompson: 'Ptolemaios and the "Lighthouse"', p. 117. But for the 'openings' in Kipling's imperial discourse, see Parry, Benita, 'The Contents and Discontents of Kipling's Imperialism', in E. Carter, J. Donald, and J. Squires (eds), *Space and Place: Theories of Identity and Location*, (London, 1993), pp. 221–240.

Chapter III

1 Morrison, Toni, *Playing in the Dark: Whiteness and the Literary Imagination*, (New York, 1992), pp. 46–47.

2 Erskine, Andrew, 'Culture and Power in Ptolemaic Egypt: The Museum and Library of Alexandria', *Greece and Rome* 42.1 (1995), p. 39.

3 Erskine: 'Culture and Power', p. 39.

4 Green: 'Alexander's Alexandria', pp. 17–18.

5 See also Babb, Valerie, *Whiteness Visible: The Meaning of Whiteness in American Literature and Culture*, (New York and London, 1998).

6 Stephens, Susan A., *Seeing Double: Intercultural Poetics in Ptolemaic Alexandria* (Berkeley, Los Angeles, and London, 2003), p. 9.

7 Theocritus, *Idyll*, 15. 44–50. Trans. T. Sargent.

8 Athenaeus, *The Deipnosophists*, 5. 196–203 describes an elaborate Ptolemaic procession from the early third century BCE; see also Rice, E. E., *The Grand Procession of Ptolemy Philadephus*, (Oxford, 1983).

9 But see discussion of Parthians in Augustan art at Rose, Charles Brian, 'The Parthians in Augustan Rome', *American Journal of Archaeology* 109.1 (2005), pp. 21–75.

10 Stam, Robert and Ella Shohat, 'Contested Histories: Eurocentrism, Multiculturalism, and the Media', in D. T. Goldberg (ed), *Multiculturalism: A Critical Reader*, (Oxford and Cambridge, 1994), pp. 303–304.

11 On the possibility of distinguishing alternative readings by female audiences in antiquity, see, for example, Osborne, Robin, 'Looking on – Greek style. Does the sculpted girl speak to women too?', in Morris: *Classical Greece: ancient histories*, pp. 80–96.

12 Dougherty, Carol, *The Raft of Odysseus: The Ethnographic Imagination of Homer's Odyssey*, (Oxford, 2001), p. 11. Cf. Dougherty, Carol, *The Poetics of Colonization: From City to Text in Archaic Greece*, (New York and Oxford, 1993).

13 Vergil, *Aeneid*, 1.279.

14 Syed, Yasmin, *Vergil's Aeneid and the Roman Self: Subject and Nation in Literary Discourse*, (Ann Arbor, 2005).

15 On Vergil's relation to the Near East, begin with Gordon, Cyrus H. 'Vergil and the Near East', *Ugaritica VI, tome 17* (Paris, 1969), pp. 267–288.

16 Vergil, *Aeneid*, 4.215–17. Cf. similar slurs after Aeneas has arrived in Italy at *Aeneid*, 12.96–100.

17 See Johnson, W.R., *Momentary Monsters: Lucan and his Heroes* (Ithaca and London, 1987), pp. 46–63. Also Thomas, Richard F., *Lands and Peoples in Roman Poetry: The Ethnographical Tradition*, Cambridge Philological Society, suppl. vol. no. 7 (Cambridge, 1982), pp. 108–123.

18 Toll, Katharine, 'Making Roman-ness and the *Aeneid*', *Classical Antiquity* 16.1 (1997), p. 41.

19 See Fitzgerald, William, 'Labor and Laborer in Latin Poetry: The Case of the *Moretum*', *Arethusa* 29 (1996), p. 397.

20 *Moretum*, 32.

21 *Moretum*, 31–35. E. J. Kenney suggests the manner of description follows conventions for describing art at Kenney, E. J. (ed), *The Ploughman's Lunch: Moretum, a Poem Ascribed to Virgil*, (Briston, 1984), p. 23, n. 32–5.

22 Snowden: *Blacks in Antiquity*, pp. 5–11.

23 On literary representations of the master/slave bond see Fitzgerald, William, *Slavery and the Roman Literary Imagination*, (Cambridge and New York, 2000). Postcolonial feminist writings might also provide helpful structures for analysis, beginning with Spivak, Gayatri Chakravorty, *In Other Worlds: Essays in Cultural Politics*, (New York, 1987).

24 Ovid, *Amores*, 1. 5. 13–23.

25 *Moretum*, 102.

26 Fitzgerald: 'Labor and Laborer', pp. 415–416.
27 Griffith, Mark, 'What Does Aeneas Look Like?' *Classical Philology* 80.4 (1985), p. 309.
28 For a broader perspective, see the multi-volume work Vercoutter, Jean, (ed), *The Image of the Black in Western Art*, (Cambridge, Mass).
29 For a general overview, see Moignard, Elizabeth, *Greek Vases: an Introduction* (London, 2006).
30 See Thomas, Bridget M., 'Constraints and Contradictions: Whiteness and Femininity in Ancient Greece', in L. Llewellyn-Jones (ed), *Women's Dress in the Ancient Greek World*, (London, Swansea, and Oakville, Connecticut, 2002), pp. 1–16.
31 Snowden: *Blacks in Antiquity*, pp. 151–153.
32 British Museum 1849.5–18.10. Reproduced at Bérard, Claude, 'The Image of the Other and the Foreign Hero', in B. Cohen (ed), *Not the Classical Ideal: Athens and the Construction of the Other in Greek Art*, (Leiden, Boston, and Köln, 2000), fig. 15.4, p. 396.
33 Bérard: 'The Image of the Other', p. 402.
34 Hall: *Inventing the Barbarian*, p. 172.
35 Snowden: *Blacks in Antiquity*, p. 25 and figs. 11–14.
36 Snowden: 'Greeks and Ethiopians', pp. 113–114.
37 Lissarrague, François, 'The Athenian Image of the Foreigner', in T. Harrison (ed), *Greeks and Barbarians*, (New York, 2002), p. 101.
38 Lissarrague: 'Athenian Image', pp. 108–109.
39 Lissarrague: 'Athenian Image', p. 110.
40 Ovid, *Amores*, 2.7 and 2.8.
41 Snowden: *Blacks in Antiquity*, p. 179.
42 See James, Sharon L., 'Slave-Rape and Female Silence in Ovid's Love Poetry', *Helios* 24.1 (1997), pp. 60–76.
43 Lissarrague: 'Athenian Image', pp. 106–107.
44 Hardwick, Lorna, 'Ancient Amazons – Heroes, Outsiders or Women?' *Greece and Rome* 37.1 (1990), pp. 28–29. Also Veness, Ruth, 'Investing the Barbarian? The Dress of Amazons in Ancient Art', in Llewellyn-Jones: *Women's Dress*, pp. 95–99.
45 But see Veness: 'Investing the Barbarian?', pp. 99–104.
46 Lissarrague: 'Athenian Image', p. 115.
47 Lissarrague: 'Athenian Image', pp. 116–117.
48 Tsiafakis, Despoina 'The Allure and Repulsion of Thracians in the Art of Classical Athens', in Cohen: *Not the Classical Ideal*, pp. 367–372.
49 For an in-depth examination of the role of both in ancient ideology, see duBois, Page, *Centaurs and Amazons: Women and the Pre-History of the Great Chain of Being* (Ann Arbor, 1982).
50 Hall: *Inventing the Barbarian*, p. 102 and *passim*.
51 Castriota, David, *Myth, Ethos, and Actuality: Official Art in Fifth-Century B.C. Athens*, (Madison, 1992), pp. 76–89.
52 McNiven, Timothy J., 'Behaving Like an Other: Telltale Gestures in Athenian Vase Painting', in Cohen: *Not the Classical Ideal*, pp. 88–89.
53 Stewart: *Faces of Power*, pp. 130–150.
54 Stewart: *Faces of Power*, pp. 142–144. Also, Stewart, Andrew, 'Alexander in Greek and Roman Art', in Roisman: *Brill's Companion to Alexander the Great*, pp. 31–66; On Roman views of Alexander more generally, see Spencer, Diana, *The Roman Alexander: Readings in a Cultural Myth*, (Exeter, 2002).

55 See DeVries, Keith, 'The Nearly Other: Attic Vision of Phyrgians and Lydians', in Cohen: *Not the Classical Ideal*, pp. 338–363.

56 Another intriguing African figure in myth is Antaeus, the son of Poseidon and Gaia, who was associated with Libya and defeated by Hercules in a wrestling match.

57 Vasunia: *Gift of the Nile*, p. 190.

58 Miller, Margaret C., 'The Myth of Bousiris: Ethnicity and Art', in Cohen: *Not the Classical Ideal*, p. 426.

59 Miller: 'Myth of Bousiris', p. 427.

60 Miller: 'Myth of Bousiris', p. 438; her interpretation is elaborated throughout pp. 430–442.

61 Boston, Museum of Fine Arts, 63.2663. Reproduced at Bérard: 'The Image of the Other', fig. 15.9, p. 403.

62 Snowden: *Blacks in Antiquity*, pp. 153–154.

63 Herodotus, *Histories*, 7.61.3.

64 Berlin, Staatliche Museen zu Berlin, Antikensammlung V.I.3238. Reproduced at Bérard: 'The Image of the Other', fig. 15.12, p. 408. For later traditions, see McGrath, Elizabeth, 'The Black Andromeda', *Journal of the Warburg and Courtauld Institutes* 55 (1992), pp. 1–18.

65 Ovid, *Heroides*.15. 35–36 and *Ars Amatoria*. 3.191; cf. *Ars Amatoria*.1. 53, in which she is said to be carried away from the 'the black Indians'.

66 Ancient descriptions of Andromeda's portrayal in art include: Achilles Tatius, *Leucippe and Clitophon*, 3.7, and Philostratus, *Imagines*, 1.29.

67 Heliodorus, *The Ethiopian Story*, 4.8.

68 Selden, Daniel, '*Aithiopika* and Ethiopianism', in Hunter: *Studies in Heliodorus*, pp. 184, 209, and 212. See also Perkins, Judith, 'An Ancient "Passing" Novel: Heliodorus' *Aithiopika*', *Arethusa* 32 (1999), pp. 197–214.

69 Bacon, Helen H., *Barbarians in Greek Tragedy*, (New Haven, 1961), pp. 89–92.

70 Hall: *Inventing the Barbarian*, pp. 54–55.

71 Hall: *Inventing the Barbarian*, p. 99.

72 See also Sancisi-Weerdenburg, Helen, 'Exit Atossa: Images of Women in Greek Historiography on Persia', in A. Cameron and A. Kuhrt (eds), *Images of Women in Antiquity*, (Detroit, 1983), pp. 20–33 and Brosius, Maria, *Women in Ancient Persia (559–331 BCE)*, (Oxford and New York, 1996).

73 Aeschylus, *Persians*, 230–45. See Goldhill, Simon, 'Battle Narrative and Politics in Aeschylus' *Persae*', repr. in Harrison: *Greeks and Barbarians*, pp. 52–56.

74 Aeschylus, *Persians*, 181–199.

75 Vasunia: *Gift of the Nile*, p. 38; on Egyptian fertility, pp. 43–47.

76 Aeschylus, *Suppliant Women*, 70–71, 154–55, 719–720, and 745.

77 Vasunia: *Gift of the Nile*, pp. 47–53.

78 On the fecundity of the Nile, see, for example, Pliny, *Natural History*, 7.3.3.

79 Vasunia: *Gift of the Nile*, pp. 40–43.

80 Vasunia: *Gift of the Nile*, pp. 37–38. See also West, Stephanie, 'Io and the Dark Stranger (Sophocles, *Inachus* F 269a)', *Classical Quarterly* n.s. 34.2 (1984), pp. 292–304.

81 Vasunia: *Gift of the Nile*, pp. 58–69.

82 Euripides, *Medea*, 1323–1350. On similar dynamics in Euripides' *Hecuba*, see Segal, Charles, 'Violence and the Other: Greek, Female, and Barbarian in Euripides' *Hecuba*', *Transactions of the American Philological Association* 120 (1990), pp. 109–131.

83 Euripides, *Medea*, 252–258. For black feminist identification with this double

exclusion of Medea, see, for example, Carroll, Constance M., 'Three's a Crowd: The Dilemma of the Black Woman in Higher Education', in G. T. Hull, P. B. Scott, and B. Smith (eds), *All the Women are White, All the Blacks are Men, But Some of Us Are Brave*, (New York, 1982), pp. 123–124.

84 Thomas: *Herodotus in Context*, pp. 133–34.

85 Euripides, *Iphigenia at Tauris*, 35–39.

86 Euripides, *Iphigenia at Tauris*, 1364–1378.

87 Euripides, *Iphigenia at Tauris*, 1174. See also Saïd, Suzanne, 'Greeks and Barbarians in Euripides' Tragedies: The End of Differences?' in Harrison: *Greeks and Barbarians*, pp. 80–81 and 86–87.

88 Long, Timothy, *Barbarians in Greek Comedy* (Carbondale and Edwardsville, 1986), p. 128.

89 Anderson, William S., *Barbarian Play: Plautus' Roman Comedy* (Toronto, Buffalo, and London, 1993), p. 139. See also the translations in Richlin, Amy, *Rome and the Mysterious Orient: Three Plays by Plautus*, (Berkeley, Los Angeles, and London, 2005).

90 Vasaly, Ann, *Representations: Images of the World in Ciceronian Oratory*, (Berkeley, Los Angeles and Oxford, 1993), p. 191.

91 Vasaly: *Representations of the World*, pp. 191–192.

92 Vasaly: *Representations of the World*, p. 194.

93 Vasaly: *Representations of the World*, pp. 198–205.

94 Shatzman, Israel, 'The Egyptian Question in Roman Politics (59–54 B.C.)', *Latomus* 30 (1971), pp. 363–369.

95 Cicero, *On Behalf of Rabirius Postumus*, 22.

96 Cicero, *On Behalf of Rabirius Postumus*, 35.

97 Cicero, *On Behalf of Rabirius Postumus*, 25–27.

98 Lewis: *Life in Egypt*, p. 196.

99 Tacitus, *Histories*. 1. 11.

100 For the Greek novels themselves, see Reardon, B.P. (ed), *Collected Ancient Greek Novels*, (Berkeley, Los Angeles, and London, 1989); a general introduction can be found at Holzberg, Niklas, *The Ancient Novel: An Introduction*, trans. C. Jackson-Holzberg, (London and New York, 1995). On Egypt in the novels, see Nimis, Stephen, 'Egypt in Greco-Roman History and Fiction', *Alif: Journal of Comparative Poetics* 24 (2004), pp. 44–55 and Sandy, Gerald N., 'Apuleius' *Golden Ass*: from Miletus to Egypt', in H. Hofman (ed), *Latin Fiction: The Latin Novel in Context*, (London and New York, 1999), pp. 81–102. For the impact of such settings on the construction of identity, see Stephens, Susan, 'Cultural Identity', in T. Whitmarsh (ed), *The Cambridge Companion to the Greek and Roman Novel*, (Cambridge and New York, 2008), pp. 56–71. Finally, the ancient Jewish novel also employs Egypt in distinct ways; for those texts, see Wills, Lawrence M. (ed), *Ancient Jewish Novels: An Anthology*, (Oxford and New York, 2002).

101 Moffitt, John F., 'The Palestrina Mosaic with a "Nile Scene": Philostratus and Ekphrasis: Ptolemy and Chorographia', *Zeitschrift für Kunstgeschichte* 60.2 (1987), p. 228.

102 Shumate, Nancy, *Nation, Empire, Decline: Studies in Rhetorical Continuity from the Romans to the Modern Era*, (London, 2006), p. 131.

103 Juvenal, *Satires*,15. 29–32.

104 Juvenal, *Satires*,15. 124–126.

105 Shumate: *Nation, Empire, Decline*, p. 139.

106 Juvenal, *Satires*,15. 110–116.
107 Juvenal, *Satires*,15. 130–131.
108 Shumate: *Nation, Empire, Decline*, p. 145. Also Alston, Richard, 'Conquest by text: Juvenal and Plutarch on Egypt', in Webster and Cooper: *Roman Imperialism*, pp. 99–109.
109 Thompson, Dorothy, 'Athenaeus in his Egyptian Context', in D. Braund and J. Wilkins (eds), *Athenaeus and His World: Reading Greek Culture in the Roman Empire*, (Exeter, 2000), p. 79.
110 Thompson: 'Athenaeus in his Egyptian Context', p. 81.
111 Cassius Dio, *Roman History*, 51.21.8; cf. Plutarch, *Life of Antony*, 86.3.
112 On the difficulty of reconstructing the precise route, see Beard, Mary, *The Roman Triumph*, (Cambridge, Mass. and London, 2007), pp. 101–105. Cf. Ovid's representation of an imagined triumph at *Tristia*, 4.2.
113 Beard: *Roman Triumph*, p. 123.
114 Vergil depicts Augustus' triumph from 29 BCE, on Aeneas' shield, including a parade of foreign captives at *Aeneid*, 8.720–728.
115 Beard: *Roman Triumph*, p. 121.
116 Beard: *Roman Triumph*, pp. 114–119.
117 Beard: *Roman Triumph*, p. 187.
118 Futrell, Alison, *Blood in the Arena: The Spectacle of Roman Power*, (Austin, 1997).
119 Beard: *Roman Triumph*, p. 45.
120 Currie, Sarah, 'The empire of adults: the representation of children on Trajan's arch at Beneventum', in J. Elsner (ed), *Art and Text in Roman Culture*, (Cambridge and New York, 1996), pp. 153–181.
121 Beard: *Roman Triumph*, p. 139.
122 Cassius Dio, *Roman History*, 43.19.
123 Ferris, I. M., *Enemies of Rome: Barbarians Through Roman Eyes*, (Sutton, 2000), pp. 7–8.
124 Ferris: *Enemies of Rome*, p. 22.
125 See also: Schneider, Rolf Michael, *Bunte Barbaren*, (Stuttgart, 1986).
126 Ferris: *Enemies of Rome*, pp. 64–65.
127 Ferris: *Enemies of Rome*, p. 88.
128 Ferris: *Enemies of Rome*, p. 98.
129 Dillon, Sheila, 'Women on the Columns of Trajan and Marcus Aurelius and the Visual Language of Roman Victory', in S. Dillon and K. E. Welch (eds), *Representations of War in Ancient Rome*, (Cambridge and New York, 2006), p. 263.
130 Dillon: 'Women on the Columns', pp. 263–67.
131 Rodgers, René, 'Female Representations in Roman Art: Feminising the Provincial "Other"', in S. Scott and J. Webster (eds), *Roman Imperialism and Provincial Art*, (Cambridge, 2003), pp. 81–92. Also Holliday, Peter J., *The Origins of Roman Historical Commemoration in the Visual Arts*, (Cambridge and New York, 2002), pp. 112–118.
132 Erim, Kenan T., 'A New Relief showing Claudius and Britannia from Aphrodisias,' *Britannia* 13 (1982), pp. 277–ii.
133 Martial, *Epigrams*, 11. 53. 1–4.
134 Cohen, Beth, 'Ethnic Identity in Democratic Athens and the Visual Vocabulary of Male Costume', in Malkin: *Ancient Perceptions*, p. 251.
135 For example, Propertius, *Elegies*, 3.6 and 4. 8. 79–80.
136 Propertius, *Elegies*, 2.18d. 23–28.

137 Ovid. *Amores,* 1.14. 45–56.

138 Cf. Martial, *Epigrams,* 5. 68; see also Balsdon: *Romans and Aliens,* p. 215 and Thompson: *Romans and Blacks,* pp. 131–132. More generally, see Levine, Molly Myerowitz, 'The Gendered Grammar of Ancient Mediterranean Hair', in H. Eilberg-Schwartz and W. Doniger (eds), *Off With Her Head! The Denial of Women's Identity in Myth, Religion, and Culture,* (Berkeley, Los Angeles, and London, 1995), pp. 76–130 and Wyke, Maria, 'Woman in the Mirror: The Rhetoric of Adornment in the Roman World', in Archer, Fischler, and Wyke: *Women in Ancient Societies,* pp. 134–151.

139 On the remoteness of Tomis, see, for example, Ovid, *Tristia,* 1.1.127–128 and 3.3.3–4, the latter where he places it in the 'outermost parts of the unknown world'.

140 See Trofimova, Anna A. (ed), *Greeks on the Black Sea: Ancient Art from the Hermitage* (Los Angeles, 2007).

141 Radulescu, Adrian, *Ovid in Exile,* trans. L. Treptow, (Iasi, Oxford, Palm Beach, and Portland, 2002), pp. 85–86.

142 For general introductions, begin with Williams, Gareth, 'Ovid's Exilic Poetry: Worlds Apart', in B. W. Boyd (ed), *Brill's Companion to Ovid,* (Leiden, Boston, and Köln, 2002), pp. 337–381 and Claassen, Jo-Marie, 'Ovid's Poetic Pontus' in F. Cairns and M. Heath (eds), *Papers of the Leeds International Latin Seminar, Sixth volume 1990,* (Leeds, 1990), pp. 65–94.

143 Ovid, *Tristia,* 3.9. 1–4.

144 Ovid, *Tristia,* 5.7.11–12, cf. 5.10.27–36; earlier he notes that any Greek spoken in the area is 'overcome with Getic tone', 5.2.67–68, cf. 5.7. 51–52.

145 For example, Ovid, *Tristia,* 1.11.31–34; 3.2.7–8; 3.3.5–8; 3.10; and 5.7.

146 Ovid, *Tristia,* 4.4.61–62.

147 Ovid, *Tristia,* 1.3 and 3.11.29–30; cf. 3.3. 53–54.

148 Ovid, *Tristia,* 3.3. 53–54; 2.201–206.

149 Claassen, Jo-Marie, 'Ovid's Wavering Identity: Personification and Depersonalisation in the Exilic Poems', *Latomus* 49 (1990), pp. 102–116.

150 Ovid, *Tristia,* 5.2. 1–8.

151 For example, Ovid, *Tristia* 3.1.17–18; 3.14.43–46; 5.1.71–74; and 5.7.55–60. In *Letters from Pontus,* Ovid claims to have learned the 'Getic and Sarmatian tongue', 3.1.40.

152 Ovid, *Tristia,* 5.10.37–38.

153 Sancisi-Weerdenburg, Heleen, 'Yauna by the Sea and Across the Sea', in Malkin: *Ancient Perceptions,* pp. 323–346.

154 Stoneman, Richard, 'The *Alexander Romance*: From history to fiction', in Morgan and Stoneman: *Greek Fiction,* pp. 118 and 122–123. Also Jasnow, Richard, 'The Greek Alexander Romance and Demotic Egyptian Literature', *Journal of Near Eastern Studies* 56.2 (1997), pp. 95–103.

155 Stoneman, Richard, (ed), *Legends of Alexander the Great,* (London, 1994), p. xii. Also Mossé, Claude, *Alexander: Destiny and Myth,* trans. J. Lloyd, (Baltimore, 2004).

Chapter IV

1 Woolf, Virginia, 'A Dialogue upon Mount Pentelicus', in S. Dick (ed), *The Complete Shorter Fiction of Virginia Woolf,* second edition (San Diego, New York and London, 1989), p. 64.

2   Woolf: 'A Dialogue', pp. 65–66.
3   A range of case-studies is considered in Stephens, Susan A. and Phiroze Vasunia (eds), *Classics and National Cultures*, (Oxford and New York, 2010).
4   Weiss, Roberto, *The Renaissance Discovery of Classical Antiquity*, second edition (Oxford and New York, 1988).
5   Cahill, Thomas, *How the Irish Saved Civilization: The Untold Story of Ireland's Heroic Role from the Fall of Rome to the Rise of Medieval Europe*, (New York, 1995).
6   Haddour, Azzedine, 'Tradition, Translation and Colonization: The Graeco-Arabic Translation Movement and Deconstructing the Classics', in A. Lianeri and V. Zajko (eds), *Translation and the Classic: Identity as Change in the History of Culture*, (Oxford and New York, 2008), pp. 203–226. Also Etman, Ahmed, 'Translation at the Intersection of Traditions: The Arab Reception of Classics', in L. Hardwick and C. Stray (eds), *A Companion to Classical Receptions*, (Malden and Oxford, 2008), pp. 141–152.
7   Bowler, Peter J., *The Invention of Progress: The Victorians and the Past*, (Oxford and Cambridge, Mass., 1989). Cf. Dodds, E. R., *The Ancient Concept of Progress and other Essays on Greek Literature and Belief*, (Oxford, 1973).
8   For Hippocrates' manuscript tradition, see Jouanna: *Hippocrates*, pp. 348–365. On his survival more generally, Smith, Wesley D., *The Hippocratic Tradition*, (Ithaca and London, 1979).
9   Jouanna: *Hippocrates*, p. 364.
10 Harrison, Mark, *Climates and Constitutions: Health, Race, Environment and British Imperialism in India 1600–1850*, (New Delhi and Oxford, 1999), p. 93.
11 Harrison: *Climates and Constitutions*, p. 92.
12 Harrison: *Climates and Constitutions*, p. 1.
13 Harrison: *Climates and Constitutions*, pp. 216–217.
14 Wheeler: *Complexion of Race*, pp. 23–28.
15 Stewart, Mart A., '"Let Us Begin with the Weather?": Climate, Race, and Cultural Distinctiveness in the American South', in M. Teich, R. Porter, and B. Gustafsson (eds), *Nature and Society in Historical Context* (Cambridge and New York, 1997), p. 249.
16 Stewart: '"Let Us Begin"', p. 249. For discussion of some of the contradictions encountered when applying theories of polygeny to the justification of slavery, see Gould: 'American Polygeny', pp. 111–114.
17 Bernal: *Black Athena, vol 1*, pp. 201–204, 215–223 and *passim*.
18 On *Black Athena*'s implications for the related field of classical philosophy, see Flory, Dan, 'Racism, *Black Athena*, and the Historiography of Ancient Philosophy', *The Philosophical Forum* 28.3 (1997), pp. 183–208.
19 For example, Young: 'Egypt in America', pp. 153–156.
20 Quoted at van Binsbergen, Wim, 'Black Athena Ten Years After: towards a constructive re-assessment', *Talanta* 28–29 (1996–1997), p. 51.
21 Bernal: *Black Athena, vol 1*, p. 22.
22 Bernal, Martin, 'Greece: Aryan or Mediterranean? Two Contending Historiographical Models', in S Federici (ed), *Enduring Western Civilization: The Construction of the Concept of Western Civilization and Its "Others"*, (Westport, 1995), p. 4.
23 Bernal: 'Greece: Aryan or Mediterranean?', p. 4.
24 Bernal: 'Greece: Aryan or Mediterranean?', pp. 9–10.
25 Bernal: *Black Athena, vol 1*, p. 21.

26 Bernal: *Black Athena, vol 1*, p. 7.
27 Bernal: *Black Athena, vol 1*, p. 21. Bernal discusses the linguistic argument at much greater length in Bernal, Martin, *Black Athena: The Afroasiatic Roots of Classical Civilization, Volume 3: The Linguistic Evidence*, (New Brunswick, 2006). Two linguists responded to the initial argument at Jasanoff, Jay H. and Alan Nussbaum, 'Word Games: The Linguistic Evidence in *Black Athena*', in Lefkowitz and Rogers: *Black Athena Revisited*, pp. 177–205. Bernal replied at Bernal, Martin, '*Ausnahmslosigkeit über Alles*: A Reply to Jay H. Jasanoff and Alan Nussbaum', in *Black Athena Writes Back: Martin Bernal Responds to his Critics*, D. C. Moore (ed), (Durham and London, 2001), pp. 107–161.
28 Bernal: *Black Athena, vol 1*, p. 17.
29 Bernal: *Black Athena, vol 1*, p. 7.
30 For more on the differences between diffusionism and isolationism, see Marchand, Suzanne and Anthony Grafton, 'Martin Bernal and His Critics', *Arion* 5.2 (1997), pp. 1–35.
31 Morris, Sarah P., 'The Legacy of *Black Athena*', in Lefkowitz and Rogers: *Black Athena Revisited*, p. 168.
32 O'Connor, David, 'Egypt and Greece: The Bronze Age Evidence', in Lefkowitz and Rogers: *Black Athena Revisited*, pp. 54–55.
33 O'Connor, 'Egypt and Greece', pp. 60–61.
34 Bernal: *Black Athena, vol 1*, p. 21.
35 Hall: *Ethnic Identity*, p. 8.
36 Scobie, Alex, *Hitler's State Architecture: The Impact of Classical Antiquity*, (University Park and London, 1990), p. 14.
37 Hall: *Ethnic Identity*, pp. 114–118.
38 Hall: *Ethnic Identity*, pp. 185–186.
39 Hall: *Ethnic Identity*, pp. 64–65.
40 Hall: *Ethnic Identity*, p. 185.
41 Bernal: *Black Athena, vol 1*, pp. 19–20 and 44–45.
42 Bernal: *Black Athena, vol 1*, pp. 88–98.
43 Hall, Edith, 'When is a Myth Not a Myth? Bernal's "Ancient Model"', in Lefkowitz and Rogers: *Black Athena Revisited*, p. 338.
44 Bernal discusses Sesostris extensively in Bernal, Martin, *Black Athena: The Afroasiatic Roots of Classical Civilization, Volume 2: The Archaeological and Documentary Evidence*, (New Brunswick, 1991), pp. 187–273. Levine, Molly Myerowitz, 'The Marginalization of Martin Bernal', *Classical Philology* 93 (1998), pp. 345–363 evaluates the reception of the second Volume as well as the negative responses to Bernal's work collected in Lefkowitz and Rogers: *Black Athena Revisited*. Bernal responds directly to his critics, including many in the Lefkowitz collection, at Bernal: *Black Athena Writes Back*.
45 For example, van Binsbergen: 'Black Athena Ten Years After', pp. 63–64. A new interdisciplinary reassessment is currently forthcoming from Oxford University Press: Orrells, Daniel, Gurminder K. Bhambra, and Tessa Roynon, (eds), *African Athena: New Agendas*.
46 Young: 'Egypt in America', p. 156.
47 Levine, Molly Myerowitz, 'Bernal and the Athenians in the Multicultural World of the Ancient Mediterranean', in R. Katzoff (ed), *Classical Studies in Honor of David Sohlberg*, (Ramat Gan, 1996), p. 16.
48 Bernal, Martin, '*Black Athena* and the APA', *Arethusa* special issue, (1989), p. 31.

49 Bernal: '*Black Athena* and the APA', p. 32.

50 Bernal: *Black Athena, vol 1*, pp. 52–53.

51 Bernal: *Black Athena, vol 1*, p. 242; cf. Herodotus, *Histories*, 2. 104. 2.

52 Bernal: *Black Athena, vol 1*, pp. 241–242.

53 Bernal: *Black Athena, vol 1*, p. 242.

54 For example, Asante, Molefi Kete, *Afrocentricity: The Theory of Social Change*, revised and expanded edition (Chicago, 2003).

55 Howe: *Afrocentrism*, p. 36.

56 Howe: *Afrocentrism*, p. 47.

57 On Du Bois and Garvey, begin with Howe: *Afrocentrism*, pp. 50–53 and pp. 74–77. Also Bell, Bernard W., Emily Grosholz, and James B. Stewart (eds), *W.E.B. Du Bois on Race and Culture: Philosophy, Politics, and Poetics*, (New York and London, 1996). On the development of 'Ethiopianism' in African–American thought, see Selden: '*Aithiopika* and Ethiopianism', pp 196–198.

58 On Blyden, see Mudimbe, V.Y., *The Invention of Africa: Gnosis, Philosophy, and the Order of Knowledge*, (Bloomington and Indianapolis, 1988), pp. 98–134.

59 Howe: *Afrocentrism*, pp. 163–92. See also Diop's succinct overview of the tenets of his work in Diop, Cheikh Anta, 'The Meaning of Our Work', in R. R. Grinker and C. B. Steiner (eds), *Perspectives on Africa: A Reader in Culture, History, and Representation*, (Oxford and Cambridge, Mass, 1997), pp. 724–727.

60 James, George G. M., *Stolen Legacy*, (Nashville, 1954), p. 7.

61 Howe: *Afrocentrism*, pp. 66–72.

62 Lefkowitz: 'Ancient History, Modern Myths', p. 22.

63 Bowersock, Glen, 'Rescuing the Greeks: A classicist defends the traditional version of Greek cultural achievement', *New York Times Book Review*, (February 25, 1996), pp. 6–7. Cf. Griffin, Jasper, 'Anxieties of Influence', *The New York Review of Books* 43 (June 20, 1996), pp. 67–73 and Lefkowitz, Mary, *Not Out of Africa: How Afrocentrism Became an Excuse to Teach Myth as History*, (New York, 1996).

64 Howe: *Afrocentrism*, pp. 270–273.

65 Appiah, Kwame Anthony, 'Europe Upside Down: Fallacies of the New Afrocentrism', in Grinker and Steiner: *Perspectives on Africa*, p. 729.

66 Young: 'Egypt in America', p. 161. See also Dain, Bruce, *A Hideous Monster of the Mind: American Race Theory in the Early Republic*, (Cambridge, Mass and London, 2002) and Trafton, Scott, *Egypt Land: Race and Nineteenth-Century American Egyptomania*, (Durham and London, 2004).

67 Young: 'Egypt in America', pp. 161–165.

68 Keita, S. O. Y, '*Black Athena*: "Race," Bernal and Snowden', *Arethusa* 26 (1993), p. 304.

69 Young: 'Egypt in America', p. 162. See also Gould: 'American Polygeny', pp. 106–111.

70 Yurco, Frank J., '*Black Athena*: An Egyptological Review', in Lefkowitz and Rogers: *Black Athena Revisited*, p. 65.

71 Howe: *Afrocentrism*, pp. 115–117.

72 Sanders, Edith R., 'The Hamitic Hypothesis: Its Origin and Functions in Time Perspective', *Journal of African History* 10.4 (1969), pp. 521–32.

73 For example, Brace, C. Loring *et al.*, 'Clines and Clusters Versus "Race": A Test in Ancient Egypt and the Case of a Death on the Nile', in Lefkowitz and Rogers: *Black Athena Revisited*, p. 130.

74 Howe: *Afrocentrism*, p. 132.

75 Yurco, Frank J., 'Were the Ancient Egyptians Black or White?', *Biblical Archaeology Review* 15.5 (September/October 1989), p. 24.

76 Young: 'Egypt in America', p. 163.

77 Morsy, Soheir A., 'Beyond the Honorary "White" Classification of Egyptians: Societal Identity in Historical Context,' in S. Gregory and R. Sanjek (eds), *Race*, (New Brunswick, 1994), pp. 175–198.

78 Levine: 'Bernal and the Athenians', p. 17.

79 Yurco: 'Were the Ancient Egyptians', p. 24.

80 Bard, Kathryn A., 'Ancient Egyptians and the Issue of Race,' in Lefkowitz and Rogers: *Black Athena Revisited*, p. 104.

81 Bard: 'Ancient Egyptians', p. 109.

82 Walker, Susan (ed), *Ancient Faces: Mummy Portraits from Roman Egypt*, (New York, 2000).

83 Bard: 'Ancient Egyptians', p. 107.

84 Bard: 'Ancient Egyptians', p. 108.

85 Keita: '*Black Athena*: "Race,"', pp. 302–305. On the Mediterranean as a term of identification, see Purcell, Nicholas, 'The Boundless Sea of Unlikeness? On Defining the Mediterranean', in I. Malkin (ed), *Mediterranean Paradigms and Classical Antiquity*, (London and New York, 2005), pp. 9–29.

86 van Binsbergen, Wim, 'Rethinking Africa's Contribution to Global Cultural History: lessons from a comparative historical analysis of mankala board-games and geomantic divination', *Talanta* 28–29 (1996–1997), p. 249.

87 See Yurco, Frank J., 'Egypt and Nubia: Old, Middle, and New Kingdom Eras,' in Yamauchi: *Africa and Africans*, pp. 28–112.

88 See Russmann, Edna R., 'Egypt and Kushites: Dynasty XXV', in Yamauchi: *Africa and Africans*, pp. 113–131.

89 See Burstein, Stanley, 'The Kingdom of Meroe', in Yamauchi: *Africa and Africans*, pp. 132–58.

90 See also Phillipson, David W., *Ancient Ethiopia: Aksum: Its Antecedents and Successors*, (London, 1998).

91 von Henneberg, Krystyna, 'Monuments, Public Space, and the Memory of Empire in Modern Italy', *History and Memory* 16.1 (2004), pp. 45–46.

92 von Henneberg: 'Monuments, Public Space,' p. 52.

93 von Henneberg: 'Monuments, Public Space,' p. 72.

94 Watkins, David, *The Roman Forum*, (Cambridge, Mass, 2009), pp. 205–209. See also Painter, Borden W. Jr, *Mussolini's, Rome: Rebuilding the Eternal City*, (New York, 2005) and Andersen, Wayne, *The Ara Pacis of Augustus and Mussolini: An Archeological Mystery*, (Geneva and Boston, 2003). On efforts prior to Mussolini's see Atkinson, David, Denis Cosgrove, and Anna Notaro, 'Empire in modern Rome: shaping and remembering an imperial city, 1870–1911', in F. Driver and D. Gilbert (eds), *Imperial Cities: Landscape, Display and Identity*, (Manchester and New York, 1999), pp. 40–63.

95 Scobie: *Hitler's State Architecture*, p. 27.

96 See also Lacoue-Labarthe, Philippe and Jean-Luc Nancy, 'The Nazi Myth', *Critical Inquiry* 16 (1990), pp. 291–312.

97 Scobie: *Hitler's State Architecture*, p. 14.

98 Losemann, Volker, 'The Nazi concept of Rome,' in C. Edwards (ed), *Roman Presences: Receptions of Rome in European Culture, 1789–1945)*, (Cambridge and New York, 1999), pp. 221–235.

99   Scobie: *Hitler's State Architecture*, pp. 37–41. For connections between Nazi film and Hollywood versions of ancient Rome, see Winkler, Martin M., *The Roman Salute: Cinema, History, Ideology*, (Columbus, 2009), pp. 122–150.

100 Schäche, Wolfgang, 'From Berlin to "Germania"': Architecture and Urban Planning', in D. Ades *et al.* (eds), *Art and Power: Europe Under the Dictators 1930–45*, (London, 1995), pp. 326–29.

101 Herminghouse, Patricia and Magda Mueller, 'Introduction: Looking for Germania', in P. Herminghouse and M. Mueller (eds), *Gender and Germanness: Cultural Productions of Nation*, (Providence and Oxford, 1997), pp. 1–8.

102 Mellor, Ronald, 'Introduction' in R. Mellor, (ed), *Tacitus: The Classical Heritage*, (New York and London, 1995), pp. xix–liv.

103 Mellor: 'Introduction', pp. xxii–xxiv; also Kelley, Donald R., '*Tacitus Noster*: The *Germania* in the Renaissance and Reformation', in T. J. Luce and A. J. Woodman, (eds), *Tacitus and the Tacitean Tradition*, (Princeton, 1993), pp. 156–163. For a different account of the passage from antiquity, see Zank, Wolfgang, 'From *Germania* to the Holy Roman Empire of the Germanic Nation', in W. Zank, *The German Melting Pot: Multiculturality in Historical Perspective*, (New York, 1998), pp. 39–54.

104 Isaac: *Invention*, p. 137. Also, Krebs, Christopher B., *A Most Dangerous Book: Tacitus's Germania from the Roman Empire to the Third Reich*, (New York, 2011). For Nazi racial ideology, see Burleigh, Michael and Wolfgang Wippermann, *The Racial State: Germany 1933–1945*, (Cambridge and New York, 1991).

105 Losemann: 'Nazi concept', p. 226.

106 Turner, Frank M., 'British politics and the demise of the Roman republic: 1700–1939', in *Contesting Cultural Authority: Essays in Victorian Intellectual Life*, (Cambridge and New York, 1993), pp. 231–261.

107 Begin with Turner, Frank M., *The Greek heritage in Victorian Britain*, (New Haven, 1981) and Jenkyns, Richard, *The Victorians and ancient Greece*, (Oxford, 1980). Also Turner, Frank M., 'Why the Greeks and not the Romans in Victorian Britain?' in G. W. Clarke (ed), *Rediscovering Hellenism: The Hellenic Inheritance and the English Imagination*, (Cambridge and New York, 1989), pp. 61–81.

108 Vance, Norman, *The Victorians and Ancient Rome*, (Oxford and Cambridge, Mass, 1997), pp. 228–30.

109 Vance: *Victorians and Ancient Rome*, p. 232.

110 Vasunia: 'Greater Rome', pp. 49–50 and Hingley: *Roman Officers*, p. 52.

111 For example, Hingley: *Roman Officers*, p. 48 and Vance: *Victorians and Ancient Rome*, pp. 238–40.

112 Hingley: *Roman Officers*, pp. 29–31. Also Vance: *Victorians and Ancient Rome*, pp. 233–235.

113 On Gandy, see Darley, Gillian, *John Soane: An Accidental Romantic*, (New Haven and London, 1999), pp. 144–147.

114 Vance: *Victorians and Ancient Rome*, pp. 234–235.

115 Vasunia: 'Greater Rome', pp. 41–42.

116 Vance: *Victorians and Ancient Rome*, p. 242.

117 Vance, Norman, 'Decadence and the subversion of empire', in Edwards: *Roman Presences*, p. 110.

118 Vance: 'Decadence', pp. 110–111.

119 Hingley: *Roman Officers*, p. 32.

120 Vance: 'Decadence', p. 121.

121 Vance: 'Decadence', p. 122.

122 Majeed, Javed, 'Comparativism and references to Rome in British imperial attitudes to India', in Edwards: *Roman Presences*, p. 106.

123 Berlinerblau, Jacques, *Heresy in the University: The Black Athena Controversy and the Responsibilities of American Intellectuals*, (New Brunswick and London, 1999), p. 60.

124 Bernal: *Black Athena, vol 1*, p. 229.

125 Majeed: 'Comparativism and references', pp. 92–98.

126 Bernal: *Black Athena, vol 1*, pp. 236–237.

127 Majeed: 'Comparativism and references', pp. 101–103.

128 Young: 'Egypt in America', pp. 165–168.

129 Majeed: 'Comparativism and references', pp. 101–103.

130 Majeed: 'Comparativism and references', p. 108.

131 Hingley: *Roman Officers*, p. 73.

132 See Oergel, Maike, 'The redeeming Teuton: nineteenth-century notions of the "Germanic" in England and Germany', in G. Cubitt (ed), *Imagining Nations*, (Manchester and New York, 1998), pp. 75–91.

133 Hingley: *Roman Officers*, pp. 63–65. Also Hines, John, 'Britain After Rome: Between Multiculturalism and Monoculturalism', in Graves-Brown, Jones, and Gamble: *Cultural Identity and Archaeology*, pp. 256–270.

134 Hingley: *Roman Officers*, pp. 72–85.

135 Vasunia: 'Greater Rome', p. 48.

136 Hingley: *Roman Officers*, p. 62.

137 Ayres, Philip, *Classical Culture and the Idea of Rome in Eighteenth Century England*, (Cambridge and New York, 1997), pp. 84–90.

138 Hingley: *Roman Officers*, pp. 12–14. For another assessment of Haverfield, see Freeman, Philip, 'British imperialism and the Roman Empire', in Webster and Cooper: *Roman Imperialism*, pp. 19–34.

139 Hingley: *Roman Officers*, pp. 113–114. See also Freeman, P. W. M., 'Mommsen through to Haverfield: the origins of studies of Romanization in late 19th-c. Britain', in D. J. Mattingly (ed), *Dialogues in Roman Imperialism: Power, discourse, and discrepant experience in the Roman Empire*, (Portsmouth, 1997), pp. 27–50.

140 Hingley: *Roman Officers*, p. 120.

141 Hingley: *Roman Officers*, p. 95.

142 Hingley: *Roman Officers*, p. 126. See also Vance: *Victorians and Ancient Rome*, pp. 238–40.

143 O'Higgins, Laurie, '(In)felix Paupertas: Scholarship of the Eighteenth-Century Irish Poor', *Arethusa* 40.3 (2007), p. 435.

144 Bernal: 'Greece: Aryan or Mediterranean?', p. 8.

145 McElduff, Siobhán, 'Fractured Understandings: Towards a History of Classical Reception among Non-Elite Groups', in C. Martindale and R. F. Thomas (eds), *Classics and the Uses of Reception*, (Malden, Massachusetts and Oxford, 2006), p. 190. Also Harris, Jason and Keith Sidwell (eds), *Making Ireland Roman: Irish Neo-Latin Writers and the Republic of Letters*, (Cork, 2009).

146 Parker, Grant, trans., *The Agony of Asar: A Thesis on Slavery by the Former Slave, Jacobus Elisa Johannes Capitein 1717–1747*, (Princeton, 2001), pp. 10–11.

147 Parker: *Agony of Asar*, p. 78.

148 Gates, Henry Louis, Jr., *The Trials of Phillis Wheatley: America's First Black Poet and Her Encounters with the Founding Fathers*, (New York, 2003), pp. 16–17.

149 Quoted at Gates: *Trials of Phillis Wheatley*, p. 20.

150 Gates: *Trials of Phillis Wheatley*, p. 31.

151 For the significance of her time abroad to her emancipation, see Carretta, Vincent, 'Phillis Wheatley, the Mansfield Decision of 1772, and the Choice of Identity', in K. H. Schmidt and F. Fleischmann (eds), *Early America Re-Explored: New Readings in Colonial, Early National, and Antebellum Culture*, (New York, 2002), pp. 201–223.

152 Walters, Tracey L., *African American Literature and the Classicist Tradition: Black Women Writers from Wheatley to Morrison*, (New York, 2007), p. 40.

153 Wheatley, Phillis, 'To Maecenas', in J. D. Mason, Jr. (ed), *The Poems of Phillis Wheatley*, (Chapel Hill, 1966), p. 4. For an early classicist's view of Terence's racial origins, see Frank, Tenney, 'On Suetonius' Life of Terence', *The American Journal of Philology* 54. 3 (1933), pp. 269–273.

154 Wheatley, Phillis, 'To the University of Cambridge, in New-England', in Mason: *Poems of Phillis Wheatley*, p. 5.

155 Wheatley, Phillis, 'To the Right Honourable William, Earl of Dartmouth, His Majesty's Principal Secretary of State for North America, & C', in Mason: *Poems of Phillis Wheatley*, p. 34.

156 Gates: *Trials of Phillis Wheatley*, pp. 7–16 discusses the individual judges.

157 Jefferson, Thomas, excerpted in W.H. Robinson (ed), *Critical Essays on Phillis Wheatley*, (Boston, 1982), p. 42.

158 Begin with Richard, Carl J., *Greeks and Romans Bearing Gifts: How the Ancients Inspired the Founding Fathers*, (Lanham, 2008).

159 Ronnick, Michele Valerie (ed), *The Autobiography of William Sanders Scarborough: An American Journey from Slavery to Scholarship*, (Detroit, 2005) and Ronnick, Michele Valerie (ed), *The Works of William Sanders Scarborough: Black Classicist and Race Leader*, (Oxford and New York, 2006).

160 For a brief overview of their relationship, see Alridge, Derrick P., *The Educational Thought of W.E.B. Du Bois: An Intellectual History*, (New York, 2008), pp. 52–55; see also Cook, William W. and James Tatum, *African American Writers and Classical Tradition*, (Chicago and London, 2010), pp. 93–124 and Provenzo, Eugene F. Jr. (ed), *Du Bois on Education*, (Walnut Creek, 2002).

161 Johnson, Karen A., *Uplifting the Women and the Race: The Educational Philosophies and Social Activism of Anna Julia Cooper and Nannie Helen Burroughs*, (New York and London, 2000).

162 Walters: *African American Literature*. For other writers, see also Cook and Tatum: *African American Writers*; also Wetmore, Kevin J. Jr., *Black Dionysus: Greek Tragedy and African American Theatre*, (Jefferson, North Carolina and London, 2003).

163 Walters: *African American Literature*, p. 13 and *passim*.

164 Rankine, Patrice D., *Ulysses in Black: Ralph Ellison, Classicism, and African American Literature*, (Madison, 2006), p. 15.

165 O'Meally, Robert G., *Romare Bearden: A Black Odyssey*, (New York, 2007). See also Davis, Gregson, 'Reframing the Homeric: Images of the *Odyssey* in the Art of Derek Walcott and Romare Bearden', in Hardwick and Stray: *Companion to Classical Receptions*, pp. 401–414.

166 See Greenwood, Emily, 'Re-rooting the classical tradition: new directions in black classicism', *Classical Receptions Journal* 1.1 (2009), pp. 87–103.

167 Goff, Barbara and Michael Simpson, *Crossroads in the Black Aegean: Oedipus, Antigone, and Dramas of the African Diaspora*, (Oxford and New York, 2007).

See also Budelmann, Felix 'Greek Tragedies in West African Adaptations', in Goff: *Classics and Colonialism*, pp. 118–146 and van Zyl Smit, Betine, 'Multicultural Reception: Greek Drama in South Africa in the Late Twentieth and Early Twenty-first Centuries,' in Hardwick and Stray: *Companion to Classical Receptions*, pp. 373–385.

168 See Gilmore, John, 'The British Empire and the Neo-Latin Tradition: The Case of Francis Williams', in Goff: *Classics and Colonialism*, pp. 92–106; Greenwood, Emily, '"We Speak Latin in Trinidad": Uses of Classics in Caribbean Literature', in Goff: *Classics and Colonialism*, pp. 65–91; Greenwood, Emily, 'Between Colonialism and Independence: Eric Williams and the Uses of Classics in Trinidad in the 1950s and 1960s', in Hardwick and Stray: *Companion to Classical Receptions*, pp. 98–112; and Greenwood, Emily, *Afro-Greeks: Dialogues Between Anglophone Caribbean Literature and Classics in the Twentieth Century*, (Oxford and New York, 2010).

169 Walcott, Derek, 'Reflections on *Omeros*,' *South Atlantic Quarterly* 96.2 (1997), p. 236.

170 Bernal: 'Greece: Aryan or Mediterranean?', p. 8.

171 St. Clair, William, *That Greece Might Still Be Free: The Philhellenes in the War of Independence*, (New York and Toronto, 1972), p. 355.

172 St. Clair: *That Greece Might Still Be Free*, pp. 28–34.

173 Quoted at Liakos, Antonis, 'Hellenism and the Making of Modern Greece: Time, Language, Space,' in K. Zacharia (ed), *Hellenisms: Culture, Identity, and Ethnicity from Antiquity to Modernity*, (Aldershot and Burlington, 2008), p. 201.

174 Herzfeld, Michael, *Ours Once More: Folklore, Ideology, and the Making of Modern Greece*, (New York, 1986), p. 144; see also Güthenke, Constanze, 'Editing the Nation: Classical Scholarship in Greece, c. 1930', in Stephens and Vasunia: *Classics and National Cultures*, pp. 121–140.

INDEX